*Women Playwrights in England*

# Women Playwrights in England

## in England

### c. 1363-1750

*Nancy Cotton*

Lewisburg
**BUCKNELL UNIVERSITY PRESS**
London and Toronto: Associated University Presses

Associated University Presses, Inc.
4 Cornwall Drive
East Brunswick, New Jersey 08816

Associated University Presses
69 Fleet Street
London EC4Y 1EU, England

Associated University Presses
Toronto M5E 1A7, Canada

**Library of Congress Cataloging in Publication Data**

Cotton, Nancy.
    Women playwrights in England, c1363-1750.

    Bibliography: p.
    Includes index.
    1. English drama—Women authors—History and
criticism.   2. English drama—17th century—History
and criticism.   3. English drama—18th century—
History and criticism.   4. Women dramatists,
English—Biography.   I.   Title.
PR635.W62C6 1980      822'009'9287      78-73155
ISBN 0-8387-2381-0

*Printed in the United States of America*

*For my sisters*
*Carol ~ Lea ~ Betty*

# Contents

# *Preface*

The professional woman author appeared in England in the seventeenth century, the great century of English drama. Not surprisingly, the first two publicly acclaimed women writers in England were both playwrights. Aphra Behn (c. 1640-1689) and Katherine Philips (1632-1664) had their first plays produced within a decade of each other; and for almost a century they were the most famous English women of letters. Their followers in the theater were women of colorful character, pioneers in a field that even today women seldom enter.

Playwrighting is in many ways the most difficult of all literary endeavors because of its public, collaborative nature. A dramatist must fit a play to a particular audience, a particular kind of theater, contemporary theatrical conventions, and, in the repertory system that obtained from Shakespeare's day until the end of the nineteenth century, a specific group of actors. Thus, theatrical apprenticeship of some sort is indispensable. The successful playwright, moreover, needs publicity, financial backing, and professional contacts. In a period when theatrical apprenticeship, money, and contacts were virtually impossible for women to obtain, in a period when, indeed, public life was improper for them, many women nonetheless wrote plays and a number of them succeeded as professional playwrights.

This study is intended as a biographical and critical survey of the women writing plays in England from the Middle Ages to the middle of the eighteenth century, many of whom are now largely unknown to students of literature. The opening chapter deals with the noblewomen of the Middle Ages and the Renaissance who were the precursors of Aphra Behn. Chapter 2 considers the career of Behn, the first woman in England to earn her living writing plays; the only woman writing for the stage in the 1670s and the 1680s, she was an often embattled minority of one. The 1690s saw lively discussion of women's intellectual abilities and advocacy of education for women by writers such as Mary Astell and Daniel Defoe. This decade produced a group of women playwrights conscious of themselves as a group with a novel place in the culture. The third chapter discusses these playwrights, labeled by their contemporaries the Female Wits. Instructed by their experiences, Susanna Centlivre, the subject of Chapter 4, achieved great theatrical popularity by adapting her talents to the decorums that the Augustan age required for women writers. Chapter 5 then looks at other women who wrote plays during the period 1670-1750. The last chapters analyze Restoration and eighteenth-century responses to women playwrights and the way in which these responses shaped not only the women's perceptions of themselves but also their subsequent literary reputations. My focus, then, is social and historical as well as biographical and critical.

Writing this essay has meant contending with unavoidable problems of research and documentation. Biography in the period, when it exists, is generalized and archetypical rather than specific and particular and has given rise to inaccurate, often sensational, statements that have been repeated by subsequent biographers until they have been accepted as facts. Much of what I have learned has been pieced together from scattered sources, such as letters, diaries, lampoons, broadsides, wills, newspapers, complimentary verses, prologues, and epilogues. To avoid a tiresome number of individual notes, I have, when feasible, summarized the state of scholarship in one omnibus footnote for each playwright. The best source of information has been the plays themselves. For the convenience of the reader, I have cited modern editions whenever these exist. I quote from early editions of unedited plays. In these cases, I have discarded nonfunctional italics for the sake of typographical simplicity and expanded speech tags for clarity. Most of these plays are in the microform collection *Three Centuries of English and American Plays*. A few women's plays are missing from this collection; I have recorded these omissions in the notes.

For the dates of premieres of plays, printed editions, and performances, for information about benefits, casting, and publication of songs, I have used *The London Stage 1660–1800*, edited by Emmett L. Avery et al., 5 pts in 11 vols., Carbondale, Illinois, 1960–68. I make a blanket citation now to this indispensable reference work in order to avoid an unwieldy number of individual notes. Plays prior to 1660 are in most cases dated according to Alfred Harbage, *Annals of English Drama 975–1700*, 2d ed., revised by S. Schoenbaum, Philadelphia, 1964. I have collated the information in these two works with G. E. Bentley, *The Jacobean and Caroline Stage*, 7 vols., Oxford, 1941–68, and Allardyce Nicoll, *A History of English Drama 1660–1900*, 4th ed., 6 vols., Cambridge, 1952–59. From these sources I have compiled a chronology of women's plays prior to 1750, which prefaces the text.

This study was supported by two grants from the Research Foundation of the City University of New York. I am grateful to the Houghton Library of Harvard University, the Beinecke Library of Yale University, and the libraries of Columbia University for making many rare volumes available to me. Baker Library of Dartmouth College kindly provided me with a study in which to write during the summers. For their advice and encouragement I am deeply indebted to Andrew V. Ettin, Johanna Ettin, Richard W. Pearse, Elizabeth Phillips, Lynne F. Sacher, and Robert N. Shorter.

Wake Forest University                              Nancy Cotton

# Acknowledgments

My thanks are due to William Heinemann Limited and Basil Blackwell Publisher Limited for permission to quote from *The Works of Aphra Behn*, edited by Montague Summers. Quotations from Nathan Comfort Starr's edition of *The Concealed Fansyes*, *PMLA* 46 (1931): 802–38, are by permission of the Modern Language Association of America. Quotations from *The Jacobean and Caroline Stage* by G. E. Bentley are by permission of Oxford University Press.

Portions of this study originally appeared in scholarly journals. Parts of chapter 1 are reprinted from "Katherine of Sutton: The First English Woman Playwright," *Educational Theatre Journal* 30 (December 1978): 475–81, by kind permission of the editor and the American Theatre Association; and from "Elizabeth Cary, Renaissance Playwright," *Texas Studies in Literature and Language* 18 (Winter 1977): 601–08, by kind permission of the University of Texas Press. Sections of chapter 3 are reprinted from "Mary Pix, Restoration Playwright," *Restoration and Eighteenth-Century Theatre Research* 15 (Spring 1976): 12–23, by kind permission of the editor.

## Chronology of Plays by Women in England to 1750

| Date | Author | Title | Type | Auspices |
|---|---|---|---|---|
| c. 1363–1376 | Katherine of Sutton | Depositio Crucis; Elevatio Crucis; Visitatio Sepulchri | Liturgical Drama | Barking Nunnery |
| c. 1550 | Lady Jane Lumley | Iphigeneia in Aulis | Tragedy (trans. Euripides) | Closet |
| c. 1561 | Queen Elizabeth I | Hercules Oetaeus (second chorus) | Tragedy (trans. Seneca) | Closet |
| 1590 | Countess of Pembroke | Antonie | Tragedy (trans. Garnier) | Closet |
| c. 1592 | Countess of Pembroke | Thenot and Piers in Praise of Astraea | Pastoral Dialogue | Ramsbury; Host: Pembroke |
| c. 1602–1605 | Viscountess Falkland | Unknown | Tragedy | Closet |
| | Viscountess Falkland | Mariam, the Fair Queen of Jewry | Tragedy | Closet |
| 1626 | Queen Henrietta Maria | Queen Henrietta's Masque | Masque | Court |
| 1635 | Queen Henrietta Maria(?) | Florimene | Pastoral | Court |
| c. 1644–46 | Lady Jane Cavendish and Lady Elizabeth Brackley | A Pastoral | Pastoral Dialogue | Closet |
| | Lady Jane Cavendish and Lady Elizabeth Brackley | The Concealed Fancies | Comedy | Closet |

15

| Date | Author | Title | Type | Auspices |
| --- | --- | --- | --- | --- |
| 1662 | Duchess of Newcastle | Plays | Dramatic Sketches | Closet |
| 1663 | Katherine Philips | Pompey | Tragedy (trans. Corneille) | Theatre Royal, Dublin |
| 1668 | Duchess of Newcastle | Plays Never Before Printed | Dramatic Sketches | Closet |
|  | Katherine Philips | Horace | Tragedy (trans. Corneille) | Court; Drury Lane |
| 1669 | Frances Boothby | Marcelia; or, The Treacherous Friend | Tragicomedy | Drury Lane |
| 1670 | Aphra Behn | The Forced Marriage; or, The Jealous Bridegroom | Tragicomedy | Lincoln's Inn Fields |
| 1671 | Elizabeth Polwhele | The Faithful Virgins | Tragedy | Lincoln's Inn Fields |
|  | Aphra Behn | The Amorous Prince; or, The Curious Husband | Comedy | Lincoln's Inn Fields |
|  | Elizabeth Polwhele | The Frolicks; or, The Lawyer Cheated | Comedy | Unacted |
| 1673 | Aphra Behn | The Dutch Lover | Comedy | Dorset Garden |
| 1675 | Aphra Behn(?) | The Woman Turned Bully | Comedy | Dorset Garden |
| 1676 | Aphra Behn | Abdelazer; or, The Moor's Revenge | Tragedy | Dorset Garden |
|  | Aphra Behn | The Town Fop; or, Sir Timothy Tawdrey | Comedy | Dorset Garden |
| 1677 | Aphra Behn | The Rover; or, The Banished Cavaliers | Comedy | Dorset Garden |

| Date | Author | Title | Type | Auspices |
|---|---|---|---|---|
| 1678 | Aphra Behn(?) | The Debauchee; or, The Credulous Cuckold | Comedy | Dorset Garden |
| | Aphra Behn(?) | The Counterfeit Bridegroom; or, The Defeated Widow | Comedy | Dorset Garden |
| 1679 | Aphra Behn | Sir Patient Fancy | Comedy | Dorset Garden |
| | "Ephelia" | Pair Royal of Coxcombs | Comedy | A Dancing School |
| | Aphra Behn | The Feigned Courtesans; or, A Night's Intrigue | Comedy | Dorset Garden |
| | Aphra Behn | The Young King; or, The Mistake | Tragicomedy | Dorset Garden |
| 1680 | Aphra Behn(?) | The Revenge; or, A Match in Newgate | Comedy | Dorset Garden |
| 1681 | Aphra Behn | The Rover, Part II | Comedy | Dorset Garden |
| | Aphra Behn | The False Count; or, A New Way to Play an Old Game | Comedy | Dorset Garden |
| 1682 | Aphra Behn | The Roundheads; or, The Good Old Cause | Comedy | Dorset Garden |
| | Aphra Behn | The City Heiress; or, Sir Timothy Treatall | Comedy | Dorset Garden |
| | Aphra Behn | Like Father Like Son; or, The Mistaken Brothers | Comedy | Dorset Garden |
| 1684 | Aphra Behn | The Wavering Nymph; or, Mad Amyntas | Pastoral | Unknown |

| Date | Author | Title | Type | Auspices |
|---|---|---|---|---|
| c. 1685 | Lady Anne Wharton | Love's Martyr; or, Wit Above Crowns | Tragedy | Unacted |
| 1686 | Aphra Behn | The Lucky Chance; or, An Alderman's Bargain | Comedy | Drury Lane |
| 1687 | Anne Killigrew | "A Pastoral Dialogue" | Pastoral Dialogue | Closet |
|  | Aphra Behn | The Emperor of the Moon | Farce | Dorset Garden |
| c. 1688 | Countess of Winchilsea | The Triumphs of Love and Innocence | Tragicomedy | Closet |
| 1689 | Aphra Behn | The Widow Ranter; or, The History of Bacon in Virginia | Tragicomedy | Drury Lane |
| c. 1690 | Countess of Winchilsea | Aristomenes; or, The Royal Shepherd | Tragedy | Closet |
| 1695 | "Ariadne" | She Ventures and He Wins | Comedy | Lincoln's Inn Fields |
| 1696 | Catherine Trotter | Agnes de Castro | Tragedy | Drury Lane |
|  | Aphra Behn | The Younger Brother; or, The Amorous Jilt | Comedy | Drury Lane |
|  | Delariviere Manley | The Lost Lover; or, The Jealous Husband | Comedy | Drury Lane |
|  | Delariviere Manley | The Royal Mischief | Tragedy | Lincoln's Inn Fields |
|  | Mary Pix | Ibrahim, the Thirteenth Emperor of the Turks | Tragedy | Drury Lane |
|  | Mary Pix | The Spanish Wives | Comedy | Dorset Garden |

| Date | Author | Title | Type | Auspices |
|---|---|---|---|---|
| 1697 | Mary Pix | The Innocent Mistress | Comedy | Lincoln's Inn Fields |
| | Mary Pix | The Deceiver Deceived | Comedy | Lincoln's Inn Fields |
| 1698 | Catherine Trotter | Fatal Friendship | Tragedy | Lincoln's Inn Fields |
| | Mary Pix | Queen Catherine; or, The Ruins of Love | Tragedy | Lincoln's Inn Fields |
| 1699 | Mary Pix | The False Friend; or, The Fate of Disobedience | Tragedy | Lincoln's Inn Fields |
| 1700 | Mary Pix | The Beau Defeated; or, The Lucky Younger Brother | Comedy | Lincoln's Inn Fields |
| | Susanna Centlivre | The Perjured Husband; or, The Adventures in Venice | Tragicomedy | Drury Lane |
| | Catherine Trotter | Love at a Loss; or, Most Votes Carry It | Comedy | Drury Lane |
| 1701 | Catherine Trotter | The Unhappy Penitent | Tragedy | Drury Lane |
| | Mary Pix | The Double Distress | Tragedy | Lincoln's Inn Fields |
| | Mary Pix | The Czar of Muscovy | Tragedy | Lincoln's Inn Fields |
| | Jane Wiseman | Antiochus the Great; or, The Fatal Relapse | Tragedy | Lincoln's Inn Fields |
| 1702 | Susanna Centlivre | The Beau's Duel; or, A Soldier for the Ladies | Comedy | Lincoln's Inn Fields |
| | Susanna Centlivre | The Stolen Heiress; or, The Salamanca Doctor Outplotted | Comedy | Lincoln's Inn Fields |

| Date | Author | Title | Type | Auspices |
|---|---|---|---|---|
| 1703 | Susanna Centlivre | Love's Contrivance; or, Le Medecin Malgre Lui | Comedy | Drury Lane |
| | Mary Pix | The Different Widows; or, Intrigue All-A-Mode | Comedy | Lincoln's Inn Fields |
| 1705 | Susanna Centlivre | The Gamester | Comedy | Lincoln's Inn Fields |
| | Mary Pix | The Conquest of Spain | Tragedy | Haymarket |
| 1706 | Susanna Centlivre | The Basset Table | Comedy | Drury Lane |
| | "A Young Lady" | The Faithful General | Tragedy | Haymarket |
| | Catherine Trotter | The Revolution of Sweden | Tragedy | Haymarket |
| | Susanna Centlivre | Love at a Venture | Comedy | New Theatre, Bath |
| | Mary Pix | The Adventures in Madrid | Comedy | Haymarket |
| | Susanna Centlivre | The Platonick Lady | Comedy | Haymarket |
| | Delariviere Manley | Almyna; or, The Arabian Vow | Tragedy | Haymarket |
| 1709 | Susanna Centlivre | The Busy Body | Comedy | Drury Lane |
| | Susanna Centlivre | The Man's Bewitched; or, The Devil to Do About Her | Comedy | Haymarket |
| 1710 | Susanna Centlivre | Mar-Plot; or, The Second Part of the Busy Body | Comedy | Drury Lane |

| Date | Author | Title | Type | Auspices |
|---|---|---|---|---|
| 1712 | Susanna Centlivre | A Bickerstaff's Burying; or, Work for the Upholders | Farce | Drury Lane |
| 1714 | Susanna Centlivre | The Perplexed Lovers | Comedy | Drury Lane |
| 1714 | Susanna Centlivre | The Wonder: A Woman Keeps A Secret | Comedy | Drury Lane |
| 1715 | Susanna Centlivre | The Gotham Election | Farce | Unacted |
| 1715 | Susanna Centlivre | A Wife Well Managed | Farce | Unacted (until 1724) |
| 1716 | Mary Davys | The Northern Heiress; or, The Humours of York | Comedy | Lincoln's Inn Fields |
| 1717 | Susanna Centlivre | The Cruel Gift | Tragedy | Drury Lane |
| 1717 | Delariviere Manley | Lucius, the First Christian King of Britain | Tragedy | Drury Lane |
| 1718 | Susanna Centlivre | A Bold Stroke for a Wife | Comedy | Lincoln's Inn Fields |
| 1719 | Mrs. Aubert | Harlequin-Hydaspes; or, The Greshamite | Mock Opera | Lincoln's Inn Fields |
| 1721 | Eliza Haywood | The Fair Captive | Tragedy | Lincoln's Inn Fields |
| 1722 | Susanna Centlivre | The Artifice | Comedy | Drury Lane |
| 1723 | Eliza Haywood | A Wife to Be Let | Comedy | Drury Lane |
| 1725 | Mary Davys | The Self Rival | Comedy | Unacted |
| 1729 | Eliza Haywood | Frederick, Duke of Brunswick-Lunenburgh | Tragedy | Lincoln's Inn Fields |

| Date | Author | Title | Type | Auspices |
|---|---|---|---|---|
| 1730 | Penelope Aubin | The Merry Masqueraders; or, The Humorous Cuckold | Comedy | Haymarket |
| 1732 | Mrs. Egleton | The Maggot | Ballad Opera | Lincoln's Inn Fields |
| 1733 | Eliza Haywood | The Opera of Operas; or, Tom Thumb the Great | Burlesque | Haymarket |
| 1735 | Elizabeth Cooper | The Rival Widows; or, Fair Libertine | Comedy | Covent Garden |
|  | Charlotte Charke | The Carnival; or, Harlequin Blunderer | Comedy | Lincoln's Inn Fields |
|  | Charlotte Charke | The Art of Management; or, Tragedy Expelled | Satire | York Buildings |
| 1736 | Elizabeth Cooper | The Nobleman; or, The Family Quarrel | Comedy | Haymarket |
| 1737 | Mrs. Weddell | The City Farce | Farce | Unacted |
| 1739 | Elizabeth Boyd | Don Sancho; or, The Students Whim | Ballad Opera | Unacted |
| 1742 | Mrs. Weddell | Incle and Yarico | Tragedy | Unacted |
| 1743 | Charlotte Charke | Tit for Tat; or, The Comedy and Tragedy of War | Puppet Show(?) | James Street |
| c. 1745 | Mary Leapor | The Unhappy Father | Tragedy | Unacted |
| 1747 | Mrs. Hoper | The Battle of Poictiers; or, The English Prince | Tragedy | Goodman's Fields |

| Date | Author | Title | Type | Auspices |
|------|--------|-------|------|----------|
| 1748 | Mrs. Hoper | *The Cyclopedia* | Farce | Haymarket |
|      | Letitia Pilkington | *The Turkish Court; or, London Prentice* | Comedy | Little Theatre, Dublin |
|      | Letitia Pilkington | *The Roman Father* (one act) | Tragedy | Unacted |
| 1749 | Mrs. Hoper | *Queen Tragedy Restored* | Burlesque | Haymarket |
| 1750 | Catherine Clive | *The Rehearsal; or, Bays in Petticoats* | Burlesque | Drury Lane |

*Women Playwrights in England*

# Women Playwrights in England

## [ 1 ]

## Renaissance Noblewomen

*The* first recorded woman playwright in England was Katherine of Sutton, abbess of Barking nunnery in the fourteenth century. Between 1363 and 1376 the abbess rewrote the Easter dramatic offices because the people attending the paschal services were becoming increasingly cool in their devotions ("deuocione frigessere"). Wishing to excite devotion at such a crowded, important festival ("desiderans ... fidelium deuocionem ad tam celebrem celebracionem magis excitare"), Lady Katherine produced unusually lively adaptations of the traditional liturgical plays.[1] Particularly interesting is her *elevatio crucis,* one of the few surviving liturgical plays that contains a representation of the harrowing of hell. In the *visitatio sepulchri* that follows, the three Marys are acted not by male clerics, which was customary, but by nuns.[2] The Barking plays are not unique, however, in showing the participation of nuns. In religious houses on the continent women sometimes acted in church dramas, and Hrotsvitha of Gandersheim and Hildegard of Bingen wrote Latin religious plays.

27

Although the destruction of liturgical texts in England at the Reformation makes certainty impossible, it is likely, in view of the uniformity of medieval European culture and the considerable authority of women who headed the medieval nunneries, that other English abbesses contributed to the slow, anonymous, communal growth of the medieval religious drama.

Katherine of Sutton was a baroness in her own right by virtue of her position as abbess of Barking.[3] Only women of similar rank wrote drama in England until the Restoration. Virginia Woolf in her fable of Shakespeare's sister in *A Room of One's Own* (New York, 1929) was of course right in her statement that no middle-class woman, however talented, could have written for the Elizabethan public theaters. But Renaissance noblewomen, although they shared some of the disabilities of middle-class women, nonetheless wrote closet dramas, masques, and pastoral entertainments.

The English Renaissance fostered rigorous classical training for ladies, who, like male humanists, translated the ancients. The earliest extant English translation of a Greek play was the work of Lady Jane Fitzalan Lumley (c. 1537–77), who made a free and abridged prose version of Euripides' *Iphigeneia in Aulis*.[4] Lady Lumley probably translated Euripides shortly after her marriage at the age of twelve. This precocious marvel worked directly from the Greek at a time when secondhand translation from Latin was much more usual. The Latin tragedies of Seneca of course found many translators. Even Queen Elizabeth, during the early years of her reign, sometime around 1561, translated the chorus of Act II of *Hercules Oetaeus*.[5]

Imitations of Senecan tragedy were popular in aristocratic and academic circles. An influential figure in this tradition was Mary Sidney Herbert, Countess of Pembroke (1561–1621).[6] Mary Sidney studied at home with private tutors and attained proficiency in French, Italian, probably

Latin, and perhaps Hebrew. At the queen's request, she lived for a time at court, which served her as a finishing school. When she was sixteen, her parents married her to Henry Herbert, Earl of Pembroke, a match economically and politically advantageous, even though the earl was nearly thirty years older than Mary. After her marriage Mary Herbert lived at Wilton House, the earl's home in Wiltshire, where she had four children, collected a notable library, and became famous as a translator, patron of literature, and editor of the *Arcadia*. The countess's dramatic activity grew out of her close relationship with her brother, Sir Philip Sidney (1554–86). In his *Defence of Poesie* Philip attacked English romantic drama, advocating instead the classical drama of Seneca. He admired a play "full of stately speeches, and wel sounding phrases, clyming to the height of Seneca his style, and as full of notable morallitie, which it dooth most delightfully teach."[7]

After Philip's death Mary translated the *Marc-Antoine* of Robert Garnier (1534–90), the most assured French Senecan dramatist, whose eight tragedies were notable for their vigorous but polished style. Written in 1590, the countess's *Antonie* transforms rhymed French alexandrines into pedestrian blank verse. Rather better are the choral lyrics, written in a variety of meters and rhymes. Here, for example, is the opening of the chorus to Act III:

> Alas, with what tormenting fire
> Us martireth this blinde desire
>    To staie our life from flieng!
> How ceasleslie our minds doth rack,
> How heavie lies upon our back
>    This dastard feare of dieng!
> *Death* rather healthfull succor gives,
> *Death* rather all mishapps relieves
>    That life upon us throweth:
> And ever to us doth unclose
> The doore, wherby from curelesse woes
>    Our wearie soule out goeth.[8]

The Countess of Pembroke had *Antonie* printed in 1592 and thus became the first woman in England to publish a play. *Antonie* was reprinted in 1595, 1600, 1606, and 1607;[9] although unacted, it was widely influential. Swayed by example, or coerced by friendship or patronage, members of the countess's circle turned out numerous Senecan imitations. Among the earliest, oddly enough, was a translation of Garnier's *Cornelie* made in 1594 by Thomas Kyd, who, as author of *The Spanish Tragedy* (1587), was the chief exponent at the time of the blood-and-thunder action drama. Presumably hoping for patronage, Kyd promised a translation of *Porcie,* but this never appeared. Samuel Daniel, long a protégé of the countess, wrote *Cleopatra* (1593) and *Philotas* (1604), the best of the plays on the Pembroke model. Samuel Brandon in 1598 published *The Virtuous Octavia.* Fulke Greville, Lord Brooke, Philip Sidney's friend and later biographer, wrote *Mustapha* and *Alaham* in the late 1590s, and in the next decade William Alexander, Earl of Stirling, published *Darius, Croesus,* and *The Alexandraean Tragedy.*

The countess also published a dramatic dialogue, which she wrote for the royal entertainment about 1592, when she was expecting a visit from the queen. A pastoral containing ten six-line stanzas, *Thenot and Piers in Praise of Astraea* was published in 1602 in the anthology *A Poetical Rhapsody,* which went through four editions by 1621. In each of the ten stanzas, Thenot's praise of Astraea (goddess of justice, a poetical name for Queen Elizabeth) is criticized by his fellow shepherd Piers. The last stanza, in a graceful turn of compliment, discloses why Piers is dissatisfied at praise of the queen:

> Thenot.   Then Piers, of friendship tell me why,
>   My meaning true, my words should ly,
>     And strive in vaine to raise her.

Piers.   Words from conceit do only rise,
            Above conceit her honour flies;
            But silence, nought can praise her.[10]

This is the first original dramatic verse written by a woman
to appear in print.

Before the Countess of Pembroke died, and probably
because of her example, an Englishwoman for the first
time wrote and published a full-length original play. This
was Elizabeth Tanfield Cary, later Viscountess Falkland
(1586–1639). More is known about Elizabeth Cary than
about most figures of the period because one of her
daughters wrote a detailed biography of her mother.[11]
Lady Falkland was the only child and heiress of a wealthy
Oxford lawyer, Lawrence Tanfield, later Sir Lawrence and
Lord Chief Baron of the Exchequer. She was startlingly
precocious, teaching herself French, Spanish, Italian,
Latin, Hebrew, and "Transylvanian" (*Life*, p. 5). She loved
to read so much that she sat up all night. When her parents
refused her candles, she bribed the maids to smuggle them
in; by the age of twelve she had run up a debt to them of a
hundred pounds "with two hundred more for the like
bargains and promises" (*Life*, p. 7), a considerable sum in
those days even for an heiress. As a child she made
translations from Latin and French and at twelve found
internal contradictions in Calvin's *Institutes of Religion*—
upsetting behavior for a child of good Protestants.

About the age of fifteen or sixteen Elizabeth Tanfield
was married to a knight's son named Henry Cary. After
the marriage had secured the Tanfield fortune, Henry
followed the custom of the times and left his bride with her
parents while he finished his military service abroad.
During this period, sometime between 1602 and 1605,
Elizabeth Cary, who, according to her daughter, loved
plays "extremely" (*Life*, p. 54), wrote two closet dramas.
Cary's first play was set in Sicily and dedicated to her

husband; the title is unknown and the play is lost. Her second play, dedicated to her sister-in-law, was *Mariam, the Fair Queen of Jewry*.

A Senecan tragedy based on Josephus's *Antiquities*, *Mariam* is carefully researched and constructed. The play is attentive to historical details but also is sensitive to dramatic effectiveness. As the play opens, rumor has just reached Jerusalem that Caesar has executed Herod at Rome. The first half of the play shows the effects of this news. Queen Mariam is torn between grief for her husband and joy. She rejoices at Herod's death because he had killed her brother and grandfather and because he had left orders for her own death in case he did not return. Pheroras, now happily freed from his brother's authority, immediately makes a love marriage with his maid Graphina. Herod's cast-off first wife Doris now hopes to unseat Mariam's children as heirs and install her own son Antipater on the throne. Only Salome regrets the loss of Herod, but her sorrow is self-interested. She wishes to marry her Arabian lover Silleus. If Herod were alive, she could accuse her husband Constabarus of treason for protecting the two sons of Baba. Salome also hates Mariam, but sees no way to remove her haughty sister-in-law. While these events are underway, constant pointers remind us that the characters believe the rumor of Herod's death because they wish to.

The reversal comes in 3.2 with the news that Herod is alive and will arrive immediately. Herod's delight as he returns in Act 4 is short-lived. Salome now has the upper hand and her machinations lead to the catastrophe. She offers to protect Pheroras and his bride if he will accuse Constabarus of treason. She tricks Herod into believing that Mariam has been unfaithful in his absence. Herod, a man of impulse, orders the executions of Constabarus, Baba's sons, and his own beloved queen. In Act 5 a nuntius recounts to Herod the noble death of Mariam. He also reports that Salome's agent in the plot against Mariam has confessed and committed suicide. Herod now realizes the magnitude of his loss and becomes frantic with grief.

The play is a sophisticated performance for a largely self-educated person of seventeen. Cary is careful with details, and the absence of anachronisms is unusual in the period. Stylistically and dramaturgically, the play is competently though conventionally Senecan. Action is discussed rather than dramatized, and the gory details of the execution are properly left to a nuntius. Cary uses literarily varied prosody instead of the dramatically supple blank verse of her theatrical contemporaries. *Mariam* is written in rhymed quatrains, with occasional couplets and sonnets inserted. Cary has, however, infused this dramatically awkward mixture of verse forms with emotional intensity at key points.

Salome, for example, is most convincing when she meditates an unorthodox method of removing Constabarus so that she can marry Silleus:

> He loves, I love; what then can be the cause,
> Keepes me f[rom] being the Arabians wife?
> It is the principles of Moses lawes,
> For Con[s]tabarus still remaines in life,
> If he to me did beare as Earnest hate,
> As I to him, for him there were an ease,
> A separating bill might free his fate:
> From such a yoke that did so much displease.
> Why should such priviledge to man be given?
> Or given to them, why bard from women then?
> Are men then we in greater grace with Heaven?
> Or cannot women hate as well as men?
> Ile be the custome-breaker: and beginne
> To shew my Sexe the way to freedomes doore. . . .
>                                   (sig. B3ʳ)

In the Renaissance this was of course villainess talk, but
villainess or not, Salome was ahead of her time in her
attitude toward equitable divorce laws.

The active and lustful Salome makes a provocative contrast with the passive and chaste Mariam, who initiates no
action whatever, not even to save her own life. As she is
facing death, she decides that her fault was a sullenness of
temper that prevented her from defending herself. She
feels guilty because she had placed her full reliance on her
chastity of body without giving her husband her chastity of
spirit; she had, then, been guilty of a certain infidelity of
mind. This seems a harsh self-accusation for a woman
whose husband had murdered two of her close relatives,
but her conclusion is nonetheless reinforced by the
chorus's strong statement of the duties of wives:

> When to their Husbands they themselves doe bind,
> Doe they not wholy give themselves away?
> Or give they but their body not their mind,
> Reserving that though best, for others pray?
>   No sure, their thoughts no more can be their owne,
>   And therefore should to none but one be knowne.
>
> Then she usurpes upon anothers right,
> That seekes to be by publike language grac't:
> And though her thoughts reflect with purest light,
> Her mind if not peculiar is not chast.
>   For in a wife it is no worse to finde,
>   A common body, then a common minde.
>                                        (sig. E4<sup>r</sup>)

These are hard beliefs for a woman who wished to be a
writer.

The vividness of Cary's treatment of Mariam and Salome
suggests that she had the range of emotional experience
and the imaginative power to appreciate both attitudes
toward experience. Cary apparently entered marriage

with an impossible idealization of wifely behavior, which she expresses through Mariam, and with an even more impossible ideal of an independent, even rebellious, intellectual life, embodied in Salome. These deeply ambivalent attitudes shaped the remainder of her life. An intellectual heiress of Catholic leanings joined with a careerist courtier in a Protestant court, Cary lived with her husband twenty years, during which she bore eleven children and was nearly always either pregnant or nursing. Her intellectual and artistic talents found their only outlet in religion. During her marriage she continued to read theology and discussed religious doctrines with distinguished prelates. At the same time, she acted out her ideals of wifely behavior. She taught her children to love their father better than their mother. She acceded to husband's wishes that she become a fashionable dresser and an accomplished horsewoman, despite her indifference to clothes and terror of horses. She mortgaged her jointure to advance her husband's career, whereupon her father disinherited her in favor of her oldest son, Lucius Cary, who also inherited his mother's literary talent. It is not surprising that she had periods of depression severe to the point of mental illness. Meanwhile, Henry Cary achieved a seat on the Privy Council, the rank of viscount, and the Lord Chief Deputyship of Ireland.

In 1626 Lady Falkland rebelled. She converted to Catholicism, nearly ruining her husband's career. He repaid her by abandoning her, taking custody of her children, and stripping her house of the bare necessities of life. Lady Falkland's poverty and suffering were severe; for long periods she lived in semistarvation. She appealed to the court for help (Queen Henrietta Maria was a French Catholic) and finally in 1627 the Privy Council ordered Lord Falkland to support his wife, although seven months later he still had not complied with the order. Lady Falkland turned again to writing, producing a life of Edward II, poems to the Virgin, and lives of saints. She translated Catholic polemics; her translation of Cardinal Perron's reply to King James was publicly burned. Lady Falkland kept her rebellious spirit to the end. In her last years she kidnapped two of her sons and, defying the Star Chamber, smuggled them to the continent to become Catholics.

Given the outward docility of Elizabeth Cary's married life until 1626, it is strange that *Mariam* was ever published. None of her other creative works were printed, and *Mariam* was not entered for publication until 1612, ten years after it was written, and did not actually appear until 1613. Her daughter claims, "She writ many things for her private recreation . . . one of them was after stolen out of that sister-in-law's (her friend's) chamber, and printed, but by her own procurement was called in" (*Life,* p. 9). This explanation is suspect for a number of reasons, not the least of which is that the Stationers' Register shows that there was nothing surreptitious about the publication of the play.[12] Moreover, Lady Falkland's daughter makes the standard excuse of the period for an aristocrat who stoops to publication. Cary herself scorns such excuses in the introduction to her translation of Cardinal Perron: "I will not make use of that worn form of saying I printed it against my will, moved by the importunity of friends."[13]

A more likely explanation is that the publication of *Mariam* was inspired by the Countess of Pembroke. Both Mary Herbert and Elizabeth Cary were well acquainted with John Davies of Hereford, the famous master of calligraphy. Davies was a protégé and intimate of the Pembroke circle; he made a beautiful manuscript of Philip Sidney and Mary Herbert's translation of the psalms. He was also Elizabeth Cary's writing master. Davies must have spoken to his brilliant young pupil about his distinguished patroness and her activities. Indeed, the immediate cause

that prompted Cary to publish her play may have been a
poem by Davies. In 1612 he prefaced his "Muse's Sacrifice,
or Divine Meditations" with a poetical dedicatory letter to
the Countess of Pembroke, the Countess of Bedford, and
Elizabeth Cary. Davies compliments the Countess of Pembroke for her psalms and then praises "Cary, of whom
Minerva stands in feare":

> Thou mak'st Melpomen proud, and my Heart great
>     of such a Pupill, who, in Buskin fine,
> With Feete of State, dost make thy Muse to mete
>     the scenes of Syracuse and Palestine.
> ...............................................
> Such nervy Limbes of Art, and Straines of Wit
>     Times past ne'er knew the weaker Sexe to have;
> And Times to come, will hardly credit it,
>     if thus thou give thy Workes both Birth and Grave.[14]

Davies then chides all three ladies because they "presse the
Presse with little" they have written. Could the woman who
wrote Salome's speech resist the appeal for publication on
behalf of her sex's honor? *Mariam* was entered for publication in December of the same year as the appearance of
Davies's poem. However *Mariam* came to be printed, and
so preserved, it was never intended for acting. Neither the
Countess of Pembroke nor Viscountess Falkland wrote
their plays for the stage; *Antonie* and *Mariam* were written
as closet drama. To write for the public stage was déclassé.
It was a queen who broke down this barrier of caste and
helped break down also the barriers against actresses.

   Queen Henrietta Maria (1609–69) arrived in England at
the age of sixteen as the bride of Charles I.[15] In 1626,
during her first year in her new country, the young
queen acted at court in a pastoral play and masque that she
herself wrote and directed. The play, which has been lost,
was written in French and performed by the French ladies

who attended the queen. Letters of Englishmen commenting on the occasion show the dismay produced even in an audience carefully handpicked: "On Shrovetuisday the Quene and her women had a maske or pastorall play at Somerset House, wherin herself acted a part, and some of the rest were disguised like men with beards. I have knowne the time when this wold have seemed a straunge sight, to see a Quene act in a play but *tempora mutantur et nos.*" "I heare not much honor of the Quene's maske, for, if they were not all, soome were in men's apparell." Ambassadors from continental courts were more sophisticated. The Venetian ambassador admired the "rich scenery and dresses" and the "remarkable acting" of the queen. "The king and court enjoyed it, those present being picked and selected, but it did not give complete satisfaction, because the English objected to the first part being declaimed by the queen." The ambassador from Florence was equally complimentary: "She acted in a beautiful pastoral of her own composition, assisted by twelve of her ladies whom she had trained since Christmas. The pastoral succeeded admirably; not only in the decorations and changes of scenery, but also in the acting and recitation of the ladies—Her Majesty surpassing all the others. The performance was conducted as privately as possible, inasmuch as it is an unusual thing in this country to see the Queen upon a stage; the audience consequently was limited to a few of the nobility, expressly invited, no others being admitted."[16] The English disapproval of the queen's performing a role on stage must have come as a surprise to Henrietta Maria. She had been reared in a court where nobility and even royalty acted in masques and plays. Her brother Louis XIII as a child led his brothers and sisters in amateur theatricals.

Although she has been suggested as the author of the anonymous lost pastoral *Florimene,* presented by the queen's ladies at court in December 1635, Henrietta Maria apparently wrote no more plays, but her incorrigible love of acting liberalized aristocratic attitudes toward actresses. After the disapproval of her 1626 court performance, she continued to have amateur theatricals in her private apartments and to dance in court masques. In 1633 she took the chief part in another play, *The Shepherd's Paradise,* written by the courtier Walter Montague for her and her ladies. Again there was a furor. Puritan William Prynne had the bad luck to publish *Histriomastix,* his attack on the stage, within a few days of the queen's performance. Prynne inopportunely denounced "Women-Actors, notorious whores": "And dare then any Christian woman be so more then whorishly impudent, as to act, to speak publicly on a Stage (perchance in man's apparel, and cut hair, here proved sinful and abominable) in the presence of sundry men and women?"[17] Prynne was condemned to have his ears cut off, the queen continued to act, amateur theatricals became common in polite circles, and by 1660 the profession of acting on the public stage was open to women. The admission of actresses to the stage was important for women playwrights because as actresses women for the first time obtained practical theatrical apprenticeship. By the eighteenth century there would be a number of actress-playwrights.

Henrietta Maria helped transform aristocratic attitudes not only toward actresses but also toward the commercial stage. She was the first English queen to attend plays at public theaters. Her considerable power over her husband caused Charles I to do what no English king had done before—he looked over scripts and even suggested plots for several plays written by others. The queen introduced from France the cults of *préciosité* and Platonic love and persuaded courtiers like Cartwright and Carlell to write plays illustrating her pet theories; thus the gentleman playwright came into existence. By the Restoration persons of the highest social rank in England were writing for the public stage.

This upper-class interest in playwrighting is seen in Lady Jane Cavendish (1621–69) and her sister Lady Elizabeth Brackley (c. 1623–63).[18] The Cavendish sisters, daughters of William Cavendish, Duke of Newcastle, were, by both upbringing and marriage, part of the world of aristocratic theatricals. Before the war their father was a patron of the playwrights Brome, Shirley, and Jonson. In 1633 and 1634 Jonson wrote entertainments for the king's visits to the Newcastle estates; perhaps Jane and Elizabeth were present. About 1640 *The Country Captain,* publicly attributed to Newcastle but largely written by James Shirley, was performed at the Blackfriars Theater. Lord Brackley, Elizabeth's future husband, in 1634 appeared with the king in Thomas Carew's masque *Coelum Britannicum.* The same year Brackley acted in Milton's *Comus* at Ludlow Castle; his sister and brother were also principal performers, their parents the chief spectators. With this background, it is not surprising that the Cavendish sisters should themselves write plays.

Sometime between 1644 and 1646, the young women, both in their early twenties, collaborated on two plays. *A Pastoral* remains in manuscript, but *The Concealed Fansyes* was published in 1931. The authors here had promising raw material but were unable to construct a coherent plot. The story line, clumsily handled, shows a sound and simple comedic pattern: Two sisters, Lucenay and Tattiney, are wooed by Courtly and Presumption. The men plan to tame their wives after marriage, but the women turn the tables and tame their husbands. The dialogue reflects the concerns of the authors as heiresses. Lucenay and Tattiney repeatedly and bluntly discuss marriage as the buying and selling of heiresses for dowries and estates.

Lucenay dreads marriage: "My distruction is that when I marry Courtly I shall bee condemn'd to looke upon my Nose, whenever I walke and when I sitt at meate confin'd by his grave winke to looke upon the Salt, and if it bee but the paireing of his Nales to admire him" (p. 815). After her marriage she describes how she escaped this servility. By refusing to keep her place, she throws her husband into a

> conflict, betwixt Anger and mallencholly not knoweinge whether my behaviour proceeded from neglect or ignorance, then hee declared himselfe by allygory and praysed a Lady, obedyent ffoole in towne, and swore hir Husband was the happyest man in the world. I replyed shee was a Very good Lady, and I accounted him happy that was hir Husband, that hee could content himselfe with such a Meachanick wife. I wishe sayd hee shee might bee your Example, and you have noe reason to sleight hir, for shee is of a noble family. I knowe that sayd I, and doe the more admire why shee will contract hir family, Noblenes and Birth, to the servitude of hir husband, as if hee had bought hir his slave, and I'm sure hir Father bought him for hir, for hee gave a good Portion, and now in sense who should obey? (pp. 834–35)

The conversational patterns are convincing; the use of indirect conversation suggests a writing skill born of epistolary, rather than dramatic, cultivation.

After collaborating with her sister in *The Concealed Fansyes,* Lady Jane Cavendish was present during the military action when the Parliamentarians captured and recaptured her home, Welbeck Abbey. She saved the art treasures of Bolsover Castle, another of the Newcastle estates. She raised money for her exiled father by selling her jewels and plate and sent him a thousand pounds of her private fortune. She refused to marry until the age of thirty-three because she refused anyone but a royalist, and at the time most royalists were in exile. After her marriage, she bore three children and continued to write, producing several volumes of verse. Nothing further is known of Lady Brackley.

The Cavendish sisters' young stepmother, Margaret Cavendish, Duchess of Newcastle (1623–73), was the first woman in England to publish collections of plays and England's first feminist playwright.[19] Her career as a prolific writer is surprising in view of her secluded upbringing and poor education. She was born Margaret Lucas, youngest of the eight children of a wealthy country gentleman who died before she was two, leaving the family affairs in the strong hands of his wife. The family was exceptionally close-knit and exclusive, drawing the sons- and daughters-in-law into the family orbit. Margaret, as the youngest, grew up painfully shy of strangers. As a child she was indulged in her habit of wearing clothes of her own flamboyant design, one of the trademarks of the "eccentricity" for which she was later notorious among her contemporaries. Her education was undisciplined. After the death of Queen Elizabeth, a reaction had set in against rigorous studies for gentlewomen. Margaret describes an education almost negative: "As for tutors, although we had for all sorts of virtues, as singing, dancing, playing on music, reading, writing, working, and the like, yet we were not kept strictly thereto, they were rather for formality than benefit; for my mother cared not so much for our dancing and fiddling, singing and prating of several languages, as that we should be bred virtuously, modestly, civilly, honorably, and on honest principles."[20] Her lack of education marred all her writing; she never absorbed some elementary principles of grammar, and the idea of revision was unknown to her. Later in life, Margaret felt keenly her lack of learning and spoke strongly for education for women.

At the age of twenty, the bashful Margaret Lucas as-

tonished her family (and her biographers) by attending
the distressed Queen Henrietta Maria as a maid of honor
and then following the queen into exile in France. The
explanation of her puzzling behavior is that Margaret was
a female cavalier, whose romantic gesture for a lost cause
was in the spirit of the age. In France she met and married
the exiled Marquis, later Duke, of Newcastle, thirty years
her senior, whom she adored with fervent hero worship.
Her marriage was an ideal one for a seventeenth-century
woman writer. William Cavendish was himself an amateur
poet and playwright, and a generous patron of writers,
philosophers, and artists. He encouraged and assisted his
young, beautiful, childless wife in her writing, her
"chiefest delight and greatest pastime" (*Plays Never Before
Printed*, 1668). She describes their relationship in a letter to
the duke in her *Philosophical and Physical Opinions* (1663):
"Though I am as Industrious and Carefull to serve Your
Lordship in such imployments, which belong to a Wife, as
Household affairs, as ever I can . . . yet I cannot for my
Life be so good a Huswife, as to quit Writing. . . . you are
pleased to Peruse my Works, and Approve of them so well,
as to give me Leave to Publish them, which is a Favour, few
Husbands would grant their Wives; But Your Lordship is
an Extraordinary Husband, which is the Happiness of
Your Lordships Honest Wife and Humble Servant Mar-
garet Newcastle."

After her marriage, she began, out of ambition, to write
with a view to publication: "I am very ambitious, yet 'tis
neither for beauty, wit, titles, wealth, or power, but as they
are steps to raise me to Fame's tower, which is to live by
remembrance in afterages."[21] This desire for fame is the
key to her personality.[22] She saw literature as the only
avenue to renown for a woman:

> I confess my Ambition is restless, and not ordinary;
> because it would have an extraordinary fame: And since

all heroick Actions, publick Imployments, powerfull Governments, and eloquent Pleadings are denyed our Sex in this age, or at least would be condemned for want of custome, is the cause I write so much.

(An Epistle to my Readers, *Natures Pictures,* 1656)

The first Englishwoman to publish extensively, the duchess produced a dozen books, including poetry, fiction, scientific and philosophical speculations, letters, and declamations. She was the first woman in England to publish her autobiography, the first to publish a biography of her husband, the first to write about science.

In 1662 the duchess published *Plays,* a collection of closet dramas written while she was abroad. The volume includes fourteen plays, several in two parts. In 1668 she brought out a smaller collection, *Plays Never Before Printed,* which includes five plays and various dramatic fragments. In these volumes are some of the most ardently feminist plays ever written. In Part II of *Loves Adventures,* for example, Lady Orphan, disguised as the page Affectionata, wins great fame as a soldier; the Venetian States make her Lieutenant-General of the army and a member of the Council of War. The Pope invites Affectionata to Rome and offers to make her a cardinal.

Another military woman, Lady Victoria, appears in *Bell in Campo.* Refusing to be left at home when her husband goes to war, Lady Victoria raises a female army and accompanies the men to battle. Victoria points out to her troops that masculine contempt for feminine ability ultimately rests on the physical weakness of women, but urges that right education could make women good soldiers, "for Time and Custome is the Father and Mother of Strength and Knowledge" (*Plays,* p. 588). She urges:

Now or never is the time to prove the courage of our Sex, to get liberty and freedome from the Female Slav-

ery, and to make our selves equal with men: for shall
Men only sit in Honours chair, and Women stand as
waiters by? shall only Men in Triumphant Chariots ride,
and Women run as Captives by? shall only men be
Conquerors, and women Slaves? shall only men live by
Fame, and women dy in Oblivion?

(*Plays*, p. 609)

Encouraged by Victoria, the woman army achieves heroic
exploits, rescuing the men from military disaster. They are
rewarded after the war with special privileges. Lady Victoria herself is given a public triumph, a suit of gold
armor, and a sword with a diamond hilt; her statue is set
up in the center of the city.

In *Youth's Glory and Death's Banquet* Sir Thomas Father
Love, over the objections of Lady Mother Love, is rearing
their daughter, Lady Sanspareille, with an education masculine and intellectual:

Mother Love. What? would you have women bred up
to swear, swagger, gaming, drinking, whoring, as most
men are?
Father Love. No, Wife, I would have them bred in
learned Schools, to noble Arts and Sciences, as wise men
are.
Mother Love. What Arts? to ride Horses, and fight
Dewels.
Father Love. Yes, if it be to defend their Honour,
Countrey, Religion; For noble Arts makes not base
Vices, nor is the cause of lewd actions, nor is unseemly
for any Sex. . . .

(*Plays*, p. 124)

Lady Sanspareille is melancholy because of her desire for
fame, which she describes in words like those that Margaret used about herself: "Know it is fame I covet, for
which were the ambitions of Alexander and Caesar joyned
into one mind, mine doth exceed them . . . my mind being

restless to get to the highest place in Fames high Tower; and I had rather fall in the adventure, than never try to climb." She despairs that she may not have "a sufficient stock of merit, or if I had, yet no waies to advance it" (*Plays*, p. 130). She resolves, with her father's consent, never to marry, but to devote herself to poetry:

> for that time which will be lost in a married condition, I will study and work with my own thoughts, and what new inventions they can find out, or what probabilityes they conceive, or phancies they create, I will publish to the world in print . . . but if I marry, although I should have time for my thoughts and contemplations, yet perchance my Husband will not approve of my works, were they never so worthy, and by no perswasion, or reason allow of there publishing; as if it were unlawfull, or against nature, for Women to have wit. . . . some men are so inconsiderately wise, gravely foolish and lowly base, as they had rather be thought Cuckolds, than their wives should be thought wits, for fear the world should think their wife the wiser of the two. . . .
>
> (*Plays*, p. 131)

In Part II Lady Sanspareille fulfills her ambitions, addressing assemblies of amazed savants on learned and literary topics. After her untimely death, her memory is preserved by statues set up in all the colleges and public places in the city.[23]

While interesting for their early feminist heroines, the Duchess of Newcastle's plays are the poorest of her works. Her plays, like those of her stepdaughters, are structurally incoherent. She produces original and arresting raw materials for plots that are never constructed; actions are discussed rather than dramatized. Her usual method of organization is to take three unrelated story lines and alternate scenes among them mechanically. Often the individual scenes have no beginning, middle, or end; one scene simply stops abruptly and an unrelated scene follows. The most common type of scene is a dialogue or trialogue in which one character orates, harangues, or lectures to the other(s). Occasionally there is a real conversation, but generally there is no interaction among characters. The characters are personified abstractions, such as The Lord Fatherly, The Lord Singularity, The Lady Ignorant; and development of such characters rarely occurs.

The duchess was aware of these obvious flaws: "Some of my Scenes have no acquaintance or relation to the rest of the Scenes; although in one and the same Play, which is the reason many of my Playes will not end as other Playes do" (To the Reader, *Plays*). She offered this poem as "A General Prologue to all my Playes":

> But Noble Readers, do not think my Playes,
> Are such as have been writ in former daies;
> As Johnson, Shakespear, Beaumont, Fletcher writ;
> Mine want their Learning, Reading, Language, wit:
> The Latin phrases I could never tell,
> But Johnson could, which made him write so well,
> Greek, Latin Poets, I could never read,
> Nor their Historians, but our English Speed;
> I could not steal their Wit, nor Plots out take;
> All my Playes Plots, my own poor brain did make
> From Plutarchs story I ne'r took a Plot,
> Nor from Romances, nor from Don Quixot,
> As others have, for to assist their Wit,
> But I upon my own Foundation writ. . . .

There is another reason for the peculiar structure of her plays. In the 1662 collection she says that she wrote her plays from her husband's example, and, indeed, the duchess's plays follow the pattern of the duke's unaided efforts. An example of his unretouched work survives, *A Pleasante & Merrye Humor off A Roge*,[24] an unstructured dramatic sketch. Professional playwrights like Dryden,

Shirley, and Shadwell turned the duke's sketches into professional plays which were then performed in the London theaters. The duchess, looking up to her husband, assumed that this was the way plays were written: "I have heard that such Poets that write Playes, seldome or never join or sow the several Scenes together; they are two several Professions." She explains that, as her plays were written while she was in exile, she was "forced to do all my self . . . without any help or direction" (To the Readers, *Plays*).

Structurally incoherent as they are, the plays of the Duchess of Newcastle are historically significant as early feminist statements. They made a statement to her contemporaries partly by their physical appearance. The two volumes of plays, like all the duchess's works, were large, handsome books with sumptuous engravings of the author's portrait. Her title pages carried the resounding ascription "Written by the Thrice Noble, Illustrious, and Excellent Princess, the Duchess of Newcastle." With princely arrogance, she sent copies to friends, protégés, and even to the libraries of the universities. And no matter how much she was ridiculed, she was too rich and powerful to be ignored. Her books, although often empty of artistic worth, existed, and the medium—handsome folios written by a woman—was the message.

Contrary to general contemporary belief, none of her plays was performed. Pepys, on 30 March 1667, recorded, "Did by coach go to see the silly play of my Lady Newcastle's, called 'The Humourous Lovers.'" A month later Pepys was still unaware that the play was a professional version of one of the duke's sketches. In April he wrote that the duchess "was the other day at her own play, 'The Humourous Lovers.'"[25] The same play was attributed to the duchess by others. In May 1667, Gervase Jaquis wrote to the Earl of Huntington, "Upon monday last the Duchess of Newcastls play was Acted in the theater in Lincolns Inne field the King and the Grandees of the Court being present and soe was her grace and the Duke her husband."[26]

Contemporary with the Duchess of Newcastle, another pioneer woman playwright did have a play performed on the public stage. This was Katherine Fowler Philips (1632–64), better known as a poet under the sobriquet "the matchless Orinda."[27] Katherine Philips was not an aristocrat but the daughter of a successful London cloth merchant. She can be considered along with the Renaissance noblewomen, however, because the pattern of her life and works was so much like theirs. She married into the gentry, moved socially among the aristocracy, and translated neoclassical French plays.

Katherine was a precocious child. John Aubrey reports on the authority of "her cosen Blacket, who lived with her from her swadling cloutes to eight, and taught her to read" and "when a child she was mighty apt to learne, and . . . she had read the Bible thorough before she was full four yeares old; she could have sayd I know not how many places of Scripture and chapters. She . . . had an excellent memory and could have brought away a sermon in her memory."[28] At eight she entered a boarding school, probably learning French and a little Italian, staying perhaps until she was fifteen. She then went to Wales to join her mother, who, widowed when Katherine was eleven, had remarried a Welsh baronet. Her mother's marriage allowed Katherine Fowler to move socially among the Welsh gentry. At sixteen she married James Philips, then fifty-four, a man of substantial property and a prominent Cromwellian. Their marriage was amiable. They lived quietly in Wales, the older husband tolerating not only his young wife's poetic activity but also her increasing episcopalianism and royalism. Philips acted as stepmother to her husband's daughter by a first marriage, but remained childless herself for seven years. Then in 1655 she gave birth to a son who died within six weeks; the next year she bore a daughter.

She "loved poetrey at schoole, and made verses there";[29] her first published poem appeared in 1651 when she was twenty. Philips was a competent cavalier poet who celebrated platonic friendships with women, whom she addressed poetically as Lucasia, Rosania, Ardelia, Philoclea. She was recognized in her own lifetime as exemplifying ideal friendship between women, the sort of ideal friendship that had long been part of the male fictive tradition. Though she was diffident, she had a gift for friendship and an ability to charm both men and women. Among her literary and personal friends were Henry Vaughan, Francis Finch, John Birkenhead, Sir Edward Dering, Henry Lawes, Jeremy Taylor, Samuel Cooper, and Abraham Cowley. She corresponded with Sir Charles Cotterell, the royal Master of Ceremonies, whom she addressed as Poliarchus; her *Letters from Orinda to Poliarchus* were published in 1705 and reprinted in 1729.

In June 1662, Philips made an extended visit to Ireland, partly to accompany Lucasia upon her marriage into the Irish peerage, partly on business for her husband. In Dublin she was taken up by the brilliant society gathered there after the Restoration. She had a sympathy with the French language, already demonstrated in some minor translations, and at this time she began work on a translation of Pierre Corneille's *Pompée*. The Earl of Orrery made himself her literary patron, and as a result of his encouragement she finished the work rapidly. Orrery was so pleased with *Pompey* that he determined to have it performed. He enlisted his friends in his project and set them an example by contributing a hundred pounds for Roman and Egyptian costumes. Dublin at this time had a finer theater than any in London, the Theatre Royal in Smock Alley, which had just been completed by John Ogilby, Master of the Revels in Ireland. Philips's *Pompey* was sumptuously premiered there in February 1663, before Dublin's elegant society, including the Duke of Ormonde, Lord Lieutenant of Ireland. Dedicated to the Duchess of York, *Pompey* was introduced by a prologue by the Earl of Roscommon, who urged the ladies in the audience to

> hear a Muse, who has that Hero taught
> To speak as gen'rously, as e're he fought.
> Whose Eloquence from such a Theme deters
> All Tongues but English, and all Pens but Hers.
> By the just Fates your Sex is doubly blest,
> You Conquer'd Caesar, and you praise him best.[30]

*Pompey* was an instant success. It gratified the fashionable taste for works French, heroic, sumptuous, and operatic—a taste cultivated by English royalists during their years of exile on the continent. An immediate Dublin edition of five hundred copies sold out quickly. A London edition and London production followed promptly. By the summer of 1663 the play was so popular in London that Sir William Davenant made Act 5 of his *Playhouse to Be Let* a spoof of *Pompey*. The music in the play contributed to its success. For the interacts Philips wrote five songs, which were set to music by various hands. All were popular, especially the first, which was the hit of the season even before the play opened. A dozen years later this song was included in *Choice Ayres, Songs, and Dialogues* (1675). The first stanza shows how cleverly Philips assessed the pleasure-loving atmosphere of the Restoration court:

> Since affairs of the State, are already decreed,
> Make room for Affairs of the Court,

> Employment and Pleasure each other succeed,
>     Because they each other support.
>         Were Princes confin'd
>         From slackening their Mind,
>     When by Care it is rufled and Curl'd,
>     A Crown would appear
>     Too heavy to wear
> And no Man would govern the World. (*Poems,* p. 12)

*Pompey,* more than any of Philips's other works, spread her fame in her own lifetime. In addition to single editions, the play was printed with her collected works in 1667, 1669, 1678, and 1710.

The Earl of Orrery's commendatory verses typify the reaction of her contemporaries:

> Who your Translation sees, cannot but say,
> That 'tis Orinda's Work, and but his Play.
> The French to learn our Language now will seek,
> To hear their greatest Wit more nobly speak. . . . (*Poems,*
> sig. b1ᵛ)

Corneille "Englished" now sounds artificial, dull, turgid. Even so, the skill of Philips's translation is beyond question. It is the first rhymed English translation of a French tragedy, and the couplet-by-couplet rendering of French alexandrines into English heroic couplets preserves the sense, spirit, rhetorical devices, and epigrammatic force. Orinda's *Pompey* is considered the best Restoration translation of a French tragedy.[31]

Exhilarated by the reception of *Pompey,* Philips began to translate Corneille's *Horace* and had reached Act 4, scene 6 before her untimely death of smallpox at the age of thirty-two. The play was finished by Sir John Denham and had a busy stage career, with musical and farcical interacts added by the comedian John Lacy. On 4 February, 1668 *Horace* was given a magnificent production at court before an exclusive audience. John Evelyn recorded his attendance: "This Evening I saw the Trajedie of *Horace* (written by the virtuous *Mrs. Philips*) acted before their *Majesties:* 'twixt each act a Masque & *Antique:* daunced: The excessive galantry of the Ladies was infinite, Those especially on that . . . Castlemaine esteemed at 40000 pounds & more."[32] The crown jewels were taken from the Tower to be worn in the performance by Lady Castlemaine, the king's mistress, who took the role of Camilla.[33] In 1669 *Horace* had a continuous run at the Theatre Royal January 16–21. The king attended on opening night; Pepys, on the third night.[34] *Horace* shows the same high level of competence as *Pompey* and was also included in the various editions of Orinda's collected works.

In the Restoration, translations were still received on equal terms with original works. While we think of Katherine Philips's translation of Corneille's *Pompée*, her contemporaries spoke of Mrs. Philips's *Pompey*. Because of this attitude, her importance in theater history far exceeds her contribution to dramatic literature. Her theatrical successes with *Pompey* and *Horace* indicated that the time was ripe for women to attempt professional playwrighting, as the chronology of the 1660s shows. In 1662 the Duchess of Newcastle's *Plays* were published. In 1663 *Pompey* was a hit. The 1667 edition of Philips's works included both her plays. In 1668 the Duchess of Newcastle's *Plays Never Before Printed* appeared, and Philips's *Horace* was performed at court. Early in 1669 *Horace* was performed publicly, and there was a new edition of Philips's works.

In the late summer of 1669 Frances Boothby, otherwise unknown, saw the public performance by the King's Company of her play *Marcelia; or, The Treacherous Friend.* This tragicomedy follows a familiar Restoration pattern, a heroic main plot juxtaposed with a manners subplot. In the first plot, mainly in heroic couplets, King Sigismund illicitly pursues Marcelia with the aid of his wicked favorite Melynet; Marcelia remains faithful to her fiancé Lotharicus, Melynet is exposed and banished, and Sigismund renews his love affair with his abandoned mistress Calinda. The prose subplot shows the rich fool Moriphanus unsuccessfully courting the witty widow Perilla, who is finally won by Lucidore, the wild gallant of the play. *Marcelia* is mediocre in language but passably well constructed.

Boothby attempted to capitalize on the novelty of her authorship. Her prologue announced *Marcelia* as a woman's play and asked the women in the audience for support:

> I'm hither come, but what d'ye think to say?
> A Womans Pen presents you with a Play:
> Who smiling told me I'd be sure to see,
> That once confirm'd, the House would empty be.
> Not one yet gone!—
> . . . . . . . . . . . . . . . . . . . . . . . . . . . . . . . . . . . . . .
> But still she hopes the Ladies out of Pride
> And Honor, will not quit their Sexes side. . . .

The dedication to her kinswoman Lady Yate appealed to her "unequal'd Eloquence and Wisdom, to appose the Censuring world, upon this uncommon action in my Sex." Although nothing more was heard from Frances Boothby, she was the first Englishwoman to have an original play produced on the public stage.

Within a year appeared a woman who was to make playwrighting her career. In September 1670 the Duke's Company produced the first play by Aphra Behn.

# [ 2 ]

# *Aphra Behn*

Had the Plays I have writ come forth under any Mans
Name, and never known to have been mine; I appeal
to all unbyast Judges of Sense, if they had not said
that Person had made as many good Comedies, as any
one Man that has writ in our Age; but a Devil on't the
Woman damns the Poet. . . . All I ask, is the Priviledge
for my Masculine Part the Poet in me.

Aphra Behn, Preface, *The Lucky Chance,* 1686

*Aphra Behn* (c. 1640-89) was a hard-driving professional
playwright, independent, bawdy, witty, and tough. She
differed from all her feminine predecessors because she
was "forced to write for Bread and not ashamed to owne
it" (To the Reader, *Sir Patient Fancy;* 4:7).[1] Nothing is
known of her background or education but myths and
guesses.[2] She was born in Wye; she was born in Canter-
bury. Her maiden name was Amis; or Johnson. She was
the daughter of a barber; or of the lieutenant-general of
Surinam. She was married to a London merchant named
Behn, of Dutch extraction; or Mr. Behn was a fiction. She
had lovers innumerable; she suffered faithfully a long
unhappy passion for a bisexual lawyer named John Hoyle.

But what is known of her life shows her one of the remarkable personalities of her age.

Her first biography, "Memoirs on the Life of Mrs. Behn," appeared in 1696 with the earliest collected edition of her novels and purported to be "Written by a Gentlewoman of her Acquaintance."[3] "One of the Fair Sex" reports Behn's early precosity "ev'n in the first Bud of Infancy," for "besides the Vivacity and Wit of her Conversation, at the first Use almost of Reason in Discourse, she wou'd write the prettiest, soft-engaging Verses in the World" (sigs. A7$^v$–A8$^r$). There is no record of her education, but her works show that she knew French, and there is presumptive evidence that she knew Spanish and Italian also.

About 1663–64 Behn traveled to Surinam, then an English colony. She describes her journey in her famous and influential *Oroonoko* (1688), sometimes called the first abolitionist novel. The facts may be embroidered— *Oroonoko* after all is a novel rather than an autobiography— but they show her adventurousness. She tells us that her stay was short in the colony "because my Father dy'd at Sea, and never arriv'd to possess the Honour design'd him (which was Lieutenant-General of six and thirty Islands, besides the Continent of Surinam) nor the Advantages he hop'd to reap by them: So that though we were oblig'd to continue on our Voyage, we did not intend to stay upon the Place" (5:177–78). She visited the Indians, who were understandably amazed at her European dress: "They were all naked; and we were dress'd, so as is most commode for the hot Countries, very glittering and rich; so that we appear'd extremely fine; my own Hair was cut short, and I had a Taffety Cap, with black Feathers on my Head; my Brother was in a Stuff-Suit, with Silver Loops and Buttons, and abundance of green Ribbon" (5:185). Behn remembered with gusto her voyage across "Three thousand Leagues of spacious Ocean" (Dedication, *The Young King;* 2: 105), recounting in *Oroonoko* her adventures searching for "tiger" cubs and eating an armadillo.

Upon her return to England, according to her biographer, she "gave King Charles the Second, so pleasant and rational an Account of his Affairs there, and particularly of the Misfortunes of Oroonoko, that he desir'd her to deliver them publickly to the World; and [was] satisfy'd on her Abilities in the Management of Business, and the Fidelity of our Heroine to his Int'rest" ("Memoirs," sig. b1ᵛ). This anecdote is as difficult to prove or disprove as any told about her life at this period, but she herself tells of presenting to "his Majesty's Antiquary's ... some rare Flies, of amazing Forms and Colours" from Surinam (5: 130). The story goes that she married Mr. Behn about this time. He disappeared rapidly from the scene, perhaps of the plague in 1665 or 1666, and was never heard of again. Behn never mentions him in any of her writings.

Everything about the character she gives of herself in *Oroonoko,* even perhaps the tale of her acquaintance with the king, is consonant with the first indisputable external evidence about her life. In 1666 she went to Antwerp as a secret agent for the English government. Her employment as a spy is documented in a series of letters preserved among official state papers.[4] Her mission was to send information about disaffected Cromwellians, now taking their turn in exile, and to relay Dutch military plans. As a secret agent she used the code name Astrea. Later, as her literary name, Astrea became as synonymous with Aphra Behn as Orinda was with Katherine Philips.

Astrea ran into debt in the Netherlands and sent urgent appeals for money to Thomas Killigrew, who had recommended her for the job, and even to Lord Arlington, Secretary of State. Finally she had to borrow money from a London merchant in order to pay her debts abroad. She arrived home in 1667, penniless and substantially in debt. Despite further appeals to those who had employed her, she ended up in debtor's prison. She wrote Killigrew the day before her imprisonment:

> I will send my mother to the King with a petition, for I see everybody are words, and I will not perish in prison from whence he [her creditor] swears I shall not stir till the utmost farthing be paid; and oh God, who considers my misery and charge too, this is my reward for all my great promises and my endeavours. Sir, if I have not the money to-night, you must send me something to keep me in prison, for I will not starve.[5]

No one knows how or when she was released from prison, but it may indeed have been someone at court who paid her debt, perhaps the king himself, for to the end of her life she was an ardent Tory, devoted to Charles II and his brother James.

"The Rest of her Life was entirely dedicated to Pleasure and Poetry; the success in which, gain'd her the Acquaintance and Friendship of the most sensible Men of the Age" ("Memoirs," sig. b6ᵛ). As to the "Pleasure," if the word means sexual pleasure as it often did in the Restoration, there is little external evidence. Her works show her sexual sophistication and won her a reputation in her own lifetime as an adept of love, who practiced what she preached: "The Passions, that of Love especially, she was Mistress of; and gave us such nice and tender Touches of them, that without her Name we might discover the Author."[6] As to the "Poetry," the incomplete edition of her collected works runs to six volumes. The determination expressed in her letter to Killigrew—"I will not starve"—is evident in all her work. She turned out plays, poems, novels, and translations to suit the marketplace. Her wide circle of friendships is documented in innumerable compliments from distinguished contemporaries. Among her literary friends were Dryden, Otway, Edward Howard,

Waller, Charles Cotton, Nahum Tate, Edward Ravenscroft, Nathaniel Lee, Thomas Creech, and probably the Earl of Rochester. She must have known all her contemporaries in the theater, both playwrights and actors. Sir Peter Lely and Mary Beale painted portraits of her. People of other professions also sought her out, and students just down from the universities haunted her rooms. She apparently was "able to write in the midst of Company, and yet have her Share of the Conversation."[7] She was noted among her friends for her witty conversation, beauty, and generosity.

No one knows how she gained an entree to the theater. In *Oroonoko*, after describing the "glorious Wreaths" of feathers made by the natives, she says, "I had a Set of these presented to me, and I gave 'em to the King's Theatre; it was the Dress of the *Indian Queen*, infinitely admir'd by Persons of Quality; and was inimitable" (5: 130). The patentee of the King's Company at this time was Thomas Killigrew, whom Behn had worked for during her career as a spy. In spite of these connections with the King's Company, her plays were produced by the rival Duke's Company. Perhaps, as has been suggested, she took her plays to the rival house because Killigrew had treated her shabbily about her expenses in the Netherlands. It has also been suggested that the Duke's Company might have been more receptive to a woman playwright because it was the more innovative of the two companies.[8] This hypothesis, however, ignores the fact that the King's Company had already produced plays by Frances Boothby and Katherine Philips in 1669. A more likely hypothesis is that the Duke's Company was competing with the King's Company by producing a woman playwright in the following year.

Whatever the circumstances, Behn entered the theater in 1670, producing, before her death nineteen years later, seventeen extant plays. Two more plays have been lost— *Like Father Like Son; or, The Mistaken Brothers* (1682) and *The*

*Wavering Nymph; or, Mad Amyntas* (1684). Four anonymous plays have been attributed to her—*The Woman Turned Bully* (1675), *The Debauchee; or, The Credulous Cuckold* (1677), *The Counterfeit Bridegroom; or, The Defeated Widow* (1677), and *The Revenge; or, A Match in Newgate* (1680).

She began her apprenticeship with *The Forced Marriage; or, The Jealous Bridegroom* (1670), a romantic tragicomedy of intrigue of the popular Beaumont and Fletcher school. In February 1671 Behn followed up with a romantic comedy, *The Amorous Prince; or, The Curious Husband,* more vivacious in language and more complex in plot. With *The Dutch Lover* (1673) Behn found her forte, the comedy of intrigue, and her style, brisk colloquial prose. Her apprentice work was finished—she had found her stage formulas. Behn typically manipulates several sources into a complexly plotted play of expert stage craftsmanship. A number of couples—eluding the unwanted marriages arranged for them—meet, bed and/or wed after innumerable intrigues, mistaken identities, duels, disguises, and practical jokes. Her plays abound in bedroom farce. Her scenes of comic lowlife are delightful, full of landladies, bawds, buffoons, and prostitutes. She provides spectacle in masquing, costuming, and dance, and uses stage machinery and other technical resources to create special effects. Behn had a fine lyric gift, and her plays are full of witty and romantic songs. These plays, although fun to read, are for the stage rather than the page. Behn was the first woman to write theatrically.

Her wit is more often in the plot than in the dialogue. Because of this, her plays are often compared unfavorably with the comedies of manners written by her contemporaries. But Behn was writing in another genre, the Spanish-type comedy of intrigue, one of the most commercially successful genres of the day.[9] Behn wrote for money and she chose the mode that suited her talents.

Behn's assessment of her own plays in the preface to *The Lucky Chance,* quoted as the epigraph to this chapter, is accurate. She wrote as well as any of her contemporaries except Etherege, Wycherley, and Dryden. And considering her prolific output, she indeed "made as many good Comedies, as any one Man" in her own age.

Behn wrote a series of fine intrigue comedies. The best of these, *The Rover; or, The Banished Cavaliers* (1677), is set at carnival time in Naples, where impoverished English cavaliers-in-exile become entangled with Spanish ladies and win their persons and fortunes. Behn's rover, Willmore, is her distinctive version of a favorite Restoration character, the wild gallant. The rover is eager for an amour anytime, anyplace, with any woman at hand. *The Rover* stayed in the repertory until the middle of the eighteenth century, the role of the witty heroine being taken by such famous actresses as Elizabeth Barry, Anne Bracegirdle, Anne Oldfield, and Peg Woffington. Behn exploited her success by continuing Willmore's adventures in *The Rover Part II* (1681). The play was dedicated to the Duke of York because of "the incouragement" he gave "the Rover at his first appearance, and the concern" he was "pleas'd to have for his second" (The Epistle Dedicatory; 1: 113). Another variant on *The Rover* was *The Feigned Courtesans; or, A Night's Intrigue* (1679). Again a group of English travelers, this time in Rome, meet, intrigue with, and marry a group of foreign ladies. Also among Behn's best is *Sir Patient Fancy* (1678), an amusing tangle of the amours of two neighboring London families, a first-rate stage play with fine scenes of bedroom farce. Behn's *Emperor of the Moon* was an instant success in 1687. A gay and extravagant combination of *commedia dell' arte,* operatic spectacle, sumptuous costuming, dance, song, satire, intrigue, and a bit of manners comedy, *The Emperor of the Moon* was performed for nearly a hundred years.

Two of Behn's plays deal centrally with her most distinctive theme, her attack on forced marriage. Announcing that theme in the title of her first play, she went on to
write *The Town Fop; or, Sir Timothy Tawdrey* (1676) and *The
Lucky Chance; or, An Alderman's Bargain* (1686)—a sentimental, then a harder treatment of the same subject. In
*The Town Fop,* the young lovers are brought near to ruin
before a fifth-act reversal dissolves a forced marriage. We
see not their witty stratagems but their bitter sufferings
when parental authority is abused. The effect, then, is
sentimental rather than comic. Ten years later *The Lucky
Chance* made a comic attack on loveless marriage, with
three pairs of lovers using their wits to escape that dreadful fate. All three heroines complain explicitly about
forced marriage. Lady Fulbank:

> Oh, how fatal are forc'd Marriages!
> How many Ruins one such Match pulls on!
> Had I but kept my Sacred Vows to Gayman,
> How happy had I been—how prosperous he!
> Whilst now I languish in a loath'd embrace,
> Pine out my Life with Age—Consumptions, Coughs.
> (1.2;3:200)

Leticia, preparing to elope with Bellmour, addresses the
absent Sir Feeble:

> Old Man forgive me—thou the Aggressor art,
> Who rudely forc'd the Hand without the Heart.
> (3.2;3:230)

Diana speaks similarly as she prepares to elope with Bred-
wel:

> Father, farewell—if you dislike my course,
> Blame the old rigid Customs of your Force.
> (5.1;3:260)

The serious tone of these complaints, made in what is essentially a farcical comedy, shows the earnestness of Behn's feeling that love should be the basis for marriage. New Comedy in general depicts the witty stratagems of young lovers who outwit their elders and thus escape unwanted arranged marriages. Behn goes beyond this to attack the arranged marriage as an institution.

She also used the stage to voice her strong opinions about the political upheavals in the latter years of Charles II's reign, when feeling ran high between Whig and Tory over the possibility of a Catholic succession through the Duke of York. In *The Roundheads; or, The Good Old Cause* (1681) Behn satirized the Parliamentarians in the turbulent days immediately preceding the Restoration. *The Roundheads* is a poor play; the satire is too gross to be telling. A few months later, in the spring of 1682, Behn produced a much better political satire in *The City Heiress; or, Sir Timothy Treat-all.* Treat-all, "an old seditious Knight, that keeps open House for Commonwealthsmen and true blue Protestants" (dramatis personae; 2:203), was clearly a satire of the prominent Whig Shaftesbury. The satire is effective and is integrated into a fast-paced intrigue comedy. That summer Behn went too far in her political outspokenness and offended the king when, for the anonymous play *Romulus and Hersilia,* she wrote an epilogue attacking the Duke of Monmouth, Charles II's natural son and potential Protestant usurper. Both Behn and the actress who spoke the epilogue were arrested. Apparently nothing much came of the arrest, but Behn had made enemies among a number of powerful Whigs and among Whig playwrights such as Shadwell.

Some of Behn's plays are not easy to categorize. She wrote one tragedy, *Abdelazer; or, The Moor's Revenge* (1676), a murderous melodrama distinguished only by its energy and the often quoted song "Love in fantastick Triumph sat." She was apparently always pressed for money, particularly during the 1680s when times were hard for playwrights, and consequently often wrote hurriedly. In 1679 she refurbished for production *The Young King; or, The Mistake,* like her earliest plays a romantic tragicomedy in the Beaumont and Fletcher mold. The dedication calls the play the "first Essay of my Infant-Poetry" (2:105) and implies that an early version was written in Surinam. The text shows signs of hasty and incomplete revision. Haste and need may also have produced *The False Count; or, A New Way to Play an Old Game* (1681), described in the epilogue as "a slight Farce, five Days brought forth with ease" (3: 175). Possibly the play was indeed written with such speed, for, although amusing, it is less complexly plotted than her other plays. Two Behn plays were produced posthumously. *The Widow Ranter; or, The History of Bacon in Virginia* (1689), set in America, unmercifully dramatizes the colonial officials as cowardly and drunken transported felons. Charles Gildon rewrote a few scenes of *The Younger Brother; or, The Amorous Jilt,* a busy intrigue comedy, and brought it out in 1696, seven years after Behn's death.

In several plays, Behn explores in distinctive ways two stock characters, the courtesan and the amazon. Critics have suggested that she gives prominence to the courtesan simply as a means of titillation.[10] Rather, she uses this character as a weapon in her thematic attack on mercenary marriage. An early example is Angelica Bianca in *The Rover.* She is so famous and beautiful a courtesan that she can sell her favors for a thousand crowns a month. In spite of her mercenary nature, she falls in love with the poor but dashing rover, Captain Willmore. He argues her into bed by upbraiding her for selling love for money. Although she is persuaded, at one point she turns the argument against him:

Pray, tell me, Sir, are not you guilty of the same mercenary Crime? When a Lady is proposed to you for a Wife,
you never ask, how fair, discreet, or virtuous she is; but
what's her Fortune—which if but small, you cry—She
will not do my business—and basely leave her, tho she
languish for you. —Say, is not this as poor?

(2.2;1:40)

Ultimately the humorless courtesan loses Willmore to the
witty maiden Hellena. Angelica Bianca mistakenly thinks
that this is due to her "lost honor," but what wins the rover
is not Hellena's "honor" but her wit. Although she loses
the love game in *The Rover,* Angelica Bianca is developed
as a three-dimensional passionate woman, a character with
real thoughts and feelings.

Two years later in *The Feigned Courtesans* the rover of the
play, Frank Galliard, woos the young Roman courtesan La
Silvianetta, while his more romantic friend Sir Harry Fil-
lamour is attracted by her companion Euphemia. The
courtesans are really Cornelia and Marcella, young ladies
of fortune and family who have run away from home in
disguise, Marcella to avoid a forced marriage, Cornelia to
avoid a convent. It is their disguise as courtesans—a role
they enjoy playing—that enables them to attract and then
win their men. Another young lady, Laura Lucretia, also
disguises as La Silvianetta in order to attract Galliard.
Inferior in wit to Cornelia, she loses the rover and must be
content with her fiancé.

The *Rover Part II,* in another two years, varies again the
pattern of Part I. Willmore, now a widower, is once more
pursued by a witty, virtuous maid—Ariadne—and a beautiful, passionate courtesan—La Nuche. Because of the
earlier play, a strong expectation is set up that Ariadne will
capture Willmore in marriage, taking him away from the
mercenary courtesan. But Ariadne's wit fails at a crucial
point. Striking up a flirtation with Willmore, she talks of

love in terms of monetary value. When he praises her charms, she says they are to be enjoyed by "one that can esteem 'em to their worth, can set a Value and a Rate upon 'em" (2.1;1:137). Wishing to impress the inconstant rover, she derides constancy because "it loses Time and Profit," because "new Lovers have new Vows and new Presents" (2.1;1:139). Willmore, who in Part I upbraided the courtesan for being mercenary, now turns the same attack on Ariadne, on honorable ladies and their marriage settlements:

> You Women have all a certain Jargon, or Gibberish, peculiar to your selves; of Value, Rate, Present, Interest, Settlement, Advantage, Price, Maintenance, and the Devil and all of Fopperies, which in plain Terms signify ready Money, by way of Fine before Entrance; so that an honest well-meaning Merchant of Love finds no Credit amongst ye, without his Bill of Lading.
>
> (2.1;1:138)

La Nuche and Willmore are attracted to each other when the play opens, and he turns the same arguments on her. Throughout five acts she wavers between love and interest while Willmore tries to win her to the rover view of love free and unconfined. Their battle of wits takes serious and comic turns, culminating in an allegorical scene (5.1) in which La Nuche in center stage hears Willmore on one side argue for her on the grounds of pure love, while Beaumond, on the other side of the stage, offers wealth for her favors. La Nuche nearly loses Willmore at this point by succumbing to Beaumond's offers, and Willmore makes her conscious of her error:

> Death, hadst thou lov'd my Friend for his own Value, I had esteem'd thee; but when his Youth and Beauty cou'd not plead, to be the mercenary Conquest of his Presents, was poor, below thy Wit: I cou'd have con-

quer'd so, but I scorn thee at that rate—my Purse shall
never be my Pimp.

(5.1;1:194)

La Nuche now realizes that she loves her rover more than
her profit and uses her wits to win him back. Knowing that
Willmore has a midnight assignation with Ariadne, she
substitutes herself for her rival. This time the courtesan
disguises as the maid. In a fifth-act surprise, Ariadne must
return to her fiancé Beaumond, while Willmore and La
Nuche pair off "without the formal Foppery of Marriage"
(5.3;1:208).

The denouement of *Rover II,* although surprising in
terms of stage convention, is carefully prepared for. La
Nuche's character is much more highly developed than
that of her prototype. La Nuche has the wit and sense of
humor that Angelica Bianca lacked. She is on stage far
more often than her rival, Ariadne, and she tends to
dominate the action. Because of her full characterization,
La Nuche elicits audience sympathy, so that her success
with Willmore is psychologically satisfying. The casting
may have added to the satisfaction of the Restoration
audience. While William Smith played Willmore in both
parts of *The Rover,* Elizabeth Barry, the most celebrated
actress of the day, played first the witty maid Hellena and
then the courtesan La Nuche. The denouement works out
a progression: in *Rover I* the witty maid wins out over the
courtesan; in *The Feigned Courtesans* the witty maid wins out
disguised as a courtesan; in *Rover II* the witty courtesan
wins out over the maid. In each case, the more generous
woman gets the man. Behn uses the series of *Rover* plays to
make in a stronger form the point she makes in her plays
against forced marriage. In those plays, heroines forced
into, or about to be forced into, loveless but profitable
marriages feel themselves prostituted. In the *Rover* series
Behn goes a step further to say that the only difference

between prostitution and marriage for money is that prostitution is the more candid, less hypocritical way for a woman to earn a living.

Another female character used to translate theme into stage action is Behn's woman warrior. This character provides a visual metaphor for the battle of the sexes and appears in both romantic and comic versions. The romantic woman warrior appears in *The Young King* as Cleomena, Princess of Dacia, who has been "bred up in War" (dramatis personae;2:108); because of an oracle, she is to inherit the throne instead of her brother. She makes her first entrance "drest like an Amazon, with a Bow in her Hand, and a Quiver of Arrows at her Back" (1.2.s.d.;2:114). Her hereditary enemy, Thersander, Prince of Scythia, for his own reasons is disguised as Clemanthis, an unknown warrior of incredible valor fighting in the Dacian army. Cleomena and Clemanthis inevitably fall in love with each other. Believing that the Scythian prince has treacherously murdered Clemanthis, the princess herself disguises as Clemanthis and fights in single combat with Thersander. Her plans for revenge are foiled when she is wounded, recognized, and carried off the field. Still bent on revenge, Cleomena next disguises as a shepherd and stabs Therander in the breast. He recovers from his near-fatal wound, the mistakes are unraveled, and the marriage of Cleomena and Thersander makes peace between the warring kingdoms. It is curious that both Cleomena and Thersander masquerade as the same person, as Clemanthis. This may support the other suggestions in the play of Cleomena's androgynous temperament. More probably, the identity of disguise suggests the identity of souls in love. The name *Clemanthis* combines the letters and sounds of the names *Cleomena* and *Thersander*.

A jolly woman warrior is the title character of *The Widow*

*Ranter*. Because the play is set in colonial America, the Widow Ranter has full scope for her unconventionality. Formerly the mistress, later the wife of old Colonel Ranter, she has been left with "fifty thousand Pounds Sterling, besides Plate and Jewels: She's a great Gallant . . . her Extravagancy is very pleasant, she retains something of her primitive Quality still, but is good-natur'd and generous" (1.1;4:229). Ranter is notorious for beginning the morning with a pipe and punch.

Ranter loves dashing Lieutenant-General Daring and intends to have him in spite of his affection for the maiden Chrisante. When Indian wars break out, Ranter disguises as a man and appears on the battlefield, with her maid Jenny dressed as a footman:

> Ranter. Why should I sigh and whine, and make my self an Ass, and him conceited? no, instead of snivelling I am resolved—
> Jenny. What, Madam?
> Ranter. Gad, to beat the Rascal. . . .
> Jenny. Beat him, Madam! what, a Woman beat a Lieutenant-General?
> Ranter. Hang 'em, they get a name in War from Command, not Courage; but how know I but I may fight? Gad, I have known a Fellow kick'd from one end of the Town to t'other, believing himself a Coward; at last forced to fight, found he could; got a Reputation, and bullied all he met with; and got a Name, and a great Commission.
> Jenny. But if he should kill you, Madam.
> Ranter. I'll take care to make it as comical a Duel as the best of 'em; as much in love as I am, I do not intend to die its Martyr.
>
> (4.2;4:288)

Daring recognizes Ranter through her disguise, and realizing that she loves him, teases her by gossiping about the widow: "Gad, I'd sooner marry a she-Bear, unless for a

Penance for some horrid Sin; we should be eternally challenging one another to the Field, and ten to one she beats me there; or if I should escape there, she wou'd kill me with drinking. . . . she'll rail and smoke till she choke again; then six Gallons of Punch hardly recovers her, and never but then is she good-natur'd" (4.3;4:290–91).

Ranter is so enraged that she draws her sword on him, and Daring, laughing, proposes to her:

> Daring. Give me thy Hand, Widow, I am thine—and so entirely, I will never—be drunk out of thy Company:—Dunce [the parson] is in my Tent,—prithee let's in and bind the Bargain.
> Ranter. Nay, faith, let's see the Wars at an end first.
> Daring. Nay, prithee take me in the humour, while thy Breeches are on—for I never lik'd thee half so well in Petticoats.
> Ranter. Lead on, General, you give me good incouragement to wear them.
>
> (4.3;4:292)

The compatibility of a marriage between these two equals in wit and war is emphasized a few minutes later. Battle breaks out in earnest, and Daring enters duelling, "Ranter fighting like a Fury by his side" (5.1.s.d.;4:295).

Behn uses the Widow Ranter to give visual, dramatic representation to the battle of the sexes. Sword combat is added to the usual wit combat of the gay couple of Restoration comedy. While the amazon was an old stage character, Behn uses her in a distinctive way. Possibly Cleomena and the Widow Ranter grew out of Behn's Surinam experience; both plays have colonial connections. *The Widow Ranter* is set in Virginia, and the first draft at least of *The Young King* was written in Surinam. Behn's woman warrior may be a colonial conception; she may also have been a feminist conception.

Certainly her creator was a feminist. During her career,

in response to the attacks of her enemies, Behn became a
staunch defender of women. She took this position gradu-
ally. She began her career confident that the novelty of
being a woman playwright would help rather than hinder
her success. A glamorous woman, widely complimented on
her beauty and wit, she intended to exploit her glamor in
the theater. She opened her first play with a flirtatious
prologue that traded on her sex as an advertisement. An
actor begins the prologue of *The Forced Marriage,* warning
the gallants that the women are planning "new Stratagems
. . . They'll join the force of Wit to Beauty." He warns that
all the ladies in the audience are spies set by the "Poetess"

> To hold you in a wanton Compliment;
> That so you may not censure what she 'as writ,
> Which done, they face you down 'twas full of Wit.

At this point an actress enters, points to the ladies, and
scoffs:

> How hast thou labour'd to subvert in vain,
> What one poor Smile of ours calls home again?
> Can any see that glorious Sight and say
> A Woman shall not Victor prove to day?
> Who is't that to their Beauty would submit,
> And yet refuse the Fetters of their Wit?
> (3:285–86)

The prologue had probably been preceded by some advance publicity, for the play opened to a full house and ran
for six nights.[11]

But as soon as it became clear to the theatrical world that
a woman was going to be a serious contender for money
and prestige, resistance set in, and a cabal formed against
Behn because of her sex. *The Dutch Lover* failed for a
number of suspiciously coincidental reasons—poor acting
(particularly in the part of the Dutch lover, played by the
comedian Edward Angel), poor costuming (which made

the mistaken identities unintelligible), and a missing epilogue (which had been promised by a friend). Behn responded with spirit in an epistle to the "Good, Sweet, Honey, Sugar-Candied Reader" in which she denounced the acting and costuming. She also turned her guns on the hostile members of the audience:

> Indeed that day 'twas Acted first, there comes me into the Pit, a long, lither, phlegmatick, white ill-favour'd, wretched Fop, an Officer in Masquerade newly transported with a Scarf & Feather out of France, a sorry Animal that has nought else to shield it from the uttermost contempt of all mankind, but that respect which we afford to Rats and Toads, which though we do not well allow to live, yet when considered as a part of God's Creation, we make honourable mention of them. A thing, Reader—but no more of such a Smelt: This thing, I tell ye, opening that which serves it for a mouth, out issued such a noise as this to those that sate about it, that they were to expect a woful Play, God damn him, for it was a woman's. Now how this came about I am not sure, but I suppose he brought it piping hot from some who had with him the reputation of a villanous Wit: for Creatures of his size of sense talk without all imagination, such scraps as they pick up from other folks. I would not for a world be taken arguing with such a propertie as this; but if I thought there were a man of any tolerable parts, who could upon mature deliberation distinguish well his right hand from his left, and justly state the difference between the number of sixteen and two, yet had this prejudice upon him; I would take a little pains to make him know how much he errs.
>
> (1:223–24)

She did not write a play, at least not under her own name, for three years. When she returned to the stage with *Abdelazer* (1676), it looks as though she made one more attempt to conciliate her enemies with flirtation. The epilogue "Written by a Friend" was spoken by "little Mrs.

Ariell" who told the gentlemen she would "intercede" for "our Poetess":

> my Sex's Cause
> Whose Beauty does, like Monarchs, give you Laws,
> Should now command, being join'd with Wit, Applause.
> Yet since our Beauty's Power's not absolute,
> She'll not the Privilege of your Sex dispute,
> But does by me submit.
>
> (2:98)

Apparently the intercession did not work, for Behn was extremely careful the following year, 1677, when she brought out two plays, possibly three, anonymously. Among them was *The Rover,* the prologue of which specifically refers to the author as a man.

After the success of *The Rover,* Behn wrote again under her own name. The next year she was forced into a defense of her fine comedy *Sir Patient Fancy.* The epilogue begins:

> I here and there o'erheard a Coxcomb cry,
> Ah, Rot it—'tis a Woman's Comedy,
> One, who because she lately chanc'd to please us,
> With her damn'd Stuff, will never cease to teeze us.
> What has poor Woman done, that she must be
> Debar'd from Sense, and sacred Poetry?
> Why in this Age has Heaven allow'd you more,
> And Women less of Wit than heretofore?
> We once were fam'd in story, and could write
> Equal to Men; cou'd govern, nay, cou'd fight.
>
> (4:115)

Behn was even blunter in the epistle to the reader: "The play had no other Misfortune but that of coming out for a Womans: had it been owned by a Man, though the most Dull Unthinking Rascally Scribler in Town, it had been a most admirable Play" (4:7).

Her enemies criticized with virulence. Shadwell, for example, complainèd:

> Such stupid humours now the Gallants seize
> Women and Boys may write and yet may please.
> Poetess Afra though she's damned to day
> Tomorrow will put up another Play. . . .[12]

Shadwell at least acknowledged that Behn wrote her own plays. Others charged her with plagiarism, an amusing charge considering that in the Restoration everyone borrowed from everyone else, and everyone pillaged French and Spanish sources. When Behn adapted Killigrew's unwieldy closet drama *Thomaso* into *The Rover,* she was forced to defend herself in the Post-Script to the published play. Her acknowledgement of indebtedness to Killigrew is deliberately incomplete: "I . . . hang out the Sign of Angelica (the only Stol'n Object) to give Notice where a great part of the Wit dwelt." She then comments accurately that "the Plot and Bus'ness (not to boast on't) is my own" and throws out a clever challenge: "As for the Words and Characters, I leave the Reader to judge and compare 'em with Thomaso" (1:107). Here Behn had her tongue in cheek, knowing that anyone with the fortitude to read Killigrew's play would see that she had transformed his "Words and Characters" infinitely for the better. She concludes by parrying the unspoken reason for accusations against her: "Had this succeeded ill, I shou'd have had no need of imploring that Justice from the Critics, who . . . wou'd doubtless have given me the whole Honour on't" (1:107). She understood quite well that the charge of plagiarism was not an attack on her use of source material but an attack on her success.

The accusation of plagiarism turned smutty. Since it was unthinkable that a woman should write good plays, then of course a man must have written them for her; and why else would a man write her plays unless he was receiving her favors? The nastiest version of this line of thinking appears in an imaginary letter to Behn by Tom Brown:

> It is no great wonder to me you should prove so witty, since so many sons of Parnassus, instead of climbing the Heliconian hill, should stoop so low, as to make your mount of Venus the barren object of their poetick fancies: I have heard some physicians say, the sweet sin of fornication draws mightily from the brain . . . if so, how could the spirit of poesy be otherwise than infus'd into you, since you always gain'd by what the fraternity of the muses lost in your embraces? . . . well might you be esteem'd a female wit, since the least return your versifying admirers could make you for your favours, was, first to lend you their assistance, and then oblige you with their applause: besides, how could you do otherwise than produce some wit to the world, since you were so often plough'd and sow'd by the kind hus-bandmen of Apollo?[13]

Although this was originally published some years after Behn's death, it reflects what others said of her during her lifetime. It was rumored, for example, that John Hoyle wrote Behn's plays:

> The censuring Age has thought it fit,
> To damn a Woman, 'cause 'tis said
> The Plays she vends she never made.
> But that a Grays Inn lawyer does 'em
> Who unto Her was Friend in Bosom. . . .[14]

Edward Ravenscroft was also suggested as the author of Behn's plays.

Another disguise for attack on Behn as a woman was the charge that her plays were obscene. This is even more amusing than the charge of plagiarism: Restoration comedy notoriously exploits sex. Behn, because she was less verbally dexterous than her famous contemporaries, was less adept at the double entendre. She was much better at erotic description of sexual delights, and she was noted for this. Dryden approved that she "so well cou'd love's kind Passion paint."[15] Others disapproved: "She'd put luscious Bawdry off for Wit."[16] Her plays offended those who are offended by bedroom farce:

> Again, for Instance, that clean piece of wit,
> The City Heiress, by chast Sappho writ,
> Where the lewd Widow comes, with brazen face,
> Just reeking from a Stallion's rank embrace,
> T'acquaint the Audience with her slimy case.[17]

The probable pun here on "case" (=vagina) shows the critic none too ingenuous.

Behn was often disingenuous herself in her defenses against the charge of obscenity, often denying double entendres or bedroom jokes where they obviously existed. But there was no reason for her to be more honest than her critics. She understood their real motives better than they themselves did. With her usual intelligent directness, she put her finger exactly on the point of the attack:

> The little Obligation I have to some of the witty Sparks and Poets of the Town, has put me on a Vindication of this Comedy from those Censures that Malice, and ill Nature have thrown upon it, tho in vain: The Poets I heartily excuse, since there is a sort of Self-Interest in their Malice, which I shou'd rather call a witty Way they have in this Age, of Railing at every thing they find with pain successful. . . . And nothing makes them so thorough-stitcht an Enemy as a full Third Day, that's Crime enough to load it with all manner of Infamy; and when they can no other way prevail with the Town, they charge it with the old never failing Scandal—That 'tis not fit for the Ladys.
>
> (Preface, *The Lucky Chance;* 3:185)

Behn saw that it was the success of her play rather than its content that offended her critics.

Attacks on Behn as a pornographer are attacks on her for writing as uninhibitedly as a man. She understood this clearly, pointing out that the jests in celebrated plays

> are never taken Notice of, because a Man writ them, and they may hear that from them they blush at from a Woman. . . . Had I a Day or two's time . . . I would sum up all your Beloved Plays, and all the Things in them that are past with such Silence by; because written by Men: such Masculine Strokes in me, must not be allow'd.
> (Preface, *The Lucky Chance;* 3:185–86)

In another place she wrote:

> I Printed this Play with all the impatient haste one ought to do, who would be vindicated from the most unjust and silly aspersion . . . which only my being a Woman has procured me; *That it was Baudy,* the least and most Excusable fault in Men writers, to whose Plays they all crowd, as if they came to no other end than to hear what they condemn in this: *but from a Woman it was unnaturall.*
> (To the Reader, *Sir Patient Fancy;* 4:7)

That goes straight to the heart of the three-hundred-year controversy about Behn's alleged pornography. Those who defend Behn from this "unjust and silly aspersion" say that she wrote exactly as her masculine contemporaries did. But this defense is precisely the reason for the attack. It is time to lay this old argument to rest, simply noting that Behn's works praise sexual pleasure and that she therefore does not display the kind of sexual nastiness found in the works of misogynists like, say, Wycherley.

During the late 1680s attacks on Behn became more viciously personal. She suffered from some painful crippling disease, she was chronically strapped for money, and her beauty had faded. Her enemies spared her on none of these misfortunes, suggesting that they were due to syphilis:

> Doth that lewd Harlot, that Poetick Quean,
> Fam'd through White Fryars, you know who I mean,
> Mend for reproof, others set up in spight
> To flux, take glisters, vomits, purge and write.
> Long with a Sciatica she's beside lame,
> Her limbs distortur'd, Nerves shrunk up with pain,
> And therefore I'll all sharp reflections shun,
> Poverty, Poetry, Pox, are plagues enough for one.[18]

Her troubles were increased by the crushing of her political loyalties, for she lived to see James II deposed in the Glorious Revolution.

Aphra Behn died 16 April 1689, reputedly at the hands of "an unskilful Physician" ("Memoirs," sig. b6$^v$), and was buried under two verses probably by Hoyle:

> Here lies a Proof that Wit can never be
> Defence enough against Mortality.

She died in poverty and out of favor politically, but she was the first woman whose pen won her burial in Westminster Abbey. Although all her life she had written to earn a living, once when defending herself against charges of plagiarism, she had complained, "I make Verses, and others have the Fame" (Post-Script, The Rover; 1:107). Later she wrote, "I am not content to write for a Third day only. I value Fame as much as if I had been born a Hero; and if you rob me of that, I can retire from the ungrateful World, and scorn its fickle Favours" (Preface, The Lucky Chance; 3:187). At the end of her life she inserted into a translation some verses of her own, an apostrophe to Daphne:

> I, by a double right, thy bounties claim,

Both from my sex, and in Apollo's name.
Let me with Sappho and Orinda be,
Oh ever sacred nymph, adorned by thee.
And give my verses immortality.[19]

She won the literary immortality she coveted. Although she died neglected, the posthumous appearance of a number of plays and novels, revivals of her plays, and dramatic adaptations of her novels established her reputation firmly. In 1691 Gerard Langbaine's *Account of the English Dramatick Poets* described "Mrs. Astraea Behn" as "A Person lately deceased, but whose Memory will be long fresh amongst the Lovers of Dramatick Poetry" (p. 17). In 1694 Thomas Southerne adapted Behn's novel *History of the Nun* into the highly successful play *The Fatal Marriage.* The next year Southerne made a hit play out of *Oroonoko,* this time making a handsome admission of his source: "I stand engaged to Mrs. Behn for the Occasion of a most Passionate Distress in my Last Play; and in a Conscience that I had not made her a sufficient Acknowledgment, I have run further into her Debt for *Oroonoko,* with a Design to oblige me to be honest; and that every one may find me out for Ingratitude, when I don't say all that's fit for me upon that Subject. She had a great Command of the Stage" (Epistle Dedicatory, *Oroonoko*). The first collection of her novels was published in 1696, and further novels were published in 1698 and 1700. In the eighteenth century the collected novels were printed repeatedly, *Oroonoko* was translated into French and German, and the collected plays went into a third edition.

Behn's success inspired a new generation of women playwrights, although at first it did not seem that this would happen. In 1689 a "Young Lady of Quality" wrote a broadside "Elegy Upon the Death of Mrs. A. Behn; The Incomparable Astrea." The elegist lamented:

Of her own Sex, not one is found
Who dares her Laurel wear,
Witheld by Impotence or Fear. . . .[20]

Six years later the elegist's fears would be assuaged when a new group of women dramatists contended for the bays.

## [ 3 ]

## *The Female Wits: Catherine Trotter, Delariviere Manley, Mary Pix*

Critick. What a Pox have the Women to do with the Muses? I grant you the Poets call the Nine Muses by the Names of Women, but why so? not because the Sex had any thing to do with Poetry, but because in that Sex they're much fitter for prostitution. . . . I hate these Petticoat-Authors; 'tis false Grammar, there's no Feminine for the Latin word, 'tis entirely of the Masculine Gender, and the Language won't bear such a thing as a She-Author.

Sullen. Come, come, you forget your self; you know 'twas a Lady carry'd the Prize of Poetry in France t'other Day; and I assure you, if the Account were fairly stated, there have been in England some of that Sex who have done Admirably.

*A Comparison Between the Two Stages,* 1702

*T*he 1695–96 theatrical season introduced four new women playwrights. An anonymous "young Lady" wrote *She Ventures and He Wins* under the nom de plume Ariadne. The other newcomers were Catherine Trotter with *Agnes de Castro,* Delariviere Manley with *The Lost Lover*

81

and *The Royal Mischief,* and Mary Pix with *Ibrahim* and *The Spanish Wives.* All these women wrote in emulation of Behn, but each was markedly different from the others.

Catherine Trotter (1679–1749) was a Scotswoman with family connections and patrons among the nobility.[1] When she was four or five, her family was left impoverished by the death of her father, a distinguished naval commander. Her mother received a pension from Charles II for a year until the king's death, but did not receive another pension until the accession of Queen Anne. During the intervening years, she and her two daughters presumably lived as poor relations. Catherine, the youngest daughter, was petite, "celebrated for her beauty," with "a remarkable liveliness in her eye, and delicacy of complexion" (*Life,* p. xlvi). She was also a child prodigy:

> She gave very early marks of her genius, and was not passed her childhood, when she surprized a company of her relations and friends with extemporary verses on an incident, which had fallen under her observation in the street. . . . She both learned to write, and made herself mistress of the French language, by her own application and diligence, without any instructor. But she had some assistance in the study of the Latin grammar and Logic, of which latter she drew up an abstract for her own use.
>
> (*Life,* pp. iv–v)

In 1693, at the age of only fourteen, she published some verses to Bevil Higgons on his recovery from smallpox and, much more impressive, an autobiographical epistolary novel entitled *Olinda's Adventures.* The novel is remarkable for its date in technique, liveliness, and charm. *Olinda's Advertures* was translated into French and went through a half dozen English editions by 1724; the editions of 1718 and 1724 carried Trotter's name.[2]

At sixteen she wrote her first play, *Agnes de Castro,* based on Aphra Behn's novel of that name. This tragedy shows a triangle of perfect lovers. The Prince of Portugal loves his wife's favorite, Agnes de Castro, but nobly conceals his illicit passion. Agnes is devoted to her mistress. The princess, although she discovers the prince's secret passion, continues unselfishly to love both her husband and her friend. This harmony enrages Alvaro and his sister Elvira, who love Agnes and the prince, and their machinations produce the catastrophe. Elvira stabs the princess in mistake for Agnes, then accuses Agnes of the murder. Alvaro, planning to rape Agnes, steals her from her jailors. Threatened by the princess's ghost, Elvira goes mad and stabs her ally Bianca, who then reveals the entire plot. At the last minute Alvaro kills Agnes in mistake for the prince, who is with difficulty prevented from falling on his sword. *Agnes de Castro* is written in weak blank verse; the lines end with one or two extra syllables. The dialogue of the play is peculiar. Although several characters occasionally appear on stage at the same time, there is almost never an actual conversation; usually there are only duologues and soliloquies. The total effect is of a Senecan tragedy a hundred years out of date.

That a beautiful girl of genteel family, at a time when it was far from respectable for a woman to be a playwright, should enter the theatrical world at the age of sixteen is astonishing. Her action must partly be taken as a measure of the economic distress of her family. She protected herself by working anonymously; in the dedication she says she "Conceals her Name, to shun that of Poetess." The title page of *Agnes de Castro* specifies that the play was written by a "Lady," and the dedication addresses the Earl of Dorset and Middlesex with easy familiarity: "This little Off-spring of my early Muse was first Submitted to Your Lordship's Judgment, whether it shou'd be Stifled in the Birth, or Preserv'd to try its Fortune in the World; and . . . 'tis from Your Sentence it has ventur'd thus far." The play's anonymity, its familiar dedication to a nobleman, its elevated subject, and its formal, bookish style publicized the author as a learned lady.

Delariviere Manley (1672–1724) had an altogether different reputation. Manley, also born a gentlewoman, was duped into scandal, and eventually turned to writing to earn her living.[3] She was the daughter of Sir Roger Manley—cavalier, soldier, and writer. Sir Roger achieved his knighthood when he left the university at sixteen to fight for Charles I. Going into exile with other cavaliers, he continued in the military as his profession, attaining before his death the rank of lieutenant-colonel. He was also a man of learning and literature, publishing a translation from the Dutch and several military histories. In 1672, at the time Delariviere was born, he was lieutenant-governor of the island of Jersey; in 1680 he became governor of Languard Fort, Suffolk. Sir Roger was by then a widower with four children. Delariviere Manley passed her girlhood at home under the care of a governess. Her only formal education was the study of French at the home of a Huguenot minister, where she was sent to recover from an adolescent infatuation. For a while it seemed that her education would be fashionably "finished" at court, but a promised position as a maid of honor to Queen Mary of Modena did not materialize because of the collapse of James II's fortunes.

At Sir Roger's death, shortly before the Glorious Revolution, Delariviere and her younger sister became the wards of their cousin, John Manley, some twenty years their senior. His father, Sir Roger's brother, had been a major in the Parliamentary army. In spite of this political difference between the brothers, Sir Roger had treated his nephew as a son and had provided his education; no doubt he thought he was leaving his young daughters in safe hands. When John Manley arrived to take custody of his wards, he "was in deep Mourning . . . for his Wife."[4] He took his cousins to London, where he persuaded Delariviere to marry him; they had a son. John's wife was still living, however, and after some years he returned to her and abandoned Delariviere, branded with the scandal of a bigamous marriage and an illegitimate child. Nearly a generation later she described her ruin in one of her novels under the character of Delia (a name she used as well as Delariviere and Dela):

> I was then wanting of Fourteen, without any Deceit, or Guess of it in others. . . .[5] To sum up all in a Little, I was marry'd, possess'd, and ruin'd. . . . the nearest remaining Relation of a Man was himself, the Traitor that had seduced me to Ruin by a specious Pretence.
>
> My Fortune was in his Hands. . . . I was young, unaquainted with the World, had never seen the Necessities of it, knew no Arts, had not been expos'd to any Hardships. My Father, a Man of true Honour and Principles, nicely Just in his Affairs with all the World, liv'd in a handsome manner, and so I had been educated. What could I do? forlorn! distressed! beggared! to whom could I run for Refuge, even from Want and Misery, but to the very Traitor that had undone me?
>
> (*Atalantis*, 2: 189, 193)

She found a refuge in the demimonde as a member of the household of the lascivious and ruthless Duchess of Cleveland. After a while, on the pretext that Manley was intriguing with her son, the duchess dismissed her. At this point Manley turned to writing to earn a living.

In 1696 she published a collection of letters, then produced a comedy and a tragedy. In March her comedy *The Lost Lover; or, The Jealous Husband* appeared under the patronage of the Duke of Devonshire and Sir Thomas Skipwith, comanager of the Drury Lane theater. *The Lost Lover* deservedly failed. The characters and dialogue are worn; the structure and motivation are poorly handled. The intrigues, vague as they are, go like this: Wilmore loves Marina; in order to secure her fortune, he becomes engaged to her mother, Lady Young-Love. He successfully circumvents the malice of his discarded mistress, prevents Marina's marriage to his father, and marries off Lady Young-Love to Sir Amorous Courtall. Wilmore's friend Wildman attempts to seduce a former sweetheart now married to a jealous old merchant; foiled, he contents himself with his present sweetheart.

Manley's preface to *The Lost Lover* is an odd mixture of apology and defiance. Her "little success," she says, was no surprise to her: "To confess my Faults, I own it an unpardonable one, to expose, after two years reflection, the Follies of seven days, (for barely in that time this Play was wrought) and my self so great a Stranger to the Stage, that I . . . in the six foregoing years, had actually been but twice at the House." Then she asserts:

> I am now convinc'd Writing for the Stage is no way proper for a Woman, to whom all Advantages but meer Nature, are refused. . . . Had I confin'd my Sense, as before, to some short Song of Phillis, a Tender Billet, and the freedom of agreeable conversation, I had still preserved the Character of a Witty Woman. . . . I think my Treatment much severer than I deserved; I am satisfied the bare Name of being a Woman's Play damn'd it beyond its own want of Merit.

She thanks Sir Thomas Skipwith for the production of her comedy and says that she has a tragedy already in rehearsal and cannot recall it.

This was *The Royal Mischief,* produced by the rival company at Lincoln's Inn Fields. The prologue appealed to the critics to give the poetess a second chance. The "royal mischief" is Princess Homais, who conceives an incestuous passion for her husband's nephew, Prince of Colchis. Aided by a former lover and her eunuch, she seduces the prince and persuades him to condemn his virtuous bride Bassima for an alleged adultery with Chief Vizier Osman. Homais is finally killed by her husband, and the remorseful prince falls on his sword. This is fairly standard tragic fare, but Manley's imagination runs away with her in the last act. Here Homais, while dying, throws her own blood and gore all over her husband and tries to strangle her lover so that they can continue their adulteries in hell. Osman begs the ultimate favor of Bassima while she is dying of poison, rather a necrophiliac touch. He is punished by being shot alive out of a cannon. His wife goes mad and (mercifully offstage) wanders about picking up bits of his smoking remains, singeing her hands.

*The Royal Mischief* is as erotic as extravagant. For example, the eunuch Acmat tells the prince of Homais's love for his portrait, the chief ornament of her bedroom:

> How often have I seen this lovely Venus,
> Naked, extended, in the gaudy Bed,
> Her snowy Breasts all panting with desire,
> With gazing, melting Eyes, survey your Form,
> And wish in vain, 't had Life to fill her Arms.
>
> (p. 17)

Again, when Homais receives news of the prince's arrival, Acmat advises her not to be "vicious." She replies:

> What to conceal desire, when every
> Attom of me trembles with it, I'le strip
> My Passion naked of such Guile, lay it
> Undrest and panting at his feet. . . .
>
> (p. 20)

Manley defended such passages in her epistle to the readers: "The principal Objection made against this Tragedy is the warmth of it . . . in all Writings of this kind, some particular Passion is describ'd, as a Woman I thought it Policy to begin with the softest. . . . when gentle love stood ready to afford an easy Victory, I did not believe it possible to pursue him too far." Apparently the objection was not entirely that the language was erotic, but, as in Behn's case, that a woman wrote it, and wrote as uninhibitedly as a man. Manley responded to this by pointing out that *Aureng-Zebe* and *The Double Discovery* (i.e., *The Spanish Friar*), both by Dryden, "have touches as full of natural fire as possible."

Whatever its extravagancies of plot and diction, *The Royal Mischief,* better structured and motivated than *The Lost Lover,* was successful.[6] The love scenes between Bassima and Osman, as played by Bracegirdle and Betterton, were undoubtedly moving on stage, and Elizabeth Barry performed the part of Homais with verve, exceeding, according to Manley, "that perfection which before she was justly thought to have arrived at." The success of the play restored Manley's self-esteem; her preface to *The Royal Mischief* shows that she felt herself launched on a successful career.

The third new woman playwright, Mary Griffith Pix (1666–1709), was different in class and background from Manley and Trotter.[7] Her father was a vicar in Oxfordshire, and her mother had good family connections, so we can assume a home of some books and learning. In 1684, at the age of eighteen, Mary Griffith married George Pix, a London merchant tailor about her own age. They had one child, who died in 1690. At the age of thirty, Mary Pix began a career as a writer, an unusual step for the wife of a London merchant. It is possible that George Pix died and that Mary Pix turned to the theater for a livelihood; perhaps the Pix family may have been economically distressed for some other reason. It is also possible that Pix wrote merely to please herself: she says in the dedication to her first comedy, *The Spanish Wives,* that from childhood she had an "Inclination to Poetry." Whatever the reasons for Pix's becoming a professional author, in 1696 she produced a novel, *The Inhuman Cardinal; or, Innocence Betrayed;*[8] a tragedy, *Ibrahim, the Thirteenth Emperor of the Turks;* and a comedy, *The Spanish Wives.*

*Ibrahim,* a historical tragedy, was produced by the patent company in late spring. The action turns on Sultan Ibrahim's rape of Morena, fiancée of General Amurat. Sheker Para, the sultan's chief mistress, instigates the rape to gain revenge on Amurat for rebuffing her amorous advances. The play ends with the political downfall and death of Ibrahim, and the suicide of Sheker Para. Morena poisons herself in emulation of Roman heroines like Lucrece, and Amurat stabs himself for grief. Although based on historical events, the play is Fletcherian in structure and language; it reads like *Valentinian* with an eastern setting. *Ibrahim* contains some stageworthy scenes. Morena kneels to the sultan and pleads piteously for her honor; she bloodies her hands snatching the sultan's scimitar in a suicide attempt; after the rape, she raves and Amurat rages. A contemporary critic gives a fair evaluation: "This Play, if it want the Harmony of Numbers, and the Sublimity of Expression, has yet a Quality, that at least ballances that Defect, I mean the Passions; for the Distress of Morena never fail'd to bring Tears into the Eyes of the Audience; which few Plays, if any since Otway's have done."[9]

*Ibrahim* was successful not only in 1696 but in later years; it was performed several times in 1704 and revived in 1715. In the dedication Pix modestly credits her success to the fact that the story was true and that the actors "gave it Life ... each maintain'd their Character beyond my hopes." She adds a preface to correct a mistake: Ibrahim was the twelfth rather than the thirteenth Turkish emperor. This self-conscious accuracy goes along with the humility she expresses, in both dedication and preface, about her sex. A close reading, she says, "will too soon find out the Woman, the imperfect Woman."

That summer Pix asked the town to "Oblige a Woman twice" in her prologue to a three-act comedy, *The Spanish Wives*.[10] A skillful double plot contrasts the situations of two young wives. The first is married to the merry old governor of Barcelona, who "gives his Wife more Liberty than is usual in Spain" (dramatis personae). His policy is vindicated. Although the governor's lady is tempted by the advances of a young English colonel, she is touched by her husband's goodness, repents, and vows fidelity. In contrast, Elenora is kept "under eleven Locks" (p. 1) by her husband, a jealous and avaricious marquess forced on her by cruel guardians. She had previously been contracted to Count Camillus, who, bent on retrieving his bride, successfully intrigues to steal Elenora from her husband and obtain a divorce for her. The marquess is comically contemptible. He regrets the loss of his wife's fortune as much as the loss of her person, crying out distractedly, "My Estate and my Wife" in the manner of Shylock's "My ducats, and my daughter." The governor is also comic, but neither foolish nor contemptible. Continually breaking into snatches of song, he is reminiscent of Old Merrythought in *The Knight of the Burning Pestle. The Spanish Wives*, though slight, is a lively and amusing farce. Some of the marital repartee is tellingly human. Music, song, dance, and disguise add to the fun and provide stage spectacle. Not surprisingly, "this Farce had the good Fortune to please";[11] performances are recorded as late as 1726. Of the plays offered by women in the 1695–96 season, Pix's are the most entertaining and stageworthy.

The plays of Trotter, Manley, and Pix had all been preceded in September by "Ariadne's" intrigue comedy, *She Ventures and He Wins*. In the main plot, an heiress named Charlot decides to find a husband who loves her for herself as well as for her money. She woos, weds, tests, and finally rewards Lovewell. In the subplot, Freeman and Urania, a vintner and his wife, revenge themselves on conceited Squire Wouldbe for attempting to seduce Urania. Wouldbe hates the "nauseous fondness" (p. 10) of his wife Dowdy, who "Crys and Snivels" (p. 9) whenever he leaves the house. He is forced to conciliate her, however, because he is dependent upon his mother-in-law, who supplies their household goods from her pawnshop. In a clumsy and incomplete denouement, Wouldbe's adulterous intentions are exposed to Dowdy. Nothing is known of the author, but she advertised herself as a follower of Behn. In the prologue "Our Author hopes indeed,/ You will not think, though charming Aphra's dead,/ All Wit with her, and with Orinda's fled." In the preface "Ariadne" confesses that her faults as a writer "could not conquer the Inclination I had for Scribling from my Childhood. And when our Island enjoyed the Blessing of the Incomparable Mrs. Behn, even then I had much ado to keep my Muse from shewing her Impertinence; but, since her death, has claim'd a kind of Privilege; and, in spite of me, broke from her Confinement."

Trotter, Manley, and Pix used the same line of advertisement; all sought advantage from the novelty of female authorship, appealing to the chivalry and amorousness of the men, and the partisanship of the women:

> To day t'incite your Charity the more,
> A Female Author does your Smiles implore;
> . . . . . . . . . . . . . . . . . . . . . . . . . . . . . . . . . . . . . . . . . . . .
> She's Dead, if Try'd by strict Poetick Laws;
> But Men of Honour can't refuse a Womans Cause. . . .
> Prologue, *Agnes de Castro*

> My last kind Wishes Ladies are for you,
> Espouse your Sexes Cause, and bravely too. . . .
> Prologue, *The Royal Mischief*

By the great Rules of Honour all Men know
They must not Arm on a Defenceless Foe.
The Author on her weakness, not her strength relies,
And from your Justice to your Mercy flies.

Epilogue, *Ibrahim*

All three women had their first plays premiered by the
patent company at Drury Lane and seem to have been
friends. They seem an oddly assorted trio—the wife of a
London merchant, a rakish cast wife, and a genteel girl of
sixteen—but the theatrical world was small and their
friendship may have been a purely literary one. Whatever
the personal relationships among them, they felt a group
identity as women playwrights and expressed that feeling
publicly in verses about their desire to fill the vacant
female laureateship. For example, Trotter's *Agnes de Castro*
appeared in print with commendatory verses from Manley:

Orinda, and the Fair Astrea gone,
Not one was found to fill the Vacant Throne:
Aspiring Man had quite regain'd the Sway,
Again had Taught us humbly to Obey;
Till you (Natures third start, in favour of our Kind)
With stronger Arms, their Empire have disjoyn'd,
. . . . . . . . . . . . . . . . . . . . . . . . . . . . . . . . . . . . . . . . . . .
O! How I long in the Poetick Race,
To loose the Reins, and give their Glory Chase;
For thus Encourag'd, and thus led by you,
Methinks we might more Crowns than theirs Subdue.

Manley's *Royal Mischief* was printed with commendatory
verses from Trotter and Pix. Trotter (still anonymous as
"the Author of Agnes de Castro") compliments Manley as
the female literary champion:

Th' Attempt was brave, how happy your success,
The Men with shame our Sex with Pride confess;

For us you've vanquisht, though the toyl was yours,
You were our Champion, and the Glory ours.
Well you've maintain'd our equal right in Fame,
To which vain Man had quite engrost the claim. . . .

Pix addresses Manley as "Pride of our Sex, and Glory of the Stage," claiming that she is "Like Sappho Charming, like Afra Eloquent."

The presumption of these verses provoked a dramatic burlesque of the three women the following September, when Drury Lane opened the season with *The Female Wits; or, The Triumvirate of Poets at Rehearsal*, written by an anonymous Mr. W. M. *The Female Wits*, although occasionally heavyhanded, is an amusing satire in the tradition of Buckingham's *Rehearsal*. Manley, under the name Marsilia, bears the brunt of the ridicule; the play in rehearsal is a point-by-point spoof of her *Royal Mischief*.

In the play-within-the-play, Lady Loveall (=Princess Homais) loves her husband's son Fastin. This is in accord with her vow to keep her wishes within her own family; she has already seduced the steward and the butler. (Homais's previous lovers were the Grand Vizier Osman and his cousin.) The maid, Betty Useful (=the eunuch Acmat), describes to Fastin his stepmother's love for his picture in language that parodies the erotic description of Homais in *The Royal Mischief*:

A Thousand tender Names all Day and Night she gives you, but you can never scape her Lips, her Curtains by me drawn wide, discover your goodly Figure; each Morn the idol's brought, eagerly she prints the Dead Colours, throws her tawny Arms abroad, and vainly hopes kisses so Divine, wou'd inspire the painted Nothing, and mould into Man.

(p. 36)

Fastin's wife Isabella years before had silently conceived a platonic affection for the steward Amorous (=Bassima and Osman). This middle-class setting incomprehensibly drifts into the storming of a castle as Marsilia announces that she has "miraculously" (p. 54) turned the play into an opera. The author spares none of Manley's absurdities in the last act of *The Royal Mischief.* Lady Loveall tries to cover her husband "with Livid Gore" (p. 60). Amorous continues to woo Isabella while they are trapped on the leads of the castle; they escape to the moon, but Marsilia had originally intended to poison Isabella and to "ram" Amorous "into a great Gun, and scatter him o're the sturdy Plain" (p. 54).

After this preposterous conclusion, Marsilia fatuously remarks, "Well, sure by this Play, the Town will perceive what a woman can do" (p. 63). Marsilia tells her fellow poetesses, "T'wou'd be but civil of the Men to lay down their Pens for one Year, and let us divert the Town; but if we shou'd, they'd certainly be asham'd ever to take 'em up again" (p. 5). She instructs the women dancers, "Pray take care, Gentlewomen, as we Poets are fain to do, that we may excell the Men" (p. 46); and during the rehearsal of the castle storming she is so discontented with the actors that she says, "I am sorry I had not this Castle taken by women" (p. 52).

*The Female Wits* depicts Marsilia as vain, catty, and morally oblique. She is so conceited about her own creation—"the Love so passionate, the Lines so strong"—that she fears "not a Female Actress in England can reach 'em" (p. 3). She repeatedly quotes her own lines to prove herself an adept of love: "My Scorching Raptures make a Boy of Jove;/ That Ramping God shall learn of me to Love" (p. 4). When a friend asks, "Won't the Ladies think some of those Expressions indecent?", Marsilia replies complacently, "I understand the Ladies better than you. To my knowledge they love words that have warmth, and fire, &c. in 'em" (p. 4). Her more practical experience

with love is also alluded to. Although she is rude to the
players, they have to put up with her because she is a
favorite with the "Masters" (p. 18). This is a reference to
Sir Thomas Skipwith, comanager of Drury Lane, who
supposedly produced Manley's first play because she was
having an affair with him. She is ridiculed for ignorantly
aspiring with rant like *The Royal Mischief* to the same
stature as Aphra Behn. While *The Emperor of the Moon* was
becoming one of the repertory's enduringly popular
farces, Marsilia foolishly claims, "Here they have talked of
the Emperour of the Moon, and the World in the Moon,
but discovered nothing of the Matter" (p. 33). Marsilia
finally becomes so enraged at the players that she leaves in
a huff, taking her play to the rival company at Lincoln's
Inn Fields. She is dismissed from the stage in the age-old
manner of farce, physical disgrace: "The wrathful Lady
has run over a Chair, shatter'd the Glasses to pieces: The
Chair-Men, to save it, fell pell-mell in with her. She has lost
part of her Tail, broke her Fan, tore her Ruffles, and
pull'd off half my Lord Whiffle's Wigg, with trying to rise
by it: So they are, with a Shagreen Air, and tatter'd Dress,
gone into the Coach" (p. 66).

The other two female wits are treated less harshly.
Catherine Trotter appears as Calista, "A Lady that pretends to the learned Languages, and assumes to her self
the Name of a Critick" (dramatis personae). The main
point of attack is conceited ignorance. " 'Tis the vainest,
proudest senseless Thing, she pretends to Grammer,
writes in Mood and Figure; does every thing methodically"
(p. 5). Calista is catty to her compatriots about their lack of
classical learning, making such lofty statements as "I read
Aristotle in his own Language: The Translation may alter
the Expression" (p. 8).[12] When conversation turns to Jonson's *Catiline,* she claims of the first speech in the play, "I
know it so well, as to have turn'd it into Latin" (p. 9). With

this one stroke the satirist ridicules both Trotter's classical learning and her stance as a drama critic.

Mary Pix is treated most gently of all, probably because she was humble about her modest gifts. She is satirized as Mrs. Wellfed, "a fat Female Author, a good sociable well-natur'd Companion, that will not suffer Martyrdom rather than take off three Bumpers in a Hand" (dramatis personae). She does, she confesses, drink "in a Morning. . . . else I had never come to this bigness, Madam, to the encreasing that inexhausted spring of Poetry; that it may swell, o'erflow, and bless the barren Land" (pp. 4–5). Although she is "big enough to be the Mother of the Muses" (p. 5), she is good-humored about her own bulk. The only poetess unaccompanied by a gallant, she thanks heaven "I'm big enough to take care of my self" (p. 15). She is humble about her lack of learning and has no pretense to friends among "Cabals of Poets and Judges" (p. 6). Although she sometimes annoys and pesters the players, on the whole she gets along with them amiably enough. Of the three female wits, Pix is the only one to receive a compliment on her work: "A bouncing Dame! But she has done some things well enough" (p. 11).

According to the preface, The Female Wits was "Acted six Days running without intermission"—apparently further performances were squelched by Manley's patron, the Duke of Devonshire[13]—and "the Auditors thought the Pictures were true, or they would have condemn'd the Person that drew 'em, in less than six Days." The satirical "Pictures" were not too unjust to Pix and Trotter. There are other contemporary references to Pix's girth and good nature;[14] the tippling may or may not have been added for more fun. Similarly, the satire of Trotter is probably only exaggerated. It is reasonable to suppose that a sixteen-year-old girl who had mastered French, Latin, and logic and had had a play produced would be somewhat conceited. But the attack on Manley was venomous. Certainly *The Royal Mischief* was an outrageously bad play that deserved a spoof, but many of the qualities attributed to Manley herself are a function of the resentment against her presumption as an outspoken feminist. She was by no means so fatuous as she was portrayed in *The Female Wits,* and she was by no means so conceited as to be insensible. After *The Female Wits,* she left the theater for ten years.

From 1696 to 1705 Manley published only a poem on Dryden's death. During this time she became the lover of a lawyer named John Tilly and joined him in get-rich-quick schemes. In 1702 she gave up Tilly so that he could repair his fortunes by marrying a rich widow. She also became the friend and correspondent of Richard Steele, who confided to her his amours and projects. She recommended her own midwife to him, and prevented his financial ruin in an alchemical scheme. She and Steele later quarreled, partly over politics, and insulted each other in print.[15] Although the spirit of the age was changing, Manley maintained her cavalier and Tory attitudes. In particular, she detested the Churchill family. This led her to her true literary medium—the political and sexual scandal novel. In 1705 she brought out the two parts of *The Secret History of Queen Zarah and the Zarazians,* an attack on Sarah Churchill, Duchess of Marlborough, and the Whig party.

She then returned to the theater in 1706 with a feminist play, *Almyna; or, The Arabian Vow.* In this tragedy, Almanzor, Sultan of the East, because his first wife was an adulteress, has concluded that women "Have mortal Souls, in common with the Brutes" (p. 2). He now marries frequently, executing each of his brides the morning after the wedding. He then meets the beautiful Almyna, who has been educated in Memphis:

What ever Greek or Roman Eloquence,

> Egyptian Learning, and Philosophy can teach;
> She has, by Application, made her own.
>
> (p. 10)

The sultan considers that her education makes her even worse than ordinary women, but falls in love with her beauty at first sight. Almyna loves Almanzor and is inspired with a plan that will make her famous: she will wed the sultan and convert him from hatred of women. She makes him an eloquent speech citing heroic ladies of the past:

> If yet thou doubt whether our Sex have Souls,
> What Presidents, my Lord, cou'd I not bring thee?
> ............................................................................................
> What was not fam'd Semiramis the Queen of Nations
> Whom mighty Alexander, emulated?
> ............................................................................................
> What was not our fair Neighbouring Judith,
> When th' Assyrian Monarch had resolv'd,
> To sweep whole Nations, like the Dust before him?
> Had she not a Soul? And an exalted one?
> That Durst alone attempt, what all Dispair'd off.
> Her Honour at the stake she rusht thro' all,
> And by one stroke, redeem'd the East from ruin.
> Or cou'd the Roman Ladies, their Virginia,
> Lucretia, Portia, Clelia, thousands more,
> Without a Soul, have gain'd such endless Fames?
> Or Cleopatra, that Heroick Queen,
> In Death, she nobly follow'd Anthony.
> But I shou'd much intrude, shou'd I but tell
> The Half of what our Sex have dar'd for Glory.
>
> (pp. 45–46)

They marry; after an ecstatic wedding night, the sultan resolves to watch Almyna die, to see if her heroic "frame of Mind be inborn to her" (p. 59). She faces death with such fortitude that Almanzor stops the execution and accepts her as his queen:

Henceforth be it not once imagin'd
That Women have not Souls, divine as we.
Who doubts, let 'em look here, for Confutation,
And reverence with us Almyna's Vertue.
(p. 64)

Meanwhile, in the subplot Almyna's sister Zoradia is pining for love of Abdalla, the sultan's brother, who has forsaken her. In the last act Abdalla and Zoradia are both killed in an abortive palace revolt; the sultan interprets this as a punishment for his custom of murdering his wives.

Although Manley was wary enough of party and personal spite to have her play performed and published anonymously, the name Almyna is an anagram of her own name.[16] The heroine reflects Manley's own wish for a better education; she had complained in the preface to *The Lost Lover* that "all Advantages but meer Nature are refused" to women. *Almyna,* which has a special interest as the first English play based on *The Arabian Nights,*[17] shows an improvement in Manley's competence both in plotting and dialogue. The casting of Betterton as Almanzor, Barry as Almyna, and Bracegirdle as Zoradia would have seemed to assure success. But, as the preface complains, it was played "at so ill-fated a Time, viz: The immediate Week before Christmas." Further performances were delayed because of the "long Indisposition" of Wilks, who played Abdalla, and the retirement of Mrs. Bracegirdle. Manley was impatient—she seems to have needed money at this time—and had the play printed, "Humbly Inscrib'd to the Right Honourable the Countess of Sandwich."

Another eleven years passed before Manley again produced a play. During this period she wrote a bestselling scandal novel, *Secret Memoirs and Manners of Several Persons of Quality of Both Sexes from the New Atalantis.* The first two volumes of this racy roman à clef appeared in 1709 and caused such a furor that the Whig government suppressed the book as well as it could and arrested the printers and the author.[18] Manley defended herself cleverly and "with an Air full of Penitence" (*Rivella*, p. 113); then, when she was released a few months later, she promptly brought out two more volumes under the title *Memoirs of Europe* (1710). Impression after impression of the *Atalantis* sold out. It was translated into French and had gone into its seventh English edition by 1736.[19] Manley also assisted Swift in writing Tory political pamphlets and succeeded him as editor of *The Examiner*. About this time she began a liaison with alderman and printer John Barber that continued until her death.[20] Also during this period a hack writing for the unscrupulous publisher Curll began a biography of Manley under the title *The History of Rivella* (to suggest Delariviere). Manley heard of this and offered Curll an autobiography instead.[21] Very shortly *The Adventures of Rivella; or, The History of the Author of the Atalantis* (London, 1714) appeared anonymously, purporting to be a translation from the French of a dialogue between the Chevalier D'Aumont and Sir Charles Lovemore. Rivella, in the old Restoration fashion, is primarily a bon vivante and only peripherally a writer: "She rarely speaks of her own Writings, unless when she wou'd expresly ask the Judgment of her Friends . . . one might discourse Seven Years together with Rivella, and never find out from her self, that she was a Wit, or an Author" (*Rivella*, p. 11). Near the close of the book Lovemore persuades her of "the Folly of a Woman's disobliging any one Party, by a Pen equally qualified to divert all" (*Rivella*, p. 116). Rivella "has accordingly set her self again to write a Tragedy for the Stage" (*Rivella*, p. 117).

Manley's tragedy, *Lucius, the First Christian King of Britain,* appeared in May 1717. By this time she had made up her quarrel with Steele; she dedicated the play to him and he wrote the prologue. The plot of this pseudohistorical play is almost too crowded to follow. In brief, Prince Lucius, son of the usurper of Britain, loves Rosalinda, widowed queen of Albany and Aquitain. Lucius, in order to win her, converts (rather perfunctorily) to Christianity, and they are secretly married. Also in love with Rosalinda are the Prince of Albany and King Vortimer of Britain. Also in love with Lucius are the Princess of Gallia and Albany's sister. The four disappointed lovers plot for five acts to separate Lucius and Rosalinda. After numerous slanders, abductions, and threatened rapes, Lucius is tricked into killing the disguised Vortimer. Aghast at his parricide, he falls into a trance. All is saved when the Prince of Cambria reveals that Lucius is the son, not of the usurping Vortimer, but of the true king of Britain. Manley, now a bestselling author, not only offered the play under her own name but used an epilogue by Prior which once again made publicity out of her sex with the same bravado that characterized her entry to the theater:

> Approve what One of us presents to Night,
> Or every mortal Woman here shall write;
> ...............................................................................
> As long as we have Eyes, or Hands, or Breath,
> We'll Look, or Write, or Talk you all to Death;
> Unless ye yield for Better and for Worse:
> Then the She-Pegasus shall gain the Course;
> And the gray Mare will prove the better Horse.

Judging from the preface, Booth and Oldfield turned in stellar performances as the romantic lovers. The play was revived and printed again in 1720,[22] perhaps in connection with Manley's publication that year of a collection of seven short novels under the title *The Power of Love*.

Manley did not bring out another play in the last seven years of her life, although she wrote at least two. Her will, proved after her last illness and death were reported in the newspapers in 1724, mentions that of her papers, "one

Tragedy called the Duke of Somerset and one Comedy named the double Mistress . . . may perhaps turn to some account."[23] These plays are lost. Nine years later, in 1733, *The Court Legacy,* an unacted ballad opera, was published; the title page claimed it was written "By the Author of the New Atalantis." Although credited to Manley in theatrical checklists, this incoherent three-act playlet is not mentioned in her will nor is it similar to her other works. Presumably the publisher was attempting to cash in on the continuing popularity of the *Atalantis.*

Of the three new women playwrights, Delariviere Manley, with only four plays produced, was the least important dramatist but the most interesting literary personality. Her plays display the same energetic exuberance as her scandal novels; *Almyna,* in particular, shows that she could have written at a respectable level for the theater had she chosen to. Manley seems to have been wary of the stage after *The Female Wits,* fearful of being roasted again in theatrical criticism. Twenty years later, her autobiography remembered the burlesque as a painful episode:

> her first Tragedy . . . was much more famous for the Language, Fire and Tenderness than the Conduct. . . . her self could hardly now bear the reading of it.
>
> Behold another wrong Step towards ruining Rivella's Character with the World; the Incense that was daily offer'd her upon this Occasion from the Men of Vogue and Wit: Her apartment was daily crouded with them. . . . Her Vanity was now at the Height. . . . and she still went on in her own Way . . . till Experience gave her enough of her Indiscretion.
>
> (*Rivella,* pp. 41-45)

*Lucius,* the only play she ever again produced under her own name, came after she had established a reputation as a novelist.

Unlike Manley, Catherine Trotter was not deterred by

*The Female Wits.* She continued to write plays and defected from the patent company to Lincoln's Inn Fields, where she became a friend and perhaps a protégée of Congreve, chief playwright for Betterton's company. In 1697 she sent Congreve some commendatory verses on *The Mourning Bride,* and he returned her a letter of thanks, regretting that the poem had arrived too late to be included in the printed edition.[24] Trotter cultivated literary friendships; she already knew Wycherley, who had written a prologue for *Agnes de Castro.*

In 1698 Lincoln's Inn Fields produced Trotter's most successful play, *Fatal Friendship.* This blank verse tragedy, less frigid than *Agnes,* depicts the misfortunes of Gramont and his friend Castalio. Before the play begins, Castalio has been wrongly declared a traitor and cast into prison; only payment of a heavy fine can release him. Meanwhile the impoverished Gramont has secretly married the equally impoverished Felicia (who is being wooed by his own father); their infant son is being held for ransom by pirates. Under pressure of financial need, he succumbs to his father's insistence that he marry the wealthy Lamira, who is, unknown to him, beloved by Castalio. Gramont refuses to consummate this bigamous marriage, but it sets off such a series of entanglements and mistakes that, in the last act, Gramont accidentally wounds Castalio and then stabs himself, just as a messenger brings too late the news of a royal pardon for all.

*Fatal Friendship* was explicitly designed to reform the stage. Trotter's dedication states that her play's "End is the most noble, to discourage Vice, and recommend a firm unshaken Virtue." There is no licentiousness and no villain; the characters are well intentioned but work at cross-purposes. Accidents bring on the disasters that Christian fortitude would have resolved. Gramont points the moral in his dying words:

O what a Wretch was I, that could not wait
Heav'ns time; the Providence that never fails
Those who dare trust it, durst I have been honest,
One day had chang'd the Scene, and made me happy.
(p. 56)

The commendatory poems praise the play's morality:

You stand the first of stage-reformers too.
No vicious stains pollute your moral scene;
Chast are your thoughts, and your expression clean.

George Farquhar sent Trotter a letter praising *Fatal Friendship* and "its beautiful author" and enclosed a copy of *Love and a Bottle* with the complaint that his play had been criticized for scandalizing the ladies. "As an argument of its innocence," he sent it "to stand its tryal before one of the fairest of the sex, and its best judge" (*Life*, p. viii).

Trotter dedicated *Fatal Friendship* to Princess Anne with an appeal for royal patronage because "when a Woman appears in the World under any distinguishing Character, she must expect to be the mark of ill Nature, but most one who seems desirous to recommend her self by what the other Sex think their peculiar Prerogative." This may be an oblique allusion to *The Female Wits*. If so, it is the only exception to the silence she maintained about the dramatic burlesque.

In 1700 Trotter made one of a group of women who wrote a collection of poems honoring Dryden after his death. In the same year she brought out her only comedy, *Love at a Loss; or, Most Votes Carry It*. According to the dedication, the play was originally intended as a subplot for one of her tragedies "when the Town had been little pleas'd with Tragedy intire." The comedy is almost as moral and reformed as her tragedies. In *Love at a Loss* each of three ladies nearly loses her man because of her own folly. Miranda's mistake is excessive coquettishness;

Lucilia's, a casual youthful flirtation that led her to write some imprudent letters; Lesbia's, consummation with her fiancé after the marriage contract but before the marriage. Although there is some intrigue, some watered-down double entendre, and some railing at marriage in the older Restoration manner, the lovers solve their problems through good sense. These sensible lovers carefully point morals. Lucilia's youthful flirtation, her "childish fault," has caused her "such dangers, such anxieties, as might warn all our Sex against those little Gallantries, with which they only think to amuse themselves; but tho' innocent, too often gain 'em such a Character of Lightness, as their future Conduct never can efface" (p. 54). The reformed rake uses logic to prove that husbands must treat their wives well:

> For treating them with rudeness, or neglect,
> Does most dishonour, on our selves reflect;
> If that respect which their own Merit drew,
> We think, by their becoming ours, less due
> And as in chusing, we their worth approve,
> We tax our Judgment, when we cease to love.
>
> (p. 56)

In the epilogue Lesbia lectures against premarital sex: "Hands, and Seals, and Oaths cannot secure/ A mind like Man's unfaithful and impure." The comedy was unsuccessful, which hardly surprises. *Love at a Loss* is more moral than merry.

The following year saw production of another highly moralized tragedy, *The Unhappy Penitent*. In this play, Charles VIII of France, long contracted to Margarite of Flanders, delays his marriage because he wishes to marry Ann of Brittanie. Margarite feels released from obligation by the delay and secretly marries the Duke of Lorrain, although the paragon Ann urges that Margarite first secure a formal release from her contract. Ann also urges

the king to fulfill his contract, in spite of her own inclination for him. Slander and confusion ensue as a result of
the machinations of the Duke of Brittanie, who hopes to
marry Margarite himself. Margarite, accused of whore-
dom, vows to enter a convent if her honor is cleared. After
the slander is exposed, her vow forbids a reconciliation
with her beloved Lorrain. The play ends with a grand
renunciation, Margarite going off to a convent in spite of
her husband's tender appeals. The king and Ann are left
not only to marry but also, considering that the king's
delay caused much of Margarite's trouble, to draw rather
priggish morals in the same haste-makes-waste spirit as
those at the end of *Fatal Friendship*. The morality of the
play is contractual. Margarite violates her contract with the
king, but redeems her mistake by keeping a contract with
heaven.

The dedication of *The Unhappy Penitent* to Lord Halifax
shows Trotter ever more serious about her moral duty as a
writer. In a tragedy, giving delight must be "Subservient"
to "forming an Instructive Moral." After a critical analysis
of the works of Dryden, Otway, Lee, and Shakespeare, she
apologizes for a defect in her play: "The Distress is not
great enough, the Subject of it only the misfortune of
Lovers, which I partly design'd in Compliance with the
effiminate taste of the Age." Rejecting love as a suitable
spring for tragedy, Trotter chose patriotism as the major
passion for her next, and last tragedy, *The Revolution of
Sweden*. This play, which did not appear until five years
later, in 1706, was the logical culmination not only of her
theories of stage reform but also of her feminism.

*The Revolution of Sweden* is a historical play depicting
Gustavus's freeing of his country from the Danes and his
election as king. Interwoven with his military exploits are
the adventures of two married couples; each wife is the
superior of her husband. Christina, wife of the traitor

Beron, disguises as a young man and fights on the Swedish side. She soliloquizes on female courage:

> Why do I dread what will enflame
> The meanest Soldiers Courage? Are our Souls too
> Like their frail Mansions of weaker frame than Mans?
> Or can the force of Custom and Opinion
> Effect this difference? 'Tis so, the Hero
> Who undaunted, faces Death midst Cannons,
> Swords and Javelins, sinks under the less
> Honourable Dangers of Pain, Disease,
> Or Poverty, below a Womans weakness:
> And we whom Custom bars this active Valour,
> Branding it with Reproach, shrink at th' Alarm
> Of War, but where our Honour's plac'd, we oft
> Have shewn in its Defence a no less Manly daring.
>
> (p. 17)

The other heroine, Constantia, is the wife of Gustavus's ally, Count Arwide. She argues theology with the archbishop while she is held captive by the Danes. When treachery causes her to doubt her husband's patriotism, she prefers public good to private love and accuses her husband to Gustavus. Arwide, when proved innocent, not only forgives Constantia but loves her the more for her patriotism:

> Yes, my Constantia, thy exalted Vertue
> Constrain'd my Admiration, tho' a Sufferer by it.
> O wou'd Men emulate thy great Example,
> Renounce all private Ends, give up their dear
> Their warmest Passions, to the publick Safety;
> Each wou'd be happy in the common Good. . . .
>
> (p. 71)

Arwide describes his wife "Not as a Woman, as a worthy Friend" (p. 24). She "has that Softness which endears/ And melts the Soul to transport: But superior/ Reason holds the Reins" (p. 25).

*The Revolution of Sweden* was unsuccessful. In 1703 Trotter had sent a rough draft or synopsis of the play to Congreve, who returned a courteous letter of detailed suggestions. The finished play ran into the very difficulties that Congreve had tactfully but frankly warned against:

> I think the design in general very great and noble; the conduct of it very artful, if not too full of business, which may either run into length or obscurity. . . . You are the best judge, whether those of your own sex will approve as much of the heroic virtue of Constantia and Christina, as if they had been engaged in some *belle passion:* for my part, I like them better as they are. . . . The last act will have many harangues in it, which are dangerous in a catastrophe, if long, and not of the last importance.
>
> (*Life,* pp. xxii–xxiii)

In the preface Trotter acknowledged that her desire to instruct her audience had caused her to neglect pleasing them also:

> I . . . cou'd never allow my self to think of any Subject that cou'd not serve either to incite some useful Virtue, or check some dangerous Passion. With this design I thought writing for the Stage, a Work not unworthy those who wou'd not trifle their time away, and had so fix'd my Mind on contributing my part towards reforming the Corruptions of it, that no doubt I have too little consider'd the present tast of the Town.

No doubt the Town would have been better pleased if the heroines, as Congreve hinted, had been "engaged in some *belle passion.*" But Trotter was sincerely single-minded in her attempt at reform and in her desire to depict heroic women.

For this reason, *The Revolution of Sweden* is interesting as an early feminist statement. It is the type of play that the Duchess of Newcastle tried to write many years earlier.

Christina is the military-patriotic lady, and Constantia fulfills the duchess's ideal of the oratorical heroine, capable of arguing theology with learned prelates. In the dedication of the play to Lady Harriot Godolphin, Trotter spoke out for women's intellectual ability:

> Encouraging Indulgence to the Endeavours of our Sex ... might incite some greater Geniuses among us to exert themselves, and change our Emulation of a Neighbouring Nation's Fopperies, to the commendable Ambition of Rivalling them in their illustrious Women; Numbers we know among them, have made a considerable Progress in the most difficult Sciences, several have gain'd the Prizes of Poesie from their Academies, and some have been chosen Members of their Societies. This without doubt is not from any Superiority of their Genius to ours; But from the much greater Encouragement they receive, by the Publick Esteem, and the Honours that are done them. . . .

Trotter here refers to the fact that in 1701 the Prix de Poésie of the Académie Française had been awarded to Catherine Durand.[25] Trotter's letters show her admiration for Durand and for other intellectual Frenchwomen such as Madame Dacier.

Catherine Trotter, herself the most intellectual of the female wits, had by this time embarked on a new literary career as a philosophical and theological writer. In this field the moralistic and didactic qualities which mar her plays found appropriate expression. Trotter had early been an admirer of Locke, and in 1703 she wrote and published anonymously her *Defence of Mr. Locke's Essay of Human Understanding*. She was closely acquainted with Bishop Burnet and his wife, who knew the secret of her authorship and revealed it to Locke himself; he sent Trotter a letter and a present of books to thank her for her championship of his theories. She also wrote religious treatises such as *A Discourse concerning a Guide in Controver-*

*sies,* which was published in 1707 with a preface by Bishop Burnet. At the same time she was a voluminous letter writer, corresponding on religious, philosophical, and literary topics. For a time she corresponded with Leibnitz. Sophie Charlotte, queen of Prussia, heard of her accomplishments and dubbed her the Scots Sappho (*Life,* p. xxv). At the age of twenty-nine, Trotter married a clergyman named Cockburn and gave up writing for twenty years. Later she wrote, "Being married in 1708, I bid adieu to the muses, and so wholly gave myself up to the cares of a family, and the education of my children, that I scarce knew, whether there was any such thing as books, plays, or poems stirring in Great Britain" (*Life,* p. xl). After rearing four children in straitened circumstances, Trotter again returned to writing: "My young family was grown up to have less need of my assistance; and beginning to have some taste of polite literature, my inclination revived with my leisure" (*Life,* p. xl). She now presented another series of theological treatises, such as *Remarks upon the Principles and Reasoning of Dr. Rutherforth's Essay on the Nature and Obligation of Virtue,* published in 1747 with a preface by Warburton. She was still concerned about the intellectual handicaps of women:

> . . . those restraints, which have our sex confin'd,
> By partial custom, check the soaring mind:
> Learning deny'd us, we at random tread
> Unbeaten paths, that late to knowledge lead;
> By secret steps break thro' th' obstructed way,
> Nor dare acquirements gain'd by stealth display.
> If some advent'rous genius rare arise,
> Who on exalted themes her talent tries,
> She fears to give the work, tho' prais'd, a name,
> And flies not more from infamy than fame.[26]

Her own "extensive" frame as a controversialist (*Life,* p. xlv) led to a two-volume subscription edition of her works after her death in May 1749, at the age of seventy-one. Her works were edited by Thomas Birch, who wrote her biography as an introduction partly because "her own sex is intitled to the fullest information about one, who has done such honour to them, and raised our ideas of their intellectual powers" (*Life,* pp. i–ii).

Like Catherine Trotter, Mary Pix was undeterred by *The Female Wits,* although she also took her plays thereafter to Lincoln's Inn Fields. In the summer of 1697, less than a year after the burlesque, she brought out a comedy, *The Innocent Mistress.* The prologue, written by Motteux, mentions without rancor Pix's change of theaters: "Twice has our Poetess kind usage found;/Change not her Fortune, tho' she c[h]ang'd her Ground." The play picks up again the theme of forced marriage used in *The Spanish Wives.* The most important of a number of interwoven plots concerns Sir Charles Beauclair, now master of a large estate, but earlier "Marrid by his Friends, to a Rich ill-favour'd Widow" (dramatis personae). He nobly endures his terrible wife and "instead of making his life easie with jolly *Bona-robas,* dotes on a Platonick Mistress, who never allows him greater favours than to read Plays to her, kiss her hand, and fetch Heart-breaking Sighs at her Feet" (p. 3). This is Bellinda, who fell in love with Sir Charles before she knew he was married. Even though their relationship is strictly platonic, her conscience afflicts her. After a high-flown renunciation scene between the lovers, Lady Beauclair is recognized and reclaimed by her first husband, long thought dead. *The Innocent Mistress* was "a diverting Play, and met with good Success, tho' acted in the hot Season of the Year."[27]

Oddly enough, it was "sociable well-natur'd" Mary Pix who a few months later was at the center of an acrimonious dispute between the rival playhouses. In September 1697 George Powell, an actor and sometimes playwright for the patent company, brought out a comedy called *Imposture*

*Defeated; or, A Trick to Cheat the Devil.* Pix protested that the play was a plagiarism. She had taken a manuscript to the Drury Lane theater when she still wrote for that house and had asked Powell to persuade the company to perform it; instead, he stole her plot. Immediately Lincoln's Inn Fields brought out Pix's original as *The Deceiver Deceived.* The prologue plays on the titles of the two comedies in order to insult Powell:

> Deceiv'd Deceiver, and Impostor cheated!
> An Audience and the Devil too Defeated!
> . . . . . . . . . . . . . . . . . . . . . . . . . . . . . . . . . . . . . . . . . . . . . .
> No, Gallants, we those tricks don't understand;
> 'Tis t'other House best shows the slight of hand. . . .

A comparison of the two plays shows that Powell lifted the main plot outline. In Pix's *Deceiver Deceived,* an avaricious old Venetian senator named Bondi counterfeits blindness in order to avoid the expense of the presidency of Dalmatia. His young wife and his daughter seize the opportunity to wear their richest jewels and clothes, to write love letters, and to entertain their gallants—all under Bondi's very nose. Unable to bear this torture, Bondi fakes a miraculous religious cure. At this point the young lovers are helped by a servant who knows the blindness was a cheat. Under threat of exposure for political and religious fraud, Bondi is forced to dower his daughter so that she can marry her poor but worthy suitor. The young wife, a sympathetic *mal mariée,* was in love with her gallant before she was forced to marry Bondi. She has flirted during her husband's "blindness" but has preserved her honor; she now gives up her gallant with the wistful hope that she may be left a young widow. In Powell's *Imposture Defeated,* Bonde also feigns blindness in order to avoid the expense of the governorship of Dalmatia. Like Bondi, Bonde, when threatened with exposure, gives up his wealth and his daughter to the daughter's suitor. Powell exploits the pretended blindness to better dramatic effect than Pix. Bonde's wife is actually lustful and dishonest, and the revelation of Bonde's pretense comes at the right moment to expose her. This is the natural and expected turn in such a plot—the moment when the "blind" husband can no longer restrain himself and exposes his own dishonesty to catch his wife *in flagrante delicto*. Pix cannot exploit this expectation because she is sentimentalizing the wife; the wife is never going to be *in flagrante delicto*. Bondi's "cure" is oddly flat. Powell handled Pix's material well but framed it in a silly plot in which a young gallant, having gambled away his estate, sells his soul to the devil for fame and fortune.

Both plays were printed in 1698. The dedications show Pix angry but dignified and Powell on the defensive. Powell says, "I stand impeacht (at least the Publick Cry is loud upon that Subject) that I have stolen a Character from a Comedy of Mrs. P——t's." He claims that he took Bonde from a novel and that he "never Read" Pix's play. He contradicts himself in the next sentence, unless he advised the company to produce plays he had not read: " 'Tis true, such a one she brought into the House, and made me a Solicitor to the Company to get it Acted, which when I had obtain'd, she very mannerly carry'd the Play to the other House; and had I really taken the Character from her, I had done her no more than a piece of Justice." The normally humble Pix used the strongest language she ever used in a dedication: "I look upon those that endeavour'd to discountenance this Play as Enemys to me. . . . I must not trouble you with the little Malice of my Foe, nor is his Name fit to be mentioned . . . he has Printed so great a falshood, it deserves no Answer." She concludes by expressing delight that she is now "pleased and treated by those who please every Spectator with a Candour and Sweetness not to be expresst."

Pix here probably refers to Betterton and Congreve, who became involved in the quarrel with Powell. Betterton had small reason to like Powell. When the Lincoln's Inn Fields troupe split off from the United Company, Powell fell heir to a number of Betterton's roles and not only imitated Betterton's style in these roles but also imitated the now aging actor's infirmities.[28] Congreve, as the chief playwright for Lincoln's Inn Fields, was an associate of Pix and a partisan in the plagiarism dispute. *Animadversions on Mr. Congreve's Late Answer to Mr. Collier* (London, 1698) by a friend of Powell's, perhaps by Powell himself, describes Congreve attending a patent company performance with "his chief Actors and Actresses, together with the two She Things, call'd *Poetesses,* which Write for his House" (p. 34). They come to damn the play, "but when they found the malicious Hiss would not take, this very generous, obliging Mr. Congreve was heard to say, *We'll find out a New way for this Spark, take my word there is a way of clapping a Play down*" (pp. 34–35). Indications are that the play was Powell's and that Congreve made up a cabal to cry down Powell's plagiarized *Imposture Defeated.*

Whoever wrote the *Animadversions* goes out of his way to mention "the insufferable Dullness of P–x" and "the Lightness both in Head and Tail of the presuming T——r" (p. 14). The book is prefixed with verse characters of contemporary playwrights; those of Pix and Trotter are libellous:

> Or could I write like the two Female things
> With Muse Pen-feather'd, guiltless yet of Wings;
> And yet, it strives to Fly, and thinks it Sings.
> Just like the Dames themselves, who slant in Town,
> And flutter loosely, but to tumble down.
> The last that writ, of these presuming two,
> (For that Queen *Ca——ne* is no Play 'tis true)

And yet to Spell is more than she can do,
Told a High Princess, she from Men had torn
Those Bays, which they had long engross'd and worn.
But when she offers at our Sex thus Fair,
With four fine Copies to her Play,—O rare!
If she feels Manhood shoot—'tis I know where.
Let them scrawl on, and Loll, and Wish at ease,
(A Feather oft does Woman's Fancy please.)
Till by their Muse (more jilt than they) accurst,
We know (if possible) which writes the worst.

Just prior to the *Animadversions* Pix had brought out the play alluded to, *Queen Catharine; or, The Ruins of Love,* for which Trotter wrote an epilogue. Pix's prologue acknowledges the presumption of writing a history play after Shakespeare, and modestly admits the inability of her "enervate voice" to "wake the mighty dead." She will therefore confine herself to the romantic rather than the martial side of history. Accordingly, her heroine is Henry V's widow. Edward IV in his youth fell in love with Catharine but she preferred Owen Tudor. Edward has since done all he could to persecute the queen and her husband, who are the model of a happy couple. The Duke of Gloucester (only perfunctorily characterized, since the audience already knows he will be the villainous Richard III) arranges for Edward to surprise Tudor and Catharine. Tudor is killed, the queen goes half-mad with grief, and Lord Dacres predicts that their children will produce a noble race of princes. In the subplot, Gloucester's schemes prevent a marriage between the Duke of Clarence and Queen Catharine's ward Isabella. This romance has naturally divided Clarence's loyalties in the ongoing civil war. The play reduces the Wars of the Roses to a quarrel over thwarted love.

In 1699 Pix wrote *The False Friend; or, The Fate of Disobedience,* announcing in the prologue her intention of participating in the reform of the stage. This purpose produced the worst of her plays. She intends to show the error of two young couples who marry secretly without parental consent, but since all are noble and wealthy, it seems likely that the father's consent would eventually have been forthcoming. The real mistake the young lovers make is trusting their false friend Appamia, who secretly loves one of the young men. Her jealous machinations lead to a fatal duel between the two husbands, the poisoning of one wife, and the madness of the other. Appamia, as she is led away to prison, counsels: "Let me for ever/ Warn my Sex, and fright 'em from the thoughts of/ Black Revenge" (p. 60). The father draws the feeble moral that children should obey their parents "Lest they are punish't such a dismal way" (p. 60).

The next year, in 1700, Pix returned to intrigue comedy and wrote one of her best, *The Beau Defeated; or, The Lucky Younger Brother*. The play is based on Dancourt's *Le Chevalier à la Mode,* and Pix is careful in the dedication to announce that "the Play is partly a Translation from the French," a point she reemphasizes in the prologue and epilogue. *The Beau Defeated* is an amusing play about two wealthy widows. Lady Landsworth, a widow of quality, resolves to marry a man virtuous and witty; he must also be poor and unaware that she is rich. She finds the man by going vizarded to the playhouse. He thinks her a prostitute; she is made to believe that he is a libertine. When the misunderstandings are cleared up, they decide to marry. In an interwoven plot, Mrs. Rich, a merchant's widow, resolves to attain quality. She assumes fashionable affectations and supports a retinue of parasites to instruct her in scandal and gaming. She plans to gain a title by marrying Sir John Roverhead. Her friends expose this beau as a disguised servant, and half-trick, half-persuade her into marrying a country squire, bumpkinish but honest and wealthy. She abandons her class pretensions, and her brother-in-law, Mr. Rich, concludes the play with an encomium of the English merchant.

In 1701 Pix wrote two more tragedies, *The Czar of Muscovy*[29] and *The Double Distress*. Like *Queen Catharine, The Czar of Muscovy* reduces history to amorous intrigue. The impostor Demetrius, successfully installed as the Russian czar, proceeds to a course of tyranny that alienates his former allies and provokes a revolution in which he is slain by the true heir, Zueski. We hear of Demetrius's political tyranny; what is dramatized is his sexual tyranny. At his wedding to Marina he falls in love with Zarrianna, Zueski's fiancée. Demetrius intends to divorce Marina and marry Zarrianna. When both ladies resist dishonor, he determines to rape Zarrianna and murder his wife. In the fifth-act finale, the ladies are rescued by Zueski and Alexander, Marina's former fiancé. The dying Demetrius regrets more than the loss of empire the loss of amorous gratification. This fast-paced prose tragedy reads like a lively acting play. There are spirited scenes of rant for the heroines, threats of rape and speeches of defiance, melting scenes between lovers in transports. Although derivative of Fletcher in content and language, *The Czar of Muscovy* is one of Pix's better tragedies. *The Double Distress* depicts the adventures of two princesses whose love affairs are snarled by the wars between the Persians and the Medes. The plot, with its mistaken identities and suggested incest, is a variant of Beaumont and Fletcher's *A King and No King;* Pix uses the name Tygranes to call attention to the borrowing. The only information about the fate of this play is Pix's comment in the dedication: "The Success answered my Expectation."

Pix's production now slowed. Her next play appeared two years later, in 1703. *The Different Widows; or, Intrigue All-A-Mode* comically contrasts two sisters, Lady Gaylove and Lady Bellmont. The idle and intriguing Lady Gaylove conceals her age by dressing her grown son and daughter in children's clothes and keeping them in total ignorance. Valentine, who wishes to marry the daughter, steals the two and enlightens them as to their age and fortunes. The daughter easily adapts to her new status, but Lady Gaylove's son remains a hopeless booby. Contrasted with her sister is Lady Bellmont, virtuous mother of the witty debauchee Sir James Bellmont. She plans to marry him to the rich and beautiful Angelica, who uses her wit to attract and then reform Sir James. The plot is extremely busy, full of complicated intrigues, disguises, and mistaken identities. Numerous subplots involve characters whose assignations end laughably with the parties hiding in closets, under couches, in chests, and under beds.

Mary Pix finished her career as a playwright with a tragedy and a comedy—*The Conquest of Spain* (1705) and *The Adventures in Madrid* (1706)—very similar to the first two plays she wrote. As *Ibrahim* had been a variant on Fletcher's *Valentinian,* so *The Conquest of Spain* is a variant on his *Loyal Subject.* Rhoderique, lascivious king of Spain, persuades the obsessively loyal general Julianus to come from retirement to fight against the Moors. The king rapes Julianus's daughter, Jacinta, but she escapes to the battlefield to tell her father. Julianus is too loyal to take revenge against the king, but Jacinta's fiancé Theomantius leads a revolution, making the Moors his allies. When the king is defeated, the Moors reveal their true purpose as allies was to conquer Spain. Meanwhile, the king has been shamed into repentance by Julianus's noble behavior, but too late. Jacinta is fatally wounded traveling through the war zone, and Theomantius falls on his sword. *The Adventures in Madrid,* like *The Spanish Wives,* is a sentimentalized intrigue comedy. Gaylove and Bellmour, two English gentlemen staying at the ambassador's house in Madrid, strike up an intrigue with two ladies in the neighboring house of old Gomez. The ladies—Laura and Gomez's wife

Clarinda—are able to play amusing and flirtatious tricks on the gallants because they know of a secret passage to the ambassador's house and also because a woman friend persuades Gomez to hire her as a servant by disguising as a eunuch. In typically Pix fashion, the seemingly erring wife is actually virtuous. As the action unfolds, we learn that Gomez's estate really belongs to his nephew, Don Phillip; Gomez had his nephew abducted by assassins, and, thinking him dead, seized the estate and forced his niece to pass as his wife by threatening her with death. Don Phillip rescues his sister and has Gomez arrested by the Inquisitor General. The young couples are happily united at the curtain.

By the end of her theatrical career, Pix had written twelve plays—six tragedies and six comedies—more than any previous woman except Aphra Behn. Pix continued the Fletcherian tradition in tragedy; three of her tragedies are imitations of Fletcher with little added to revivify old plots. Her tragedies point forward in the increasing prominence given to the heroine and to the fatal accidents to love. Her one overt attempt at stage reform, *The False Friend,* was a muddle of melodrama and moralizing. The theaters probably continued to produce these plays because Pix had a knack for alternating scenes of rant with melting love scenes in which a mighty hero languishes at his lady's feet. However silly such scenes seem on the page, they act well, and audiences continued to like them. *The Czar of Muscovy* is important in a formal element that looks forward to the future. While the medium of her other tragedies was inflated prose lined out in print as blank verse, *The Czar of Muscovy* was printed in prose.

Pix's best works are her comedies, lively intrigue plays full of stage business, bustle, and surprises. The dialogue is usually flat, but the action never flags. The comedies contain pleasant songs, some by Pix, some by Motteux, and these, set to music by Purcell or Eccles, were published separately or in contemporary anthologies. Her encomium of the English merchant in *The Beau Defeated* suggests Lillo and the bourgeois drama of the next generation. Forced or unhappy marriages appear frequently in the comedies; they are prominent in *The Spanish Wives, The Deceiver Deceived, The Innocent Mistress,* and *The Adventures in Madrid.* Pix uses the forced marriage as a plot device, but unlike Behn, does not crusade against it in strong thematic statements. Pix's treatment of the unhappily married person is sentimentalized. Either the *mal mariée* is rescued and married more satisfactorily, as in *The Spanish Wives* and *The Adventures in Madrid* (this also happens in a tragedy, *The Czar of Muscovy*); or, as in *The Deceiver Deceived* and *The Innocent Mistress,* the seemingly errant wife or husband is really virtuous. Pix's use of sentimentalized characters in intrigue actions causes oddities of plotting. Generally her comedies show the changing temper of the times in that there is less emphasis on cuckoldry and more on virtuous love. Pix's attempt to write both hard and soft comedy at the same time is characteristic of playwrights at the turn of the century under pressure for stage reform.

Mary Pix achieved some modest recognition. The dedicatees of her plays are first gentlemen, then baronets, then a countess, a viscount, and a duchess. *The Conquest of Spain* was the first new play acted at Vanbrugh's theater in the Haymarket.[30] She had no illusions, however, about her talents. Her prologues, epilogues, and dedications always speak humbly of her efforts; they are "worthless trifles" (Dedication, *Deceiver Deceived*). Her insistent modesty may have been due partly to her fear of attack as a woman playwright. Certainly the only two times she was publicly abused were because of her sex. Had she been the only new woman playwright of the 1695–96 season, her existence alone would not have provoked *The Female Wits.* Similarly, George Powell probably stole from her play because she looked a likely victim, one whose sex as well as social class made her seem too insignificant to protest. Except for these two occasions, her public and personal life was inconspicuous. She worked quietly for ten years as a minor, although professional, playwright of modest abilities.

When Mary Pix died in 1709, a benefit performance for her estate was given of the hit play *The Busy Body*, written by her friend Susanna Centlivre. Centlivre was a contemporary of Pix, Manley, and Trotter, but began writing plays somewhat later than the Female Wits. Her work belongs to the Augustan Age.

# Susanna Centlivre

My Bookseller . . . told me, of a Spark that had seen
my *Gamester* three or four times, and lik'd it extremely: Having bought one of the Books, ask'd who
the Author was; and being told, a Woman, threw
down the Book, and put up his Money, saying, he had
spent too much after it already, and was sure if the
Town had known that, it wou'd never have run ten
days. No doubt this was a Wit in his own Eyes. It is
such as these that rob us of that which inspires the
Poet, Praise.

Susanna Centlivre, Dedication, *The Platonick Lady*,
1706

*S*usanna Centlivre was the most successful of England's
early women playwrights, perhaps the best comic playwright between Congreve and Fielding. She wrote
prolifically, producing, in addition to numerous letters
and topical poems, sixteen full-length plays and three
short farces.[1] Four of her plays became stock pieces. *The
Gamester* (1705) was performed for fifty years and initiated
a series of plays about gambling. *The Busy Body* (1709), *The
Wonder: A Woman Keeps a Secret* (1714), and *A Bold Stroke for
a Wife* (1718) entered the permanent repertory as peren-

nial favorites, in America as well as in England, for over 150 years, until the end of the nineteenth century.

The origins of this remarkable woman are wholly obscure. Biographical accounts written by her contemporaries are contradictory and apocryphal.[2] The traditional early life ascribed to her by an impossible amalgamation of these contradictory reports goes as follows: Susanna Centlivre was a gentlewoman, daughter of a Mr. Freeman of Holbeach, Lincolnshire, a zealous Parlimentarian who lost his estate at the Restoration. (Alternatively, her maiden name was Rawkins and her birth was mean.) She was precocious, composing a song before she was seven, and self-educated, with a flair for languages, mastering French before she was twelve. She was orphaned young, her father dying when she was three and her mother before she was twelve; nonetheless, she had a wicked stepmother who drove her at the age of fourteen to run away from home with a company of strolling players or, alternatively, with Anthony Hammond, who dressed her in boy's clothes and took her with him to Cambridge for several months as his lover. At the same time, or shortly thereafter, she married, "or something like it,"[3] a nephew of Sir Stephen Fox and was widowed in a year. She then married an army officer named Carroll, who was killed in a duel eighteen months later. Destitute and beautiful, she turned (or returned) to provincial acting (winning the heart of Joseph Centlivre by playing in breeches) and then to playwrighting.

Little of this has been proved or disproved.[4] The *Flying Post* for June 21–23 1716 refers to "Mrs. Centlivre, who was Born at Holbeach."[5] Her frequent visits to that town support the tradition that she was born there,[6] although no birthdate has been definitely established. As for her education, her use of French sources in some of her plays indicates that she knew that language. She was not beautiful, at least not in a conventional manner. Allusions in 1703 and 1704 refer to her having a squint,[7] and she was later described as having "a small Wen on her left Eye lid."[8] During her lifetime no scandalous amours attached to her reputation. That none of the tales of her adventures can be documented has not deterred literary historians from repeating the most sensational of them as fact right up to the present.

Centlivre's life can be documented with some accuracy after 1700, when she first appeared in print under the name Susanna Carroll. She was engaged in epistolary writing, then fashionable and saleable. Her letters, dated early in 1700, just prior to the appearance of her first play, appeared in *Familiar and Courtly Letters Written by Monsieur Voiture* (London, 1700), Volume II of Voiture's letters (London, 1701), and *Letters of Wit, Politicks and Morality* (London, 1701). She is associated in these volumes with a wide circle from the theater and grub street—Tom Brown, Ned Ward, Abel Boyer, Captain William Ayloffe, Jane Wiseman, William Burnaby, and George Farquhar. Her correspondence with Celadon and Damon suggests a love affair between Centlivre and Farquhar.[9] This intrigue, however, may have been merely epistolary and fictional—publication of such letters of gallantry was conventional and profitable. A poem she wrote in 1700 indicates that she was already acquainted with other women playwrights of the time. In September she was a contributor to *The Nine Muses,* a collection of elegies on Dryden's death.[10] The other contributors were Manley, Trotter, Pix, Lady Sarah Piers, and Mrs. Sarah Field (Mrs. Sarah Fyge Egerton). Her letters and incidental verses show her a woman of charm—lively, frank, affectionate, and affable. A contemporary described her attractive personality: "She had much Vivacity and good Humour; she was remarkably good-natured and benevolent in her Temper, and ready to do any friendly Office."[11] These qualities no doubt attracted Joseph Centlivre, whom she married on 23 April 1707. Joseph, a widower with a son and a daughter, was yeoman of the mouth to Queen Anne; he had been a royal cook since the reign of King William. In 1713 the Centlivres moved to Buckingham Court, where they lived the rest of their lives.[12] After her marriage, Susanna Carroll wrote as Susanna Centlivre.

She continued all her life to attract a wide circle of friends. Her closest friend among the players was apparently Anne Oldfield, for whom she wrote some complimentary verses on a flyleaf of a book she had borrowed from the actress.[13] Many friends contributed prologues and epilogues to her plays. Among them were Farquhar, Burnaby, Nicholas Rowe, Thomas Baker, Thomas Burnet, Colley Cibber, Charles Johnson, Ambrose Philips, and Dr. George Sewall. Steele failed to deliver a promised prologue on time, and she sent him an amusing verse letter to "supplicate him with prayers most fervent,/ That he would not baulk, Sir, Your most humble Servant."[14] Her dedication of *The Cruel Gift* to Eustace Budgell shows her sincere pride in their friendship. She may have been associated for a time in an informal literary club with the novelist Eliza Haywood, the poet Martha Fowke, Anthony Hammond, the attorney Philip Horneck, and perhaps Defoe.[15] Nicholas Amhurst, poet and journalist, complimented her in his *Poems on Several Occasions* (London, 1720). In the same year, engravings of her portrait were advertised for sale.[16] Of all her friends Centlivre seems to have most admired Rowe. In 1718, while in Holbeach, she wrote "From the Country, To Mr. Rowe in Town," a poem of affectionately extravagant praise, hoping "that the next Age, may my Happiness know,/ That I Liv'd, and was

known to the excellent Rowe."[17] At the laureate's death
she contributed "A Pastoral to the Honoured Memory of
Mr. Rowe" to the group of elegies published as *Musarum
Lacrymae.*[18]

Centlivre not surprisingly found her friends among the
Whig faction, for she was herself an ardent Whig. Her
sentiments appear early in her plays. *The Beau's Duel*
(1702) makes slighting references to Jacobites. In *The
Basset Table* (1705) Sir Richard Plainman and Captain
Hearty repeatedly express hatred of the French. Farquhar's prologue to *The Platonick Lady* (1706) praises the
Battle of Ramillies, and the epilogue refers to "cow'd Gaul"
and "humble Lewis" (2).[19] When an epilogue compli-
menting the Duke of Marlborough and Prince Eugene of
Savoy was not licensed in time for the first performance of
*The Perplexed Lovers* (1712), the audience hissed. Centlivre
responded by printing the play with a poem in heroics to
Prince Eugene and with the epilogue, which had been
licensed in time for the second performance. She declared
in the preface that

> there was a Rumour spread about Town that it was a
> notorious whiggish Epilogue; and the Person who de-
> sign'd me the Favour of speaking it [Anne Oldfield], had
> Letters sent her to forbear, for that there were Parties
> forming against it, and they advis'd her not to stand the
> Shock; here was a second Blow greater than the first:
> The sinking of my Play cut me not half so deep as the
> Notion I had, there cou'd be People of this Nation so
> ungrateful as not to allow a single Compliment to a Man
> that has done such Wonders for it. I am not prompted
> by any private sinister End, having never been oblig'd to
> the Duke of Marlborough, otherwise than as I shar'd in
> common with my Country. . . . I know not what they call
> Whigs, or how they distinguish between them and To-
> ries: But if the Desire to see my Country secur'd from
> the Romish Yoke, and flourish by a firm, lasting, Hon-
> ourable Peace, to the Glory of the best of Queens, who

deservedly holds the Ballance of all Europe, be a Whig,
then I am one, else not.

(2)

Centlivre went on to jeopardize her career and her
husband's job by declaring for the House of Hanover in
the dedication to *The Wonder* in the spring of 1714. Luckily
for the Centlivres, George I acceded to the throne within a
few months. Six years later Centlivre wrote humorously
about her dedication:

> . . . spight of Steele's Advice I did it;
> Nay tho' my Husband's Place forbid it;
> . . . . . . . . . . . . . . . . . . . . . . . . . . . . . . . . . . . . . . . .
>   This made Spouse stare like any Spectre,
> And as he was my Head—to hector.
>   Madam, said he, with surly Air,
> You've manag'd finely this Affair;
> Pox take your Schemes, your Wit, and Plays,
> I'm bound to curse 'em all my Days:
> If out, I'm by your Scribbling turn'd,
> I wish your Plays and you were burn'd.
>   That I believe, my Dear, quoth I;
> But if one—you know who, shou'd Die,
> And Brunswick o'er these Jacks prevail,
> You'll tell me then another Tale:
> When all the Whigs in Post you see,
> You'll thank, instead of chiding me.[20]

The Whig press praised Centlivre for her stand, but the
benefits she anticipated from the Hanoverian succession
were in the event slight, consisting of command performances of various plays, presumably accompanied by gifts,
by members of the royal family.[21] As she wrote later,
"Anna Resign'd, and Brunswick Came,/And yet my Lot is
still the Same."[22] Meanwhile she had alienated many To-
ries, among them distinguished literary figures like Pope.
Although Pope included Centlivre in the *Dunciad,* the

worst his malice ever found to say of her was only snide: "The Cook's Wife in Buckingham Court."[23] Her loyalty was nonetheless undaunted. She continued to turn out a string of poems in praise of members of the royal household and letters in defense of Protestantism.

Centlivre died in her own home on 1 December 1723, and obituaries appeared in a number of newspapers. She was buried at St. Paul's, Covent Garden; there is no monument on her grave.[24] When her works were published in 1761, the anoymous introduction began in outrage that "neither the Nobility nor Commonalty . . . had Spirit enough to erect in Westminster-Abbey, a Monument justly due to the Manes of the never to be forgotten Mrs. Centlivre" (1:vii). The author's anger is justified by Centlivre's career as a dramatist.

She began writing plays at a difficult time. Theatrical taste was uncertain as the century swung, somewhat erratically, from the Restoration to the Augustan temper. Audiences were increasingly bourgeois, attracted by sentimental and 'reform' plays and at the same time by the plays of Farquhar and Vanbrugh. In a period inauspicious for a beginner, Centlivre had to succeed; like Behn, she wrote to eat. Her prologues, epilogues, and prefaces show a keen concern for author's benefit nights. Her dedications are obvious bids for gifts; patently fulsome, they are the least attractive things she wrote. Her economic motive did not cease at marriage, although it may have shifted to a middle-class desire for security and material accumulation. Her dedication of *The Man's Bewitched* to the Duke of Devonshire, the Lord Steward, seems a bid for Joseph Centlivre's advancement: "Since my Husband has the Honour to serve Her Majesty, under the Command of Your Grace, as he did the late King of glorious Memory, under that of your noble Father, I cou'd not be prevail'd upon to alter my Resolution of prefixing your Grace's

Name in the front of this Poem . . . to shew my Gratitude."
Writing humorously of her husband (she is probably ex-
aggerating because she is begging for South Sea stock), she
pictures him as an acquisitive bourgeois:

> . . . my Spouse who understands
> Nought to be good, but Bills and Bonds,
> The ready Cash, or fruitful Lands,
> Begins new Quarrels ev'ry Day,
> And frights my dear-lov'd Muse away:
> Nor Day, nor Night I know no Ease,
> Accosted still with Words like these.
>
>   Deuce take your scribling Vein, quoth he,
> What did it ever get for me?
> Two Years you take a Play to write,
> And I scarce get my Coffee by't.[25]

Tradition has it that she received handsome gifts from her
dedicatees,[26] but these came for her later plays, after she
was established as a playwright and also married. In 1700
she had to survive by her pen and so had a compelling
need to hit the uncertain taste of the Town. The first half
of her career, from 1700 to 1709, was checkered with
successes and failures, until she established herself and
found a dramatic mode that suited both her talents and
eighteenth-century taste.

She got off to a false start in the fall of 1700 with an
unsuccessful tragicomedy, *The Perjured Husband; or, The
Adventures of Venice.* In the first plot, Count Bassino's
determination to commit bigamy leads to the deaths of his
wife, his mistress, and himself. In the second, a young wife
tries to take a lover, while her elderly husband simultaneously woos the maid. Centlivre was careful that neither of
the intrigues in the comic subplot was consummated, and
was apparently surprised at the Town's disapproval. She
retorted in a spirited preface to the "snarling" critics who

had objected to her language as "loose," defending herself on the standard anti-Collier ground of dramatic decorum, arguing that it is not "reasonable to expect a Person, whose inclinations are always forming Projects to the Dishonour of her Husband, should deliver her Commands to her Confident in the Words of a Psalm" (1).

Her next two plays, although neither had any particular success, showed that her real talent lay with intrigue comedy. *The Beau's Duel; or, A Soldier for the Ladies* (1702) has the ingredients for success—two sets of lovers working at cross purposes, idiosyncratic fops and beaus, sword-rattling, and disguise—but some sections move slowly.[27] Centlivre had not yet achieved the rapidity of action that distinguishes her most successful plays. An unusual character is Mrs. Plotwell, who has inherited a large estate, making it unnecessary for her to continue as a kept woman; her reformation is accepted without question by the other characters. *The Stolen Heiress; or, The Salamanca Doctor Outplotted* (1702) has two parallel plots, one comic and one tragicomic, concerning the love of Lavinia and Lucasia for two poor youths, Francisco and Palante. The lovers avoid marriages arranged by two heavy fathers. The tragicomic plot, in pallid blank verse, is often embarrassingly bad,[28] but the comic plot has amusing turns, as when Francisco cleverly impersonates his pedantic rival, and when the sprightly Lavinia saves herself by falsely claiming to be pregnant by Francisco.

In June 1703, Centlivre produced her first solid commercial success in *Love's Contrivance; or, Le Medecin Malgre Lui*. With Molière as her source, she wrote a fast-paced sequence of farcical scenes designed to keep the audience laughing nonstop. *Love's Contrivance* is an acting play full of business and verve, a vehicle for a half dozen juicy comic roles. The preface shows her pleasure at finally hitting a pleasing style—"Humour lightly tost up with Wit, and drest with Modesty and Air"—in a period of uncertain taste: "Writing is a kind of Lottery in this fickle Age, and Dependence on the Stage as precarious as the Cast of a Die; the Chance may turn up, and a Man may write to please the Town, but 'tis uncertain, since we see our best Authors sometimes fail" (2). She acknowledges herself "infinitely obliged to the Players" (2). She herself, however, had provided them with sure-fire comic parts; *Love's Contrivance* shows Centlivre's strength as a farceur. The play continued to be acted at intervals through 1706. Often the last act alone was played as an afterpiece. In the season of 1723–24 this act was one of a medley of popular scenes that Tony Aston was performing at taverns around London. Perhaps as a result of the publicity, the full-length play was revived again in 1724.

Early in 1705 Centlivre followed with a smash hit in *The Gamester*, a topical play about a major eighteenth-century vice. The plot is busy but not complex: Valere, because of his addiction to gaming, faces poverty and lovelessness, but the rich and resourceful Angelica reclaims and marries him. Ostensibly writing sentimental reform comedy, Centlivre solemnly announced in the dedication that "the Design of this Piece" was "to divert, without that Vicious Strain which usually attends the Comick Muse, and according to the first intent of Plays, recommend Morality." This espousal of *utile* over *dulce* was an attempt to please the same audiences who liked Cibber's *Love's Last Shift* formula—a hero who (rather unconvincingly) reforms after being "lewd for above four acts." *The Gamester* actually caters to audience interest in gaming. Valere's penitence is far less convincing than his obsession. When he loses at play, "he swears between his Teeth" (1:135) and suffers from insomnia: "I can no sooner shut my Eyes, but methinks my evil Genius flings Arm's Ace before me" (1:136). When he wins, he rages because his winnings are not greater and refuses to pay his debts, concealing his gold to squander in further play. A born loser, he lives by gamblers' superstitions and sees only the bright side of gaming: "A Gamester's Hand is the Philosopher's Stone, that turns all it touches into Gold" (1:163). The liveliest scene in the play, 4.4, depicts the sharpers and suckers hot over the gaming table, absorbed in their own colorful jargon. This scene is also the dramatic turning point: Angelica, disguised as a man (a breeches part for Mrs. Bracegirdle), reduces Valere to desperation by winning his money, watch, ring, and finally her own portrait set with diamonds, a love token that Valere had solemnly sworn never to part with. He is then rescued by Angelica's forgiveness, a wish-fulfilling denouement.[29] Centlivre accurately calculated her audience's interest. *The Gamester* became a stock piece and was performed regularly for fifty years. It was one of the plays that established her reputation during her lifetime.

After this success, Centlivre's fortunes turned downward. *The Basset Table* (1705), produced within the year, was an unsuccessful attempt to exploit the formulas of *The Gamester*. The major variation is that the gambler is a woman, Lady Reveller, who keeps a public basset table in her home. The moralist of the piece, Lady Lucy, emphasizes the plan of the sequel: "Oh Shame to Virtue, that Women should copy Men in their most reigning Vices" (1:231). Resemblances between the two plays are many. Both have a lively gambling scene using the jargon of the game; in both the gambler is rescued from the (partly contrived) consequences of vice and married to a partner who disapproves of gaming. Both plays open with a dawn scene of servants sleepy because of the gentry's habit of all-night play; both emphasize the miseries of tradesmen whose debtors, ruined by play, default. As Sir Thomas Valere in *The Gamester* intends either to reform or disinherit his son, so in *The Basset Table* Sir Richard Plainman intends either to reform his niece or turn her out of his home.

While *The Gamester* entered the permanent repertory, only a few performances of *The Basset Table* are recorded. This may have been due to the eclipse that often overtakes sequels. More probably, audience expectations were disappointed. *The Basset Table* has more talk about than action at cards. While Valere is more convincing as a gamester than a lover, Lady Reveller is less a gambler than a vain coquette. She maintains a gaming table primarily to draw visits of numerous admirers. The title's unfulfilled promise of a gambling exposé probably caused a backfire in audience reaction. *The Basset Table* is actually a comedy of love intrigue and a good one. Some of the best scenes are Lady Reveller's comic quarrels with her disapproving but fascinated admirer, Lord Worthy, and Ensign Lovely's attempts to win Valeria, "the little She philosopher" (1:210). *The Basset Table* deserved greater success. It marks an advance in Centlivre's stagecraft; confining the action to a single house, she manipulates rapid and plausible entrances and exits of the characters in varying comic combinations.

Centlivre's next play, *Love at a Venture* (1706), was denied London production and plagiarized by Colley Cibber. It is a highly plotted comedy of intrigue in which the hero, Belair, assumes two disguises to woo two ladies. The ladies join forces and send invitations that require his presence in both disguises at the same time. Belair's stratagems to appear as two persons at once, his continual shifts of disguise, his energetic pursuit of a side intrigue with Lady Cautious in his spare moments, his servant's confused attempts to remember which role his master is playing at any given time—these are the comic highlights of the play. Occasionally a scene is too prolonged, and the fop Wou'dbe is neither funny nor functional, but as a whole the play is lively and amusing. Centlivre took *Love at a*

*Venture* to Cibber for approval. When her play was turned down, she took it to Bath with the Duke of Grafton's players.

The anonymous author of *The Laureat: or the Right Side of Colley Cibber* (London, 1740) describes the plagiarism:

> There was at this Time a certain Poetess in Rome, called Fulvia, who had sometimes succeeded in Characters of Humour on the Stage; she offer'd a Play to the Perusal of Aesopus; in this play she had drawn the Character of a very impudent fellow, who in this same Play acted under his own Appearance two different Persons, and Persuaded his Mistress to believe him not to be himself in Opposition to her Senses; this Character Aesopus scouted extremely. Why, Madam, said he, this would be putting upon the Audience indeed; they will never bear it; 'tis extravagant, it is outraging Nature, it is silly, and it is not ridiculous. The poor Lady was beat out of her Design; but as our Corrector had the Play left sometime in his Hand, he culled out this very Character, mix'd it with some other Felonies of the same Nature, which he had committed, and acted it as his own the very next Year.
>
> (p. 112)

Cibber's play was *The Double Gallant; or, The Sick Lady's Cure* (1707), a combination of Burnaby's *Reformed Wife* (1700), his *Ladies Visiting Day* (1701), and Centlivre's *Love at a Venture*. Cibber's Atall, wooing two women in two different disguises while intriguing with a married woman, is Centlivre's Belair.[30] *The Double Gallant* became a stock piece that had some two hundred performances by the end of the century. "But the credit," as F. W. Bateson says, "is really due, not to Cibber, but to Mrs. Centlivre and to Burnaby."[31]

The plagiarism was recognized and criticized immediately. Cibber, in his autobiography over thirty years later, was still defending himself, claiming that *The Double*

*Gallant* was "made up of what little was tolerable, in two, or three others, that had no Success, and were laid aside, as so much Poetical Lumber. . . . As I was only the Compiler of this Piece, I did not publish it in my own Name; but as my having a Hand in it, could not be long a Secret, I have been often treated as a Plagiary on that Account."[32] Cibber is disingenuous. The play was printed as "Written by Mr. Cibber."[33] Moreover, he was noted for being lightfingered with other dramatists' works.[34] There is no record of a quarrel between Centlivre and Cibber over this play. She was still having her ups and downs in establishing herself as a playwright and could hardly afford to alienate the powerful actor-manager. She continued to write parts for him, and he wrote an epilogue for her a few years later.

In the same year as *Love at a Venture* Centlivre wrote another comedy, *The Platonick Lady* (1706). The playwright's ingenuity runs away with her in this play, and the result is mixed. She produces endless mistakes and cross-purposes among the characters and arranges inapropos entrances and exits, but much of the stagecraft is employed seemingly for its own sake and is unnecessary to advance the main action. Moreover, stolen heirs and long-lost lovers from seventeenth-century romance are incongruously inserted into eighteenth-century comic intrigue. On the other hand, there are several good acting roles. Sharper, the bankrupt, cowardly, fortune-hunting gambler, and his servant Equipage are engaging. The heroine, Isabella, employs multiple comic disguises as an erring wife, a country wench, and a discarded lady. Four performances only are recorded. Three consecutive plays had had little or no success.

Centlivre's first seven years in the theater, in spite of the popularity of *Love's Contrivance* and *The Gamester*, had been difficult. Part of her poor success was due to the fact that her early works are often flawed, although they compare well to the general poverty of early eighteenth-century plays; part of her poor success was due to sexual hostility. Centlivre had made her plays genteel, relative to the taste of the times, for she seems to have been prepared for hostility against a woman's writing like a man. She was unprepared for hostility against a woman playwright per se. The prologue to her first play confidently advertised the sex of the author, and the play was printed with her name on the title page. After *The Perjured Husband* her plays were printed anonymously. The prologue of her second play, however, refers to "Our Female Author" (1), and the epilogue decorously characterizes her as a humble petitioner; but the prologue of her third play refers to the author as a man, and the fourth, her successful *Love's Contrivance,* was printed as written by "R.M." *The Gamester* was anonymous, and subsequent plays were printed as "By the Author of the Gamester." Deprived of praise for her work, Centlivre adopted a feminist stance. She contributed commendatory verses to a volume of poems by Mrs. Egerton, urging her friend to show "Ambitious Man what Womankind can do."[35]

Finally, when *The Platonick Lady* was printed, Centlivre made an angry appeal "To all the Generous Encouragers of Female Ingenuity." She writes, she says, because of "the Usage I have met on all sides," because "the Vulgar World . . . think it a proof of their Sense, to dislike every thing that is writ by Women." Their "Carping Malice" forces anonymity:

A Play secretly introduc'd to the House, whilst the Author remains unknown, is approv'd by every Body: The Actors cry it up, and are in expectation of a great Run; the Bookseller of a Second Edition, and the Scribler of a Sixth Night: But if by chance the Plot's discover'd, and the Brat found Fatherless, immediately it flags in the Opinion of those that extoll'd it before, and the Bookseller falls in his Price, with this Reason only, *It is a Woman's.* Thus they alter their Judgment, by the Esteem they have for the Author, tho' the Play is still the same.

She illustrates with the anecdote of the spark and *The Gamester*, quoted as the epigraph to this chapter.

And it is such as these made him that Printed my Comedy call'd, *Love's Contrivance; or, Medicin Malgre lui*, put two letters of a wrong Name to it; which tho' it was the height of Injustice to me, yet his imposing on the Town turn'd to account with him; and thus passing for a Man's, it has been play'd at least a hundred times.

Some of these same types "have arm'd themselves with resolution not to like the Play they paid to see; and if in spite of Spleen they have been pleas'd against their Will, have maliciously reported it was none of mine, but given me by some Gentleman."

And why this Wrath against the Womens Works? Perhaps you'll answer, because they meddle with things out of their Sphere: But I say, no; for since the Poet is born, why not a Woman as well as a Man?

After this outburst, Centlivre left the theater for over two years. When she returned, she met again the prejudice against women playwrights, but this time she established herself as "the Celebrated Mrs. Centlivre."

Her return to the theater with a new play in 1709 began inauspiciously, according to contemporary accounts: "This Play, when it was first offered to the Players, was received very cooly, and it was with great Difficulty that the Author could prevail upon them to think of acting it. . . . At the Rehearsal of it, Mr. Wilks had so mean an Opinion of his Part . . . that one Morning in a Passion he threw it off the Stage into the Pit, and swore that no body would bear to sit to hear such Stuff."[36] *The Female Tatler* (10 October 1709) said that Wilks "in great dudgeon flung his Part into the Pitt for damn'd Stuff, before the Lady's Face that wrote it." The story continues that there "had been scarce any thing mentioned of it in the Town before it came out, and those who had heard of it, were told it was a silly thing wrote by a Woman."[37] On the first day the audience was small but was "agreeably suprized, more and more every Act, till at last the House rung with as much Applause as was possible to be given by so thin an Audience. The next Day there was a better House, and the third crowded for the Benefit of the Author, and so it continued till the thirteenth."[38] This hit was *The Busy Body* (1709), which continued a repertory favorite until the end of the nineteenth century.[39]

*The Busy Body* is a beautifully proportioned intrigue comedy in which two young couples outwit two comic old men. There are numerous amusing disguises and intrigues, but the special ingredient of the comedy is the character of Marplot, the busybody. In his impertinent but good-natured eagerness to discover his friends' secrets, Marplot repeatedly brings the young lovers near to disaster. The plot sets up a clever tension: the audience sympathizes with the lovers and at the same time with the idiotic Marplot. Thus, as the lovers must outwit not only their enemies but also their friend, the audience is in a continual state of anxious hilarity. Marplot takes the place of the usual fop in an intrigue plot; however, he is not the butt of satirical ridicule but of amused exasperation. This gives a sunny tone to the whole play.

*The Busy Body* and all her following plays were printed as "Written by Mrs. Susanna Centlivre." She was never again forced into anonymity, nor did she again feel it necessary to publish any feminist salvoes. Prejudice against women may have continued to irritate her (she occasionally referred to the poverty of women's education), but it no longer adversely affected her career. In fact, as the feminist sentiment of the seventeenth century waned and the eighteenth century grew increasingly antifeminist, Centlivre exploited public prejudice. For example, she satirized the supposed foibles of her sex in the title *The Wonder: A Woman Keeps a Secret.* The prologue to *The Cruel Gift* appealed for indulgence because the play was a woman's and for sympathy because, unlike male playwrights, she had no "Clubs of clapping Friends" (2). Centlivre's subsequent theatrical quarrels, such as the one that engulfed her next play, turned on politics rather than sex.

Seven months after *The Busy Body,* Centlivre brought out a lightweight but pleasant comedy, *The Man's Bewitched; or, The Devil to Do About Her* (1709). After a slow exposition of Constant's plan to gain money and his sweetheart by circulating a false report of his father's death, the play picks up speed. Act 4 is amusing farce as Faithful and Laura fake exorcism and demonic possession to escape from Sir David Watchum, a guardian on the pattern of Sir Francis Gripe in *The Busy Body.* Act 5 is built around the comic responses to Sir Jeffrey Constant, believed to be a ghost. During rehearsal, Cibber suggested shortening the scene of the ghost in the last act, and Centlivre complied. Then, she says in her preface, "When Mr. Estcourt sliced most of it out, I could not help interposing my Desires to the contrary . . . and I had the Satisfaction to see I was not deceived in My Opinion, of its pleasing" (3). The difference of opinion between Centlivre and the actors was blown up into a serious quarrel by *The Female Tatler.* When the play opened on December 12, that paper described the playwright attacking the actors:

> Mrs. Centlivre told 'em, that 'twas much easier to Write a Play than to get it Represented; that their Factions and Divisions were so great, they seldom continued in the same mind two Hours together; that they treated her,

(tho a Woman) in the Masculine Gender; and as they do all Authors with Wrangling and Confusion, which has made most Gentlemen that have a Genius to Scribling, employ their Pens another way; that to show their Judgment in Plays, they had actually cut out the Scene in the Fifth Act, between the Countryman and the Ghost, which the Audience receiv'd with that wonderful Applause; and 'twas with very great strugling the Author prevail'd to have it in again; one made Faces at his Part, another was Witty upon her's: But as the whole was very well perform'd at last, she has Condescention to pass over the Affronts of a Set of People, who have it not in their Natures to be grateful to their Supporters.

The actors resented this report and stopped the run after the third night.

The prologue by a friend, apparently a last-minute attempt to save the play, disclaimed that Centlivre had any part in a "lampoon" and urged the audience to "spare her for the Busie-Body's sake" (3). When this failed, Centlivre immediately printed the play with a preface admitting that she "happen'd to mention" the dispute "among [her] Acquaintance" but categorically denying a charge that she herself wrote the offending paragraph: "No reasonable Person will believe I could be guilty of so much Folly" because of "the Injury it must of course do me, in the Run of my Play, by putting those People out of Humour, whose Action was to give Life to the Piece" (3). The prologue had pointed to Delariviere Manley as the author of the article: "Why shou'd tender Delia tax the Nation;/. . . Who always gave a Loose, herself, to Inclination?" (3) and Centlivre's preface points to Manley's motive: "the Malice of Parties" (3). Manley and Centlivre, formerly associates in *The Nine Muses,* must by this time have fallen out over politics.[40] *Female Tatler* or no, Centlivre was angry that the actors "stop'd the Run, upon any Pique whatever. 'Tis small Encouragement to write for the Stage, when the Actors, according to the Caprice of their Humours, maugre the Taste of the Town, have power to sink the Reputation of a Play; for if they resolve not to act it, the Town can't support it" (3). That the run should have continued is indicated by the success of the disputed scenes, which not only pleased at the premiere but also were made into a two-act farce, *The Ghost*, which was performed regularly throughout the second half of the century.[41]

During 1710–12 Centlivre wrote three modest plays that had modest success. *A Bickerstaff's Burying; or, Work for the Upholders* (1710) is a short farce about the customs of the island of Casgar, where widows and widowers are reluctantly buried alive with their dead spouses. The play spoofs protestations of conjugal affection beyond the grave. At the conclusion, the Emir's wife flees to England, "where Widow-hood is happy" (3:278). The title takes off from Steele's persona as *Tatler* author and his essay proposing that worthless men are in effect dead men. Centlivre's dedication "To the Magnificent Company of Upholders" wittily satirizes expensive funerals; poets, however, are in no danger from undertakers, who "are not overfond of Paper-Credit" (3). She then wrote *Marplot* (1710), a sequel to *The Busy Body*. This poor piece looks poorer by comparison with the earlier play. Centlivre reproduces the same plot structure; the still obtuse Marplot continually interrupts and imperils the amours of two of his friends. The important difference is that the lovers, and consequently the audience, do not seriously care about the intrigues. The third play of this group was *The Perplexed Lovers* (1712), a cloak-and-dagger comedy with a plot in perpetual motion. Constantia, in love with Colonel Bastion, must elude both father and brother, each of whom plans another match for her. In helping her, Camilla repeatedly risks her own romance with Belvil. The loyalty between the two heroines was a sketch for Centlivre's next, enormously successful play, *The Wonder: A Woman Keeps a Secret,* which appeared two years later, in April 1714.

*The Wonder* is a masterpiece of comic theater. The action turns on Violante's promise to protect the secret of Isabella's runaway and romance. Violante keeps her friend's secret to the point of passionate quarrels with her beloved Felix. Every event conspires to make Violante appear false. Whenever Felix calls, Isabella's lover is either tapping at the window or hiding in the bedroom; Violante no sooner leaves the house than she is mistaken for Isabella on her way from an assignation. The seemingly pointless exposition of Felix's duel prepares the audience for a proud and impetuous lover, and, sure enough, at every crisis, he brandishes sword or pistol at his supposed rival. Around this pair of lovers revolve delightful minor comic characters—the affected servant Lissardo wooing two lady's maids at once; the Scots Gibby vaporing about in Highland dress and incomprehensible dialect; the comically venal Alguazil. The plot and dialogue are tightly packed, once the action begins to roll in Act 2, so that a surprising 'turn' occurs every few minutes. But *The Wonder* is no shallow intrigue comedy in which the mistakes of a night are resolved at the end by a discovery. Violante, believing that true love does not admit doubt, insists on Felix's trust as a precondition of unraveling the secret. Their relationship is believable beyond the stage, and the best scenes are their irrational quarrels—which ring authentic—and their fumbling attempts at reconciliation. Because of Felix and Violante, the play has emotion as well as motion, and as a result delighted theatergoers for generations. The role of Don Felix was one of Garrick's triumphs, and he chose it for his farewell performance in 1776.

In the year after *The Wonder,* the year of the Jacobite

rebellion, Centlivre was again embroiled in political controversy when she wrote two satirical farces. *A Gotham Election* (1715) is heavyhanded satire of Tory corruption in a local election, and *A Wife Well Managed* (1715) mocks Catholicism in the person of a lustful priest. Neither was acted. Centlivre published them immediately with an explanatory preface and a dedication to James Craggs, then cofferer to the Prince of Wales, later Secretary of State, who had "generously espous'd" her interest when she dedicated *The Wonder* to the Duke of Cambridge. The first farce, she explained, was not licensed because "the Subject being upon Elections, the Master of the Revels did not care to meddle with it." As for the other, "it was said there would be Offence taken at the exposing of a Popish Priest. Good God! . . . Is not their very Profession Treason in any Subject in Great Britain?" Rumor of her new works "immediately furnish'd out a Thousand scandalous Stories," and she "was become the Subject of every Coffee-House in Town." She sought Cragg's protection because her "two Petites Pieces . . . were persecuted by those that did not know 'em. If they had gone thro' a legal Course of Theatrical Justice, tho' it might have been partial, yet I should have submitted to it, as others had done before me." She was right to complain of injury. Although *A Gotham Election* would have been clapped down as violently partisan, it would have introduced the novel subject of provincial politics to a stage crowded with hackneyed material. *A Wife Well Managed,* a tightly plotted dramatic fabliau, was acted as an afterpiece in 1724, after Centlivre's death. In 1732 it was adapted, without acknowledgement, into a ballad opera called *The Disappointment.*[42]

Centlivre wrote three more full-length plays, two of them poor and one ingenious. *The Cruel Gift* (1716) dresses in eighteenth-century gentility the bloody old story of

Tancred and Ghismonda. This tragedy is inane, and the blank verse is flat; however, audiences attended six nights and a command performance. *The Artifice* (1722), a comedy clumsy in characterization and tone, contains more plot material than can be worked out. There are a few memorable scenes in which Fainwell, disguised as the footman Jeffrey, exasperates Widow Heedless with his seeming obtuseness, but these are set into a play that is, on the whole, dreary.

*A Bold Stroke for a Wife* (1718), however, is a comic delight. The play turns on a single premise. Colonel Fainwell, in order to marry Anne Lovely, must gain the consent of four amusingly different guardians—a beau, a virtuoso, a businessman, and a Quaker. He wins the lady by assuming five successive disguises, the last being an impersonation of the real Simon Pure, adding that expression to the language. There is some social satire of the four types represented by the guardians, who are monomaniacal humour characters, but the tone is genial and lighthearted throughout. *A Bold Stroke for a Wife* has no depth but is an excellent stage play. The exposition is gracefully handled so that the action gets underway rapidly and continues briskly. The character parts provide superb acting roles. The play entered the permanent repertory, growing in popularity with each generation, and was performed repeatedly until the end of the nineteenth century.

The continued success of Centlivre's plays was due to her finding a dramatic mode that suited her talents, the times, and acceptable standards of decorum for a woman writer. The characteristic Centlivre play is a farcical comedy of intrigue. The intrigues further love and marriage rather than sexual adventure. There are no cuckoldings, those few liaisons alluded to (e.g., between Sir James Courtly and Mrs. Sago in *The Basset Table*) having ended before the play begins. The romantic hero is usually a soldier. Centlivre began this practice in her second play, *The Beau's Duel,* in which both the male leads are army officers; the epilogue announces, "A Soldier is her darling Character" (1). This choice of a blunt soldier rather than a witty beau for a hero, a choice perhaps made from political sentiment, affected the characterization, tone, and language of her plays.[43] Because the hero is blunt and honest, Centlivre creates as his suitable dramatic mate the forthright, sensible heroine. These two waste little time in witty sparring, for they are both decided on marriage from the beginning. The thrust of the play, then, is toward action rather than verbal wit.

Centlivre's language, inoffensive to Augustan taste, uses little double entendre. This suits her talents, for she is a writer of small verbal distinction. She did, however, have a good ear for jargon, slang, religious cant, dialect, and foreign accents. The lack of verbal flash and grace makes the plays read poorly, and modern critics find them flat, "the railway reading of Georgian England."[44] This is unduly harsh. What Centlivre's language offers in place of wit is a wide topical allusiveness,[45] which, although lost on modern readers, must have amused the original audiences. She creates not witty dialogue but witty situations that would still appeal to theatergoers today.

Centlivre was a superb stage technician, adroit at moving characters on and off stage plausibly and rapidly. Her plays are, eminently, acting vehicles, with dozens of comic roles that continued favorites of such distinguished actors as Garrick and Kitty Clive. Centlivre was particularly adept at creating clever servants. In connection with her stagecraft, it would be interesting to know if she was, as tradition has it, a strolling actress. This tradition did not appear in print until a generation after her death,[46] and the only corroboration during her lifetime is *Love at a Venture* (1706). When that comedy was performed at Bath, the prologue apologized "Lest any here shou'd blame our Author's Toil,/ For strolling with her Brat a Hundred Mile" (1). These lines seem to indicate at least a brief career as a stroller, but as her *Platonick Lady* was performed at the Haymarket in November of the same year, she was probably attending rehearsals in London at that time. There is no record of her acting in London. However she obtained her theatrical apprenticeship, she was like her contemporaries in using a wide variety of sources, ranging over earlier English drama, Spanish cloak-and-dagger plays, French drama (especially Molière, Regnard, and Thomas Corneille), Boccaccio, and *The Arabian Nights*. Whenever she translated from or adapted French or Spanish plays, she acknowledged her indebtedness, and no charges of plagiarism were ever brought against her as were laid to Aphra Behn.

Centlivre was careful to modify her sources to the taste of the new century. If her Marplot is, as is usually claimed, based on Dryden's Mar-All, her *Busy Body* is a measure of how far she had moved from Restoration taste. Although she wrote only two explicitly labeled reform plays, she had a habit of concluding plays with rhymed moral tags. These moral verses seldom had much to do with the action of the play, but presumably they satisfied audience taste. Centlivre's contemporaries were aware of the genteel tone she achieved. The author of the prologue to her *Man's Bewitched* described her mode as a "harmless hum'rous Play" (3), and *The Female Tatler* (14 December 1709) commended "the Pains she is daily taking, so Wittily and Innocently to Entertain." This innocent tone to a great extent contributed to the success of her works in her lifetime; it also allowed the continued stage life of the plays in spite of the increasing verbal prudery of the Victorian period.

Hazlitt typifies nineteenth-century attitudes toward Centlivre's plays. He reviewed performances in 1816 of

*The Busy Body* and *The Wonder* and commented that "the dialogue . . . is so light and careless, as only to occasion a succession of agreeable alarms to the ears of delicacy."[47] His remarks on these two plays are repeated in a more organized form in *Lectures on the English Comic Writers* (London, 1819):

> Her plays have a provoking spirit and volatile salt in them, which still preserves them from decay. . . . Their interest depends chiefly on the intricate involution and artful *denouement* of the plot, which has a strong tincture of mischief in it, and the wit is seasoned by the archness of the humour and sly allusion to the most delicate points. . . . The Wonder is one of the best of our acting plays. The passion of jealousy in Don Felix is managed in such a way as to give as little offence as possible to the audience. . . . The ambiguity of the heroine's situation, which is like a continued practical *equivoque*, gives rise to a quick succession of causeless alarms, subtle excuses, and the most hair-breadth 'scapes. The scene near the end, in which Don Felix . . . forces his way out of Don Manuel's house . . . by producing his marriage contract in the shape of a pocket-pistol, with the terrors and confusion into which the old gentleman is thrown by this sort of *argumentum ad hominem*, is one of the richest treats the stage affords, and calls forth incessant peals of laughter and applause. . . . The Busy Body . . . is full of bustle and gaiety from beginning to end. The plot never stands still; the situations succeed one another like the changes of machinery in a pantomime. The nice dovetailing of incidents, and cross-reading in the situations, supplies the place of any great force of wit or sentiment. The time for the entrance of each person on the stage is the moment when they are least wanted, and when their arrival makes either themselves or somebody else look as foolish as possible. The laughableness of this comedy, as well as of the Wonder, depends on a brilliant series of mistimed exits and entrances. Marplot is the whimsical hero of the piece, and a standing memorial of unmeaning vivacity and assiduous impertinence.
>
> (pp. 314–17)

Of *The Wonder* Richard Cumberland commented in his anthology *The British Drama* (London, 1817) that "few plays of its date have been so frequently before the public; and very few, I believe, who have been present at its representation, ever departed from the theatre dissatisfied with the writer of it" (7:iv). *The Wonder* was played at Daly's Theatre in 1893–94, and the introduction to the printed acting version commented that "a signal denotement of the vital practical merit of the piece is the fact that although it was produced one hundred and eighty years ago it is not discarded yet. . . . Centlivre possessed the art of dramatic construction, and 'The Wonder' is a felicitous example of it."[48] Cumberland predicted that *A Bold Stroke for a Wife* might "live for a hundred years to come" (10:v) because of "the harliquinade of the plot" and because the character of Fainwell is such a superb acting part. He pointed out the happiness of the conclusion, "how much more natural the acquiescence of the guardians is made to appear by the triumph which every one successively furnishes to all the rest, when he makes discovery of the trick by which he has been duped" (10:vii). The title may have been proverbial for a while, judging from Susan Ferrier's novel *The Inheritance* (1824). When Colonel Delmour seats himself next to the Countess of Rossville at dinner, Miss Pratt remarks, "There's a bold stroke for a wife playing there."[49] *A Bold Stroke for a Wife* exceeded Cumberland's prediction: in June 1954, it was revived successfully at the Questors Theatre, Ealing.[50] In August of the same year a revival of *The Wonder* at the Theatre Royal, Bristol, was filmed for a British television series, *Stage by Stage*.[51]

Centlivre's success, together with that of Behn before her, established the professional woman playwright as a familiar figure. She achieved her popularity by adapting her talents to changing taste, in which she more nearly resembles Cibber and Steele than the Female Wits. Trotter and Pix did not have Centlivre's theatrical skill; Manley looked back to the Restoration in her cavalier, Tory, and feminist attitudes. Centlivre's success did not, however, inspire an important new group of women dramatists, for it came at the time when the English stage was entering its long decline. More and more frequently, writers of ability would turn their talents to the novel. Not until our own century would the English drama produce women playwrights to compare with Aphra Behn and Susanna Centlivre.

# [ 5 ]

# Minor Women Playwrights 1670–1750

*B*etween 1670, the year of Behn's first play, and 1750, many other women wrote plays. Little or nothing is known of some of these women; others are remembered among the remarkable personalities of the age.

In the 1670s two women, otherwise unknown, wrote stage plays. Elizabeth Polwhele's *The Frolicks; or, The Lawyer Cheated* (1671) is a lively London comedy in which a gay couple, Rightwit and Clarabell, steal a marriage against a backdrop of cuckolding and horseplay. In an interesting scene Rightwit enters with two of his bastards tied to his back. Although unacted, *The Frolicks* was written for performance. Polwhele dedicated the play to Prince Rupert, describing herself as "young, no scholar" and commenting, "I question not but I shall be taxed for writing a play so comical, but those that have ever seen my *Faithful Virgins* and my *Elysium* will justify me a little for writing this."[1] Her *Elysium* has not been identified, but *The Faithful Virgins* is a rhymed précieuse tragedy in the Caroline mode performed about 1670 by the Duke's Company. A few years later, about 1678, a woman who used the pen name Ephelia wrote *Pair Royal of Coxcombs,* which was acted at a dancing school. The play is lost except for the prologue, epilogue, and two songs printed in her *Female Poems on Several Occasions* (London, 1679).[2]

In the next two decades three aristocratic ladies wrote in the tradition of closet drama characteristic of Renaissance noblewomen. The first was Anne Lee Wharton (1632?–85), daughter of a baronet and a considerable heiress, married late in life and unhappily to Thomas, later Marquis of Wharton. The friend and correspondent of Dr. Gilbert Burnet, she was a poet whose verse was complimented by Dryden and Waller. Wharton left in manuscript an unacted tragedy in blank verse, *Love's Martyr; or, Wit Above Crowns* (c. 1685), about Ovid's love for Julia.[3] Anne Killigrew (1660–85), the poet and painter memorialized in Dryden's well-known ode, was a maid of honor to Mary of Modena, Duchess of York.[4] Her father was chaplain to the Duke of York, and she was herself noted for sincere piety and religion. Her posthumous *Poems* (1686) contain three pastoral dialogues, in couplets, about virtuous love. The third and longest, somewhat reminiscent of Fletcher's *Faithful Shepherdess*, has speeches of varying lengths, attention to setting, and interaction among a number of characters. In view of Anne Killigrew's family, it is interesting to speculate whether her dialogues would have developed further if she had not died young of smallpox. She was related to the theatrical Killigrews, and her father, before he became a cleric, had written a play. Her piety and her social position would of course have precluded her writing for the public stage. In fact, Dryden's ode contrasts contemporary poets who "increase the steaming Ordures of the Stage" and the innocent "vestal" Anne Killigrew (*Poems*, n.p.).

The third and most notable of these aristocratic amateurs was Anne Kingsmill Finch (1661–1720), after 1712 the Countess of Winchilsea, an able minor poet of pre-Romantic sentiments.[5] The daughter of an ancient, distinguished family, she was orphaned young, and nothing is known of her childhood or education. In 1683 she was, along with Anne Killigrew, a maid of honor to Mary

of Modena. In 1684 she left this post when she married
Heneage Finch, army officer and courtier, a younger son
of Lord Winchilsea. Their marriage was exceptionally
happy; she describes him as the "much lov'd husband, of a
happy wife" (*Poems*, p. 19), a husband who "indulg'd her
Verse" (*Poems*, p. 21). The Finches were both loyal adher-
ents of James II; after the Revolution of 1688 they
remained loyal Jacobites, and consequently Heneage was
excluded from public preferment. For a few years after
the revolution they took refuge with various friends and
relations and finally became permanent guests of
Heneage's nephew Charles, the Earl of Winchilsea, at his
Eastwell estate. There they devoted themselves to the quiet
pursuits of country retirement. Heneage Finch, who
eventually succeeded his nephew to the earldom, became a
noted antiquarian, and Anne Finch became a noted poet
on the basis of manuscript circulation of her poems. Using
the pen name Ardelia, she produced a sizeable body of
work, including plays, odes, fables, songs, and verse
paraphrases of the Bible. Her nature poems were greatly
admired by Wordsworth. Like Orinda, she wrote poems to
friends using various pastoral names. Rowe was a literary
friend, as were Swift and Pope. During her lifetime a few
of her poems appeared unsigned in poetical miscellanies
and, finally, after she had become a countess, she published a selection as *Miscellany Poems on Several Occasions*
(London, 1713). Much of her work, however, including
one of her plays, remained in manuscript until this century.

In 1709 Swift wrote a poem "To the Honourable Mrs.
Finch," in which Apollo gives her the gift of poetry but,
balked of reward, lays a curse upon her: "Of Modest Poets
thou be first."[6] Indeed, her fear of publication was morbid.
Although she began writing when she was young, she did
not, she says, "lett any attempts of mine in Poetry, shew

themselves whilst I liv'd in such a publick place as the Court, where every one wou'd have made their remarks upon a Versifying Maid of Honour" (*Poems*, pp. 7–8). She was keenly sensitive to the "prejudice, if not contempt" (*Poems*, p. 8) that greeted the work of female authors: "A woman's way to charm is not by writing" (*Poems*, p. 338). She developed this idea in the introductory poem to her works:

> Alas! a woman that attempts the pen,
> Such an intruder on the rights of men,
> Such a presumptuous Creature, is esteem'd,
> The fault, can by no vertue be redeem'd.
> (Poems, pp. 4–5)

She concluded that "the dull mannage, of a servile house/Is held by some, our outmost art, and use" (*Poems*, p. 5). This conflict between her desire to write and the expectations of her sex was exacerbated by her fear that women were not, after all, capable of much achievement. She deprecates herself as "of the weaker kinde" (*Poems*, p. 14), confined "to female Clay" (*Poems*, p. 13), although she saw that women were "Education's, more than Nature's fools" (*Poems*, p. 6). Self-doubt and conflict led her to the brink of mental illness. She suffered all her life from the spleen, which she described, in an ode well known in her own time, as characterized by discontent, panic, insomnia, nightmares, religious doubts, weeping, and depression. Her illness caused her to feel that her poetry was "useless Folly, or presumptuous Fault" (*Poems*, p. 250).

The countess was particularly sensitive about her two plays, *The Triumphs of Love and Innocence* (c. 1688) and *Aristomenes; or, The Royal Shepherd* (c. 1690). The first of these she excuses as "only an Essay, wheither I cou'd go throo' with such a peice of Poetry" (*Poems*, p. 11). *The Triumphs of Love and Innocence* is a tragicomedy set in

Rhodes, where the exiled Queen of Cyprus has taken political refuge. General Lauredan, previously a supporter of the usurper, loves the queen, who secretly reciprocates his feeling; he intends to restore her to the throne, but political machinations create mutual suspicion between them. In the second plot, Blanfort, hopelessly in love with the queen, has forsaken his betrothed, Marina, who follows him to Rhodes disguised as a page to Aubusson, the Master of Rhodes. Rivalto, rebuffed in his suit to Marina and jealous of his leader, exposes her sex in order to disgrace both with the accusation of fornication. Eventually, as the title promises, Aubusson's reputation is cleared, the queen and Lauredan are affianced, and Blanfort returns to Marina. This is a remarkable first play, noticeably weak only in the characterization of Rivalto, whose villainy is pasteboard, and of the comic soldier, whose humor is forced. Much better are the virtuous heroines, the fearful queen and the self-abnegating Marina. These two give the play its tone of elevated sentiment and pathos.

*Aristomenes* the countess justified as an attempt to write a play "moral and inciting to Vertue" (*Poems*, p. 11). It is a semihistorical tragedy based on Pausanias. The royal shepherd is the prince of Rhodes, who takes a pastoral disguise to fulfill an oracle that he will wed the daughter of the best of men. He loves and wins Herminia, daughter of Prince Aristomenes, the focal character. Aristomenes is shown courageous in captivity and magnanimous in victory, giving consent that his beloved son Aristor marry the enemy princess. At Aristor's death, Aristomenes, in grief a Christianized Lear, overcomes despair with fortitude.

The Countess of Winchilsea's two closet dramas are stageworthy, remarkably so considering that she wrote them very early in her career and that she had no theatrical training. Both are skillfully plotted and competently versified. She uses blank verse interspersed with couplets and songs; the style, as in her poems, is unadorned and unaffected. The virtuous characters are virtuous without being priggish, and their reverses are due to accident rather than character. The Countess of Winchilsea left *The Triumphs of Love and Innocence* in manuscript, and she revealed *Aristomenes* diffidently at Eastwell, comparing it to "Eastern Beautys, which are only shown/To the dear spouse, and family alone" (*Poems*, p. 411). She had been encouraged in poetry by the head of the family, the young Lord Winchilsea. Accordingly, she first read the play to him "by a good winter's fire" (*Poems*, p. 337), with a self-deprecating prologue describing herself as "the ign'rant Author" (*Poems*, p. 337). She added an equally self-deprecating epilogue "To lett the Audience know when this was writt,/'Twas not for praise, or with pretense to witt" (*Poems*, p. 411). She concluded by promising never to write another play and reiterated this resolve in the preface to her poems. She kept her word not to write further plays, and, although she included *Aristomenes* in the 1713 volume, she left with the manuscript of the two plays a strict "Advertisement":

> not being able, longer then my own life, to protect either of them, from . . . being expos'd, censured, and condemn'd, I prefix these few lines, which will accompany them as long as they are to have a being, to assure all that shall peruse them, that a more terrible injury cannot be offer'd me, then to occasion, or permitt them ever to be represented. . . . did I not hope by my entreaty, to be secure of prevailing in this particular, I wou'd assure myself of itt, by a total suppression, of what I have suffer'd to be coppy'd.
>
> (*Poems*, p. 271)

Her antipathy to public exposure was a pity. The plays are far better than many tragedies produced on stage at the turn of the century, and they might well have appealed to the taste for tragedy of elevated sentiment and fatal accident.

Women less restricted by caste and temperament sought theatrical success. Jane Wiseman wrote *Antiochus the Great; or, The Fatal Relapse,* a blank verse tragedy performed at Lincoln's Inn Fields in 1701. Antiochus wavers between his former mistress Leodice (and their infant son) and his new queen Berenice, who is herself drawn toward her former fiancé Ormades. These divided loyalties end disastrously. Leodice poisons herself and the king, Ormades stabs himself, and Berenice renounces the crown to live a recluse. *Antiochus* is mediocre, but the role of Leodice, written to Mrs. Barry's talent for tragic rant, was probably effective in performance. Wiseman's dedication speaks of the play as "the first Fruits" of her muse. She accedes to the critics' objections to "want of Business," promising "more hurry next time," but defends the psychological truth of Antiochus's character. She is optimistic about her future in the theater: "The Reception it met with in the World, was not kind enough to make me Vain, nor yet so ill, to discourage my Proceeding. . . . I'll add to my Diligence, and with more eagerness pursue the Chace; and sure there's a necessity that all resolv'd like me, should meet success at last." In spite of her determination, nothing more is heard of Jane Wiseman. Giles Jacob's account in *The Poetical Register* (London, 1719), if correct, may explain why she wrote no more plays: "She was a Servant in the Family of Mr. Recorder Wright of Oxon, where, having a pretty deal of leisure Time, which she spent in Reading Novels and Plays, she began a Play . . . call'd, Antiochus . . . acted . . . with Applause. She married a young Vintner, whose Name was Holt; and with the Profits arising from her Play, they set up a Tavern in Westminster" (1:301).

Three women novelists—Mary Davys, Penelope Aubin, and Eliza Haywood—wrote also for the stage. Mary Davys

(1674–1732),[7] born in Dublin, was happily married to the Reverend Peter Davys, headmaster of the free school at St. Patrick's and a friend of Swift. When he died young in 1698, she was widowed and without means at the age of twenty-four. She went to England and tried writing. In 1700 she made an unsuccessful "first Flight to the Muses" (*Works*, 1:v) with a novel, *The Lady's Tale*, for which she received three guineas. She then settled in York for fifteen years. Although she was helped occasionally by Swift, it is not known how she eked out a living during this period. About the age of forty-one, this "Female Muse, from Northern Clime" (Prologue, *The Northern Heiress*) took her first play to London and got it performed at Lincoln's Inn Fields.

*The Northern Heiress; or, The Humours of York* (1716) has many features conventional to prose intrigue comedy—two sets of lovers, an heiress who pretends to lose her fortune in order to test her suitor's affection, a foolish country squire, a fop tricked into marrying a maid, the familiar opening scene of a beau reading, in this case "Humble Cowley" (p. 9). The unusual features give the play its interest. It is set in the country, in a boardinghouse in York. The country characters who display the humours of York are an egregious trio of wives of former lord mayors who insist on being addressed as "lady": Lady Swish, a brewer's wife, Lady Cordivant, a glover's wife, and, chief among them, a chandler's widow, Lady Greasy, who is landlady to the upper-class characters of the main plot. These three breakfast together, waxing nostalgic over former graft as they put away "four Quarts of Country Ale" and "one of strong Beer" (p. 28), and then insist on paying their hostess and tipping her maid. Lady Greasy is given to malapropisms, warning her daughter's suitor "to come no more salivating [i.e., serenading] under our windows" (p. 20). The lively, vigorous prose of the play is characterized by homely diction and specific details of domestic life—teakettles, sciatica, muslin aprons, and rolling pins.

This vein of comic country realism, popular in her later novels, took Davys to a profitable author's benefit. Her preface expresses her pleasure: "The Success it met with the third Night, was (considering the Time of Year, and my own want of Acquaintance) infinitely above what I had Reason to expect; and as the Town, and the Ladies in particular, have been pleas'd to favour my first Attempt, it will make me more industrious to promote their Diversion at a more convenient Season." Her success came in spite of

> how industrious some of the York Gentlemen were to damn this Play. . . . The first Night, in which lay all the Danger, was attended with only two single Hisses; which, like a Snake at a Distance, shew'd a Resentment, but wanted Power to do Hurt. The one was a Boy, and not worth taking Notice of; the other a Man who came prejudic'd, because he expected to find some of his Relations expos'd. But both his Fears, and his ill Nature, were groundless. . . . I think this angry Gentleman would have shewn a greater Contempt, had he said, This is a Woman's Play, and consequently below my Resentment.

Presumably with the profits from this play, Davys opened a coffeehouse in Cambridge, where she lived until her death in 1732. In 1725, encouraged by gentlemen in Cambridge, she printed her *Works* in a two-volume subscription edition. In addition to six novels, her *Works* included, as she had promised in the preface to *The Northern Heiress*, a second play, *The Self Rival: A Comedy. As it should have been Acted at the Theatre-Royal In Drury-Lane.* This second play is also written in lively prose, although it is weaker than her first in characterization and humor. The hero, Colonel Bellamont, in order to foil the mer-

cenary objections of his sweetheart's father, woos Maria
disguised as his rich old uncle, Lord Pastall. He is forced to
be his own rival when Maria pretends not to recognize him
through his disguise and accepts the suit of the supposed
uncle. An unusual character is Mrs. Fallow, a "good-
natur'd old Maid" (dramatis personae), who is contrasted
with the more predictable sour old maid, Lady Camphire
Lovebane. Mrs. Fallow believes that people should marry
young; she is a "Predestinarian" about marriage, having
astutely observed "so many Men and Women go together,
that, in all probability, could never have met" (p. 51).
Although the play is set in London, Davys makes some
slight use of her Cambridge experience for details. The
second male lead is a student at Cambridge, also Bellamont's alma mater. Barnaby, the colonel's servant, is an
adept at quoting poetry because while his master drank his
way through Cambridge, Barnaby studied his master's
books. These details, however, are peripheral. It is a pity
that Davys did not depict the comic humours of university
life as she had done before of York.

The prefatory material in the *Works* shows Davys's attitudes toward her writing. In spite of her coffeehouse
trade, her "Purse is (by a thousand Misfortunes) grown
wholly useless to every body" (*Works*, 2:6). She writes from
need and is angry at criticism for doing so:

> Perhaps it may be objected against me, by some more
> ready to give Reproach than Relief, that as I am the
> Relict of a Clergy-man, and in Years, I ought not to
> publish Plays, &c. But I beg of such to suspend their
> uncharitable Opinions, till they have read what I have
> writ, and if they find any thing there offensive either to
> God or Man, any thing either to shock their Morals or
> their Modesty, 'tis then time enough to blame. And let
> them consider, that a Woman left to her own En-
> deavours for Twenty-seven Years together, may well be
> allow'd to catch at any Opportunity for that Bread,

which they that condemn her would very probably deny
to give her.

*(Works,* 1:vii–viii)

Davys estimates her plays accurately: "I never was so vain,
as to think they deserv'd a Place in the first Rank, or so
humble, as to resign them to the last" *(Works,* 1:vii).

Little is known of Penelope Aubin (c. 1685–1731),[8]
although in the 1720s she wrote seven novels of didactic
plot and exotic setting. She was also a translator, an editor
of some moral works, and author of political odes in 1707
and 1708. In 1729 she was preaching from her own
oratory in the York Buildings. The preface to her collected
*Histories and Novels* (London, 1739) describes her in conventional terms: "She had no contemptible Share of
Learning, surpassing what is usual in her Sex: She had
excellent natural Talents, which were improved by Reading and Observation, as well as by Conversation with
Persons as much distinguished by their Rank as for their
good Understanding." Aubin's own prefaces are religious
and patriotic, espousing a didactic theory of the novel.

The didacticism of her prose and the romanticism of her
novels are in odd contrast to her intrigue comedy, *The
Merry Masqueraders; or, The Humorous Cuckold,* performed
at the Haymarket in December 1730. Aubin herself spoke
the epilogue at the author's benefit. The play is one long
allusion to the use of masquerades to further sexual adventures. To avoid such town dangers, Megrim, a miserly,
forgetful old hypochondriac, has removed his household
to his country home. Here Major Archipole and Captain
Sprightly masquerade as devils and haunt Megrim at
night. Archipole thus intends to cuckold Megrim, and
Sprightly intends to wed and bed Megrim's ward,
Clarinda. They are suspected not only by Megrim but also
by Archipole's fiancée, Miranda, a rich young widow. She
and Megrim themselves secure costumes as devils, and the

masqueraders, unknown to each other, converge on the house at night. Archipole uses the darkness to give Megrim a sound beating, and he manages to convince Miranda, offstage, that all is a harmless frolic to cure Megrim's jealousy. The sentiments of the play seem dated in 1730. Mrs. Megrim is only too willing to cuckold her husband; the other characters, including the virtuous Clarinda, sympathize with her intention; Archipole prefers this intrigue to marriage with Miranda. *The Merry Masqueraders,* although it went through three editions, is mediocre, only slightly enlivened by the slapstick of Megrim.

The most colorful of these three novelists was Eliza Fowler Haywood (c. 1693–1756).[9] The daughter of a London shopkeeper, she was married young to Valentine Haywood, a clergyman some years older than herself. Their son was christened in 1711. Marital troubles soon followed when, in 1715, her name was connected in the newspapers with an Andrew Yeatman. She must then have separated from her husband, because she appeared as an actress that year in Dublin, where she continued acting until 1717, when she reappeared in London performing at Lincoln's Inn Fields. Thereafter she acted sporadically, appearing as late as 1737 in Fielding's *Eurydice Hissed* and *The Historical Register.* In a letter of 1720 she says she gave up the stage because of its "not answering my Expectation, and the averseness of my Relations to it."[10] Her clergyman husband must have been "averse" to her acting, and her next professional venture may have caused him jealousy. In 1719 both husband and wife published books: the clergyman wrote a dull, respectable theological treatise, and his wife published an enormously successful romance, *Love in Excess.* Whether or not literary rivalry caused further marital discord, Eliza Haywood eloped from her husband in late 1720, and in January 1721 he printed an announcement of this in the newspapers, disclaiming all further financial responsibility. She went on to become the most prolific woman writer of her time, producing before her death some fifty popular novels. She also wrote poems, scandalous romans à clef, and, from 1744 to 1746, *The Female Spectator*; in 1742 she ventured briefly as a publisher. She was widely known. Fielding satirized her as Mrs. Novel in *The Author's Farce* (1730), and Pope pilloried her in the 1728 *Dunciad*, in which she and a jordan are the prizes in the games in honor of the monarch of dullness:

> See in the circle next, Eliza plac'd;
> Two babes of love close clinging to her waste
> ...............................................................................
> Pearls on her neck, and roses in ther hair,
> And her fore-buttocks to the navel bare.[11]

She is called a "Juno of majestic size,/ With cow-like udders, and with ox-like eyes."[12] Whether or not the two babes of love existed, and if so, who fathered them, is unknown. Pope's personal attack on Haywood at least partly damaged her literary reputation. She died obscurely after publishing anonymously some of her best works late in life. During her career she made the transition from sensational romance to the domestic novel, and is best remembered for several of the latter, particularly *Betsy Thoughtless* and *Jemmy and Jenny Jessamy*.

Her four plays were only a minor part of her prodigious literary output. The first was a tragedy in blank verse, *The Fair Captive* (1721), which, as she explains in an "Advertisement to the Reader," was a revision of a play originally written by Captain Hurst. In rehearsal it was found "so unfit for Representation" that Rich asked Haywood to rewrite it. She emphatically denied all pride in the composition: "I cannot say my Inclination had much share in my Consent; knowing well, that the Consequence of altering a Manuscript, is to dare the Tongue of Censure without the least View of acquiring Reputation." Indeed, the play is very bad. In Constantinople the Grand Vizier plots against the chastity of Isabella, a Spanish lady imprisoned by the Turks. Alphonso attempts to rescue her by entering the seraglio in disguise. The Grand Vizier discovers and nearly destroys the lovers but is confounded by domestic upheaval and a revolution. Isabella, with her virtue still intact, escapes from Constantinople with Alphonso.

Two years later Haywood wrote a much better play, a prose comedy called *A Wife to Be Let* (1723). The plot is busy, with three sets of romantic lovers and a widow wooed by a footman disguised as a knight. The title character is Mrs. Graspall, the virtuous young wife of a conscienceless miser. Her husband, Graspall, offers to rent his wife to an admirer for £2,000. Mrs. Graspall is outraged, but pretends to comply in order to arrange a comic exposure of her husband's disgusting avarice in front of the whole country. Haywood's growing reputation as a novelist was used to promote the play. She herself acted the part of Mrs. Graspall, and the prologue advertised the author as "A dangerous Woman-Poet":

> Measure her Force, by her known Novels, writ
> With manly Vigour, and with Woman's Wit.

In spite of these puffs, the play ran only three nights, although it was printed several times.

In 1729 Haywood presented a historical tragedy in blank verse, *Frederick, Duke of Brunswick-Lunenburgh* and dedicated it to Frederick Lewis, Prince of Wales, himself Electoral Prince of Brunswick-Lunenburgh. The hero of this dull piece is portrayed as the perfect man and emperor, brought down by the evil machinations of venal lords who fear his honesty. The play concludes with a lengthy "vision" of Frederick's descendants, especially "One . . . Supreamly Great!":

> On him alone shall Peace and War depend;
> His Voice contending Monarchs shall obey
> And the glad World confess a Brunswick's Sway.
>                                          (p. 56)

Haywood's egregious bid for royal notice was ignored, and the play expired after the third night. She complained in the preface that hers was the only new play of the season not attended by any member of the royal family. This is hardly surprising, since two years earlier in her *Court of Carimania* she had exposed the liaison between George II and Henrietta Howard.

Haywood's most successful theatrical production was an adaptation, *The Opera of Operas; or, Tom Thumb the Great* (1733). She and her collaborator William Hatchett, with the most minimal changes, turned Fielding's *Tragedy of Tragedies* into a popular ballad opera. Set to music by Arne and later by Lampe, *The Opera of Operas* was performed repeatedly in 1733 and 1734 and was revived again in 1740. Considered as a group, Eliza Haywood's plays were mediocre; they were peripheral to her novels, into which she directed her primary energies.

There are a number of women of whom little or nothing is known except their sporadic theatrical efforts. An anonymous "Young Lady" in 1706 adapted Fletcher's *Loyal Subject* into a tragedy called *The Faithful General*, which was performed at the Haymarket. In 1719 Mrs. Aubert's *Harlequin-Hydaspes; or, The Greshamite* was performed at Lincoln's Inn Fields and published anonymously. The preface claims that the play was written by a gentleman who "risks too much upon the Success of it" to displease anyone and hopes to write further plays. Presumably Mrs. Aubert was in economic distress and turned to the theater in an attempt to earn money. *Harlequin-Hydaspes,* however, a negligible three-act mock opera, had no success, and Mrs. Aubert wrote nothing else. Mrs. Egleton, the actress who created the role of Lucy Lockit in *The Beggar's Opera* (1728), for her benefit night in 1732 wrote and acted in an afterpiece called *The Maggot.* This two-act ballad opera was not published. Mrs. Egleton was married to an actor who styled himself "Baron Egleton," and, according to William Cooke's *Memoirs of Charles Macklin* (London, 1804), "like a second Ariadne, she died enamoured of Bacchus, about the year 1734" (p. 49).

Two women published plays that were not performed. Elizabeth Boyd, also author of a novel and some poems, wrote a two-act ballad opera, *Don Sancho; or, The Students Whim* (1739). Boyd's "Advertisement" thanks Chetwood for introducing the play in the green room where it was "kindly approved of"; she explains that it would have been performed "had the Season been earlier, and Benefits not so thick." She printed the play with a dedication to Lord North and a prologue addressed to Pope. The play is odd. In Oxford three students persuade Don Sancho to raise the spirits of Shakespeare and Dryden, who offer curious literary advice: "Wou'd you merit lasting Bays,/ Goodness practise more than Praise" (p. 13).

A Mrs. Weddell published two unacted plays, a farce and a tragedy, both prefaced with a mixture of sense, nonsense, and dramatic criticism. *The City Farce* (1737) carries a lengthy address "To the Gentlemen of the Pit" explaining that plays should be published before presented. In this way audiences can demand any piece that pleases, "without the Author's being subjected to the many Discouragements which attend an Application to a Manager" (p. v). Contradictorily, she cannot "admit of making the People's Taste the Rule of Writing, while it is known to all who consider the Intention of a Theatre, That its peculiar Business is to correct a wrong Taste, instead of complying with it" (p. ix). Accordingly, weary of pantomime and ballad opera, she proposes in her "first Attempt of a Dramatick kind" (p. viii) to revive "the Spirit of our old English Farce, which was designed to yield some Benefit as well as Diversion" (p. vii). Fortunately for Weddell, her "Bread" had "not any Dependence on [her] Pen" (p. ix), for her play offers neither benefit nor diversion, only lengthy discourses about various city foibles.

Weddell's second play, *Incle and Yarico* (1742) is a three-act tragedy of rather better quality. She tried to get a performance for this play, and her preface expresses bitterness at "these Playhouse Criticks," who "kept the Copy . . . a tedious while" and at last returned it with "only a supercilious Objection to its Shortness." The players were wise to refuse *Incle and Yarico,* although it has some interest because of its anti-slavery sentiment. Based on an essay in the *Spectator,* the tragedy, in a blank verse of sorts, depicts Incle shipwrecked on the coast of Africa:

> Where the Remembrance of the Multitudes
> Borne hence, to Slav'ry, by our Countrymen,
> Must make each Man we meet an Enemy.
> (p. 9)

The princess Yarico falls in love with and rescues this Englishman. In return, he gets her pregnant and sells her into slavery in Jamaica; this harsh treatment causes her to die in premature childbirth. Incle and the Jamaicans are vicious hypocrites, reflecting smugly upon Yarico's luck in having "fall'n 'mong us Christians" (p. 48). In her preface Weddell reminds her countrymen that they are "a wise People, and fond of Liberty, who consider all Men as Denizens of the Earth's plenteous Blessings, nor think the casual Tincture of the Skin, differing from the European

Hue alienates any from the indubitable Right they are naturally entitled to, as Fellow Creatures." She adds some pedestrian drama criticism in "A General View of Dramatic Poetry."

Dramatic criticism is also the subject of Mrs. Hoper's burlesque, *Queen Tragedy Restored* (1749). "Depravity of Taste" (p. 18) has sent Queen Tragedy into a decline. Although a lord advises that her physicians treat the public, they attempt to cure the queen by presenting various entertainments. She rejects an Italian opera because she cannot understand the language, but is assured that "Understanding is by no ways concerned" (p. 21). Dr. Drollery recommends relieving tragic scenes with the ludicrous "lest a polite Audience might be incommoded by a moral Reflection" (p. 25). The patient is finally cured by the spirit of Shakespeare. Othello, Hamlet, Falstaff, and Richard II are singled out for special praise: "The Stage shall flourish, Tragedy shall thrive,/ And Shakespear's Scenes ne'er die whilst They survive" (p. 46). Mrs. Hoper, a minor actress, played the title role herself. The prologue describes her as a needy widow who has turned to the stage for support in spite of her scandalized friends: "Is playing meaner, than to run in Debt?" The prologue also describes *Queen Tragedy Restored* as the "Firstling of her Quill," although Hoper is credited with two earlier plays—a tragedy, *The Battle of Poictiers; or, The English Prince* (1747), and a farce, *The Cyclopedia* (1748). Neither of these plays was published.

Another widow who turned to the stage was Elizabeth Cooper, whose husband had been an auctioneer and/or bookseller.[13] She is remembered now for her pioneer interest in early English poetry. In 1737 Cooper brought out the first volume of *The Muses Library; Or a Series of English Poetry, From the Saxons, to the Reign of King Charles II.* The dignified and intelligent preface shows a serious con-

cern about the changes in the language and the loss of
older writers. The first volume of extracts ends with
Samuel Daniel; the second volume never appeared. Oddly
enough, this learned woman made her debut as a writer
with a comedy, *The Rival Widows; or, Fair Libertine* (1735).
The rival widows are Lady Lurcher and her cousin Lady
Bellair, both enamoured of Freelove. Lurcher affects
prudery; she has cheated Bellair out of her estate and now
sets her creditors upon her. In contrast, Bellair is generous
"because Money is of no Value till 'tis used" (p. 37) and
frank about sex: "We can talk of Murder, Theft, and
Treason, without blushing: and surely there's nothing
a-kin to Love that's half so wicked" (p. 23). She exposes
Lurcher, regains her estate, and wins Freelove. Lady Bellair is the "fair libertine" of the title, and Cooper is using
this phrase in a special sense: "She's Gay without Levity,
Libertine without Scandal, Generous without Design, and
Well-bred without Affectation" (p. 14). Cooper in her
preface feels that the ladies will be pleased with a heroine
"capable of thinking for herself, and acting on the Principles of Nature and Truth." Apparently she was right, for
the play had a successful run at Covent Garden, with
Cooper herself playing the part of Bellair on her benefit
nights. *The Rival Widows* shows the imprint of Cooper's
poetic and scholarly interests. Both the title page and the
prologue quote Congreve. In the preface she prides herself on observing the unities and aiming at "Regularity and
Decorum. 'Tis what we Women-Authors, in particular,
have been thought greatly deficient in; and I shou'd be
concern'd to find it an Objection not to be remov'd." The
most notable evidence of regularity is that the printed play
uses the classical principle of scene division according to
the entrance or exit of any character. The next year
Cooper wrote another comedy, *The Nobleman; or, The Fam-*

*ily Quarrel,* performed three nights at the Haymarket but not published.

Some curious figures of the age wrote plays. Among them was the precocious, self-taught poet Mary Leapor (1722–1746), daughter of a Northamptonshire gardener.[14] "Mrs. Leapor from a Child delighted in reading, and particularly Poetry, but had few Opportunities of procuring any Books of that kind" (To the Reader, *Poems,* 1). Among the few books she did obtain were the works of Dryden and Pope; her verses in imitation of Pope attracted attention. After her death of the measles at the age of twenty-four, her *Poems Upon Several Occasions* "in Compliance with her dying Request" were "published for the Benefit of her Father" (To the Reader, *Poems,* 1) in two subscription volumes, in 1748 and 1751. Volume 2 contains a tragedy in blank verse, *The Unhappy Father.* The play is set in the country house of Dycarbas, who sends away his two sons, Lycander and Polonius, because they are rivals for the love of his ward, Terentia. Habitual quarrels between his daughter, Emilia, and her husband, Eustathius, lead to his quick belief in a slander of her fidelity. Eustathius stabs Emilia and is accidentally killed by his brother-in-law Lycander, who is himself mortally wounded. Dycarbas sends for his remaining child; when he learns that Polonius has been eaten by a shark, the unhappy father dies of grief. Terentia is about to commit suicide when she is saved by Polonius, who has escaped death after all. *The Unhappy Father* is better than this summary suggests. In a passage remarkable for its date, Emilia laments the training that turns girls into "unhappy Wives":

> Our servile Tongues are taught to cry for Pardon
> Ere the weak Senses know the Use of Words:
> Our little Souls are tortur'd by Advice;

And moral Lectures stun our Infant Years:
Thro' check'd Desires, Threatnings, and Restraint
The Virgin runs; but ne'er outgrows her Shackles
They still will fit her, even to hoary Age.
(*Poems,* 2:189–90)

Apparently Leapor hoped to see her play performed. In "To a Gentleman with a Manuscript Play" (*Poems,* 1:267–70) she commends her work "to its Patron's Care," comparing herself to a grave rural matron who fearfully sees her daughter preferred to service in London.

Another remarkable figure was Letitia Pilkington (1712–50), whose *Memoirs,* a major source of anecdotes about Swift, are fascinating, entertaining autobiography.[15] She was born Letitia Van Lewen, daughter of a Dutch obstetrician living in Dublin. Her early precocity, punished by her mother, was rewarded by her father, and she began writing verses when she was a child. At seventeen or eighteen she made a love match with a penniless parson named Matthew Pilkington and bore a child almost every year of their brief marriage. Both the clergyman and his wife wrote verse, and Matthew became vicious when Letitia's were preferred to his. Swift befriended the couple, obtaining for Matthew the mayoral chaplaincy in London. When Letitia visited him, he was intriguing with an actress and tried to sell his wife's favors to James Worsdale, a portrait painter. After Matthew's repeated infidelities, Letitia also took a lover. Matthew, assisted by a group of armed men, surprised the couple in her bed-chamber, turned her out with only the clothes on her back, and sued for divorce. After the divorce, he refused to pay the agreed maintenance and treated their children with extreme cruelty; he remained a clergyman and later re-married. Driven by need and scandal, Letitia Pilkington went to England, took lodgings directly opposite White's Club, and lived by writing, begging, shopkeeping (for a time), and perhaps prostitution. She was imprisoned for debt, but was befriended by many, including Colley Cibber and Samuel Richardson. Finally she sank into desperate poverty—one night she slept in Westminster Abbey, another she attempted suicide in St. James Park—and begged enough money to return to Dublin. There she caused another scandal by publishing the first two volumes of her *Memoirs* (1748), recounting her adventures in detail and naming names. She detailed the cruelties of her ex-husband, and the two attacked each other in a pamphlet war. She died in 1750, and the third volume of her *Memoirs* was published posthumously, in 1754.

Pilkington included most of her writings in her autobiography. An exception was a comedy, *The Turkish Court; or, London Prentice*, performed in Dublin in 1748. "It is the Opinion of several Persons that saw it acted," reported Chetwood, "that if it had better Performers, and proper Decorations, the Piece would have given great Satisfaction."[16] The play was not printed. Pilkington also began a tragedy, *The Roman Father*, based on the story of Appius and Virginia; the first act is included in Volume 2 of her *Memoirs*. At one point she says she discontinued the tragedy because "at the same time there were two bad plays wrote on that subject" (*Memoirs*, p. 273); later she says she did not finish it because Sheridan "would never permit it to be played, merely because it was mine" (*Memoirs*, p. 322). Whatever her reason, it is just as well that she did not complete *The Roman Father*, for the sample she printed is verbose and frigid. Pilkington also wrote prologues and epilogues for various occasions. An interesting feature of her work for the theater is the ghostwriting she did after her divorce. For Benjamin Victor she wrote the first act of a comedy. She ghosted for Worsdale off and on, both in Dublin and London, writing for him, in addition to numerous poems and odes, three ballad operas. At one point she lived in "a little room ... within-side of his painting-room," where she "was a prisoner all the morning, and might fast and write till three o'clock in the day" (*Memoirs*, p. 363). She wrote one of the operas "on the story of the old song *A Pennyworth of Wit*. . . . I am sorry I have not the opera, but Worsdale was too cunning for me, and seized it, sheet by sheet, as fast as I wrote it" (*Memoirs*, pp. 362–63). Pilkington's autobiography raises the possibility that other women engaged in theatrical ghostwriting.

The life of Charlotte Cibber Charke (1710–60) is also known in detail because of her autobiography.[17] *A Narrative of the Life of Mrs. Charlotte Charke, Youngest Daughter of Colley Cibber* (London, 1755) is an amazing memoir of an eighteenth-century transvestite. From infancy she clearly wanted to be a man. The earliest event she describes is her dressing in her father's clothes at the age of four, "having, even then, a passionate Fondness for a Perriwig" (*Narrative*, p. 17). At eight she went for two years to a boarding school where she received an education "sufficient for a Son instead of a Daughter" (*Narrative*, p. 17), studying Latin, Italian (she already knew French), geography, music, singing, and dancing. She passed the rest of her childhood in the country where she became an expert shot, hunting daily until a "strait-lac'd, old-fashion'd Neighbour" (*Narrative*, p. 29) put a stop to this unladylike diversion. She rode, gardened, worked in the stables, and doctored the gullible with medicines of her own invention, one of the most successful being made of boiled snails. "Many and vain Attempts were used" to make her learn household skills, but she could not "bear to pass a train of melancholly Hours in poring over a Piece of Embroidery, or a well-wrought Chair, in which the young Females of the Family (exclusive of my mad-cap Self) were equally and industriously employed; and have often, with inward Contempt of 'em, pitied their Misfortunes, who were, I was well assured, incapable of currying a Horse, or riding a Race with me" (*Narrative*, p. 33).

She was married young to Richard Charke, a musician in the theater, who had more interest in being Colley Cibber's son-in-law than Charlotte's husband. He spent the first year of their marriage among the prostitutes of Drury Lane and, after the birth of their daughter, he and Charlotte separated. He abandoned all responsibility for their child and eventually left the country. To support herself and her daughter, Charlotte Charke followed her father and her brother Theophilus into the theater. She began acting at Drury Lane with some success; she was a quick study and sometimes at the last minute replaced an indisposed actress in a principal role. In a few years she began to play men's roles as well. In 1737 she was with Fielding's company at the Haymarket, where she played both male and female parts. Sometime during her stormy career as a London actress she was summoned to a family conference about her misbehavior; her family turned her out and her father never spoke to her again.

Charlotte Charke now habitually dressed as a man and entered on a series of fantastic, picaresque adventures. For a time she hung about the fringes of the London theaters, picking up occasional acting jobs and giving puppet shows. She had a brief fling at management of the Haymarket. A mysterious second marriage to a man whose name she vowed never to reveal[18] was the "Fatal Cause" (*Narrative*, p. 89) of her subsequent poverty, which was shared by her small daughter until the child herself became an actress. She was courted by an heiress, who was heartbroken when Charke revealed her sex, and held and failed at an endless number of jobs—grocer, valet, waiter, sausage-seller, public house keeper, farmer, pastry cook, proofreader, prompter at a Bath theater. She became a strolling player for nine years under the name of Mr. Brown, traveling with a woman she referred to as Mrs. Brown. As her father had described the London theater in his *Apology,* so Charke in her *Narrative,* in anecdotes amusing and sordid, described the provincial theater: "I have had the Mortification of hearing the Characters of Hamlet, Varanes, Othello, and many more Capitals, rent in Pieces by a Figure no higher than two Six-penny Loaves, and a Dissonancy of Voice, which conveyed to me a strong Idea of a Cat in Labour" (*Narrative,* p. 189). Her nine years on the road convinced her that "it wou'd be more reputable to earn a Groat a Day in Cinder-sifting at Tottenham-Court, than to be concerned with" the strolling players (*Narrative,* p. 187). Finally she returned to London resolved to earn a living by writing. After publicly and unsuccessfully appealing for her father's forgiveness in her autobiography, which she wrote in a pitiable slum, she published several novels before her death.

In 1735, while she was still a young actress in London, Charke wrote two plays. (She was the author of *Tit for Tat* in 1743, but this may have been a puppet show rather than a legitimate play.) She acted in her own comedy *The Carnival; or, Harlequin Blunderer,* performed for her benefit on 5 September at Lincoln's Inn Fields. This play was not printed but was performed again on 17 September at the Haymarket. Charke had taken "a French Leave" of Charles Fleetwood, the new Drury Lane manager, because of a "Dispute about Parts" (*Narrative,* p. 62). Fleetwood then fired her on the grounds of immorality, an interesting charge from a company in which, the previous May, Charles Macklin had killed a fellow actor in a dispute over a wig. Charke's second play, *The Art of Management; or, Tragedy Expelled,* responded to her dismissal by attacking Fleetwood and Macklin under the names of Brainless and Bloodbolt. The setting is Drury Lane Theatre, where Brainless mismanages money, fires all players who have "more Wit than himself," and rehearses *"The Union of the Bear and Monkey,"* to be performed by "Merry Andrews, Monkies, Bears, and Prize-Fighters" (p. 12). Bloodbolt intends to frighten the Town into liking this entertainment. Bad as things are, all are surprised at the dismissal of Mrs. Tragic (Charke; she played the role herself), who turns for solace to Headpiece (Theophilus). Headpiece is about to lead an actor's revolt when he receives the patent to the house because Brainless has been imprisoned for debt. The play ends with extravagant praise for Headpiece.

*The Art of Management* seems fatuous when considered from the perspective of theatrical history,[19] because Fleetwood was manager for another decade while Charlotte and Theophilus both sank into scandal and poverty. From the perspective of 1735, however, it is easier to see why Charke's play ends the way it does and why it was well received by audiences. Fleetwood was a pleasant young man with a large fortune, but it was not impossible that he might have become bankrupt. According to Benjamin Victor in *The History of the Theatres* (London, 1761) he had gambled away his estate before he became manager (1:34–35). Colley Cibber had only recently retired from his long career as manager of Drury Lane, and Theophilus thought the theater his by hereditary right. With this motive, he had already led a successful actors' revolt against Highmore in 1733. Charlotte, equally possessive of the theater, deplored that "so many, who have good Trades, should idly quit them, to become despicable Actors. . . . Those who were bred up in the Profession, have the best Right to make it their Calling" (*Narrative,* pp. 187–88). She puts similar sentiments into the mouth of Headpiece when Brainless complains that management is a troublesome business. Headpiece replies: "I don't see any Business you had to Undertake what you did not understand; all who are bred and born in it, must necessarily know more of it than a Man of Fortune, who never appear'd but in a Side-Box, or behind the Scenes" (p. 20). Charke expresses this idea of birthright again in the prologue, which she spoke, comparing herself "from ancient Drury expell'd/Why I know not, yet helpless to be repeal'd" to the grief-stricken Adam and Eve expelled from paradise. Audiences who say the play at the York Buildings also apparently thought of Drury Lane as the home of the Cibbers. The *Daily Advertiser* reported of the first performance that "Mrs. Charke . . . drew Tears from the whole Audience in her Prologue, which she spoke very pathetically; and the new Farce . . . was very much applauded."[20] In the preface to *The Art of Management* Charke defended her "publick Proceedings" about her discharge: "While my Follies are only hurtful to my self, I know no Right that any Persons, unless Relations, or very good Friends, have to call me to Account. I'll allow private Virtues heighten publick Merits, but then the Want of those private Virtues wont affect an Actors Performance." She added an ironical dedication to Fleetwood, who attempted to suppress the play by purchasing the entire printing. After the fracas, surprisingly enough, Fleetwood rehired Charke at Colley Cibber's request. Even more surprising, after the scandals of the next twenty years, the indomitable Charlotte Charke was back on the boards again, playing at minor houses from 1754 to 1759.

The last play written by a woman in this period was also the work of an actress, the celebrated comedienne Catherine (Kitty) Clive (1711–85).[21] She was the daughter of an Irish lawyer, William Raftor, who married into a prosperous London family after losing his property for supporting James II. Her family was large and her education scanty. At twelve she was stagestruck and at seventeen she began acting at Drury Lane as Miss Raftor. She immediately achieved great popularity because of her vivacity and fine singing; during her forty years on the stage she was distinguished for character parts, especially intriguing chambermaids. About 1733 she married George Clive, a barrister of excellent family; the marriage ended shortly in separation. Kitty Clive was noted both for benevolence and hot temper. She helped support her family, particularly her brother James, and engaged in sharp theatrical quarrels, such as the public dispute with Susanna Cibber over the part of Polly in *The Beggar's Opera*. She and Garrick quarreled repeatedly and were fast friends. For her farewell appearance, in 1769, she chose one of her most popular roles, that of the maid Flora in Centlivre's *The Wonder*. She retired to Twickenham and lived the remaining sixteen years of her life in a house given to her by her friend Horace Walpole.

For her benefit night in March 1750, Clive wrote *The Rehearsal; or, Bays in Petticoats*, a two-act farce designed as a showcase for her abilities as a comic and singer. With music by Boyce, it was a popular afterpiece; it was published in 1753 and performed as late as 1762.[22] *Bays in Petticoats* is a satire of a woman playwright written by a woman, and Clive herself took the role of the affected lady author, Mrs. Hazard, whose play is in rehearsal at Drury Lane. Clive's most prolonged spoof, and the one that must have entertained the audience the most, was of herself. Mrs. Hazard is in a rage because Mrs. Clive is late to rehearsal, then sends "word, that she can't possibly wait on you this Morning, as she's oblig'd to go to some Ladies about her Benefit" (p. 24). The playwright decides to rehearse the missing actress's role herself, but cannot wear Clive's costume because, as she observes smugly, "I happen to be a Head taller, and I hope something better made" (p. 25). Mrs. Hazard is writing a new play, with a part for Mrs. Clive:

I wish she don't spoil it; for she's so conceited, and insolent, that she won't let me teach it her. You must know when I told her I had a Part for her in a Performance of mine, in the prettiest manner I was able, (for one must be civil to these sort of People when one wants them) says she, Indeed Madam, I must see the whole Piece, for I shall take no Part in a new thing, without chusing that which I think I can act best. I have been a great Sufferer already, by the Manager's not doing Justice to my Genius; but I hope I shall next Year convince the Town, what fine Judgment they have: for I intend to play a capital Tragedy Part for my own Benefit. . . . I desir'd Mr. Garrick wou'd take her in hand; so he order'd her the Part of the Mad-woman directly.

(pp. 14–15)

In its satire of the woman playwright, *Bays in Petticoats* makes an interesting comparison with *The Female Wits,* the satire of Manley, Pix, and Trotter over fifty years earlier. The later farce, although shorter and necessarily more sketchily developed, follows exactly the plot of the earlier. It opens with Mrs. Hazard dressing to attend her rehearsal. She was "once a sweet-temper'd Woman" but now "the Muses . . . have turn'd her Head" (p. 5). She conceitedly repeats her own lines while drinking tea and scolds the maid for interrupting her creative musings. She is visited and accompanied at the playhouse by a flattering fool named Witling. Her play costs her her fiancé. At the playhouse she lectures and bullies the players, and, when she is baited by a group of onlookers, leaves in a foolish rage. *Bays in Petticoats,* although it repeats the plot line of *The Female Wits,* puts the criticism of the female playwright into the mouths of fools. Witling reports that she is the town laughingstock for writing a play; unaware of the contradiction, he also reports that it is believed that her play was actually written by a man. Her fiancé, who is, suggestively, named Surly, has broken off their engagement because Hazard is going to publicly "expose herself"; writing a play is worse than sexual misbehavior:

> there is not ten Women in the Creation that have Sense enough to write a consistent N. B.—Marry her! I would sooner marry a Woman that had been detected in ten Amours, than one, who, in Defiance to all Advice, and without the Pretence that most People write for, (for every body knows she's a Woman of Fortune) will convince the whole World she's an Ideot.
>
> (pp. 10–11)

Sir Albany Odelove, the most fatuous fool in the piece, pompously advises:

> If Men, who are properly graduated in Learning, who have swallow'd the Tincture of a polite Education, who, as I may say, are hand and glove with the Classics, if such Genius's as I'm describing, fail of Success in Dramatical Occurrences, or Performances, ('tis the same Sense in the Latin) what must a poor Lady expect, who is ignorant as the Dirt.
>
> (p. 38–39)

Clive's *Bays in Petticoats* simultaneously spoofs and exploits some of the clichés about women playwrights that had been current since Aphra Behn's day, and even before. A closer look at these criticisms, together with an examination of England's early women playwrights as a group, reveals the combination of fact and fiction that shaped the literary history and the literary life of women.

## [ 6 ]

# *The Salic Law of Wit*

When Women write, the Criticks, now-a-days,
Are ready, e'er they see, to damn their Plays;
Wit, as the Men's Prerogative, they claim,
And with one Voice, the bold Invader blame.
Tell me the Cause, ye Gallants of the Pit,
Did Phoebus e'er the Salique Law admit?
                    Mary Davys, Prologue, *The Self Rival,* 1725

*The* professional woman writer was a new figure in the seventeenth century and was a subject for lively admiration and debate. The woman playwright, in particular, because of the public nature of the drama, was highly visible and came in for a good deal of praise and abuse. All this comment was preoccupied with gender; indeed, literary criticism in the Restoration and eighteenth century, when it deals with women playwrights, is basically a continuation of the age-old *querelle des femmes.*

The amazement and admiration that the new women writers aroused is manifested in the numerous "phoenix" compliments showered on them. Behn was frequently addressed as "the Phoenix, wonder of the Age,/ The Glory of your Sex,"[1] "Thou Wonder of thy Sex!"[2] Again: "Oh, wonder of thy Sex! Where can we see,/ Beauty and Knowledge join'd except in thee?"[3] Astrea was "incomparable," Orinda "matchless," and Centlivre "celebrated."

An unwritten "Salic law of wit," which, on the analogy of the law excluding women from the French throne, excluded women from Parnassus, was waived in cases of superior merit. Cowley allowed Philips to "cancel great Apollo's Salick Law."[4] George Jenkins declared that Behn "spight of their Salick Law, shall reign."[5] Commendatory verses to Trotter on her *Fatal Friendship* asserted, "Our Salique law of wit you have destroy'd," and Prior's epilogue to Manley's *Lucius* proposed "To damn this Salique Law, impos'd on Wit." At Dryden's death Abel Boyer wrote Centlivre: "The Muses despair of ever finding him a Successor among the Men Poets; but as the Salick Law has no more Force in Parnassus than in England, I dare prophesie the Bays will fall to your share" (*Letters of Wit*, p. 359).

On the other hand, literary critics who disliked women playwrights insisted on the Salic law of wit, depicting its operation in various "sessions" of the poets. This genre of literary criticism and lampoon, originated by Trajano Boccalini in Italy in 1612, found numerous translators, adaptors, and imitators in seventeenth- and eighteenth-century England.[6] In these "sessions" the poets assemble and are then praised or damned by Apollo. For example, *A Journal from Parnassus* (c. 1688) describes "amorous Afra, the Sappho of the Age":

Apollo seeing a body of a more than female size wrapt up in Hoods & Petticoats ... was about to appoint a Committee of Muses to examine her Sex: but being assured by severall Members there present that to their certain knowledge she was a Woman, & fearing lest by the Priviledge of her Sex she should wast an Hour's time in setting forth her Parts, he thought it best to prevent her by telling her that his distrust of her Womanhood proceeded not only from the unweildiness of her Person, but from the immodesty of her Writings, which he thought, not so much for their Witt as for their Lewdness, no Woman could have been Author of. . . . the Constitutions of this Assembly . . . would hardly allow a Precedent for the introducing among them a Sex that, if it were once encourag'd, wou'd soon endeavour a Monopoly of Witt. . . . in short, since her Works had neither Witt enough for a Man, nor Modesty enough for a Woman, she was to be look'd upon as an Hermaphrodite, & consequently not fit to enjoy the benefits & Priviledges of either Sex, much less of this Society.[7]

Apollo derides the Duchess of Newcastle as a madwoman in "The Session of the Poets, to the Tune of Cook [sic] Lawrel."[8] *The Session of the Poets, Holden at the Foot of Parnassus-Hill* (London, 1696) arraigns Manley and Pix in nearly identical passages. Manley is "Indicted by the Name of D. M. Spinster, in that she very peremptorily, *mutatis mutandis,* against an express Form in that case made and provided by Apollo and the Muses, has Sacrilegiously usurp'd that Province of Poetry no ways belonging nor appertaining unto her, for few Sappho's or Orinda's appear now upon the Stage" (p. 39). An adaptation of Boccalini by N. N. in 1704 is scurrilous:

The Literati having, some few Months since, admitted Orinda, Mrs. Behn, Mrs. Manly, and several other Poetesses, into Parnassus, contrary to their Ancient Customs; It was observ'd that the Virtuosi were more assiduous at their Exercises than formerly; and being more Inspir'd by the Beauty of these Ladies, then by the Muses, made such Excellent Performances in Poetry, that even Apollo wondred at 'em: But it was not long, 'ere his Majesty smelt a Rat; wherefore he gave orders no more Ladies should be admitted, and that these should be Banish'd out of Parnassus. For he . . . foresaw, that the Learned Exercises, which the Virtuosi and these Ladies perform'd together, would end like the Playing of Dogs, in getting upon one another's Backs.[9]

In 1738–39 "The Apotheosis of Milton" appeared at irregular intervals in *The Gentleman's Magazine.* In this "session" the spirits of the poets buried in Westminster Abbey assemble with Chaucer as president. Although laundered in expression, the prohibition against women is as firm as ever. Aphra Behn is not allowed to join the assembly: "Observe that Lady dressed in the loose *Robe de Chambre* with her Neck and Breasts bare; how much Fire in her Eye! What a passionate Expression in her Motions! And how much Assurance in her Features! Observe what an Indignant Look she bestows on the President, who is telling her, *that none of her Sex has any Right to a Seat there.*"[10]

The Salic law of wit was sometimes enforced by audiences who heckled women's plays because of the author's sex. Prologues and epilogues refer frequently to this. Behn's epilogue to *Sir Patient Fancy,* for example, begins, "I here and there o'erheard a Coxcomb cry,/Ah, Rot it—'tis a Woman's Comedy" (4:115). Similarly, Trotter's epilogue to *Fatal Friendship* asks the audience to be "just" in judging the play, "Not with grimace, and words all noise, and huff,/Damn it, a woman's! that must needs be stuff" (*Works,* 2:552). Behn was not describing an unfamiliar figure when she spoke of the "wretched Fop" who entered the pit at the premiere of *The Dutch Lover* to tell the audience "that they were to expect a woful Play, God damn him, for it was a woman's" (1:223–24). Davys records the two hecklers at the opening of *The Northern Heiress* who came to hiss "like a Snake at a Distance" (Preface). The organized heckling of hostile cabals is also recorded. Charles Gildon in the dedication of Behn's *Younger Brother* protested the "unjust Sentence this Play met with before very partial Judges"; he describes the "Faction that was made against it, which indeed was very Evident on the First day, and more on the endeavours employed, to render the Profits of the Third, as small as could be" (4:316-17). Davys's assertion in the prologue to *The Self*

*Rival* that critics were "ready, e'er they see, to damn" women's plays is also illustrated by the advance report of Centlivre's *Busy Body,* which nearly failed on opening night because "those who had heard of it, were told it was a silly thing wrote by a Woman."[11] It is hardly surprising, then, that women playwrights so often turned to other women for support. Many dedicated their plays to women of rank, and the appeal to the women in the audience became a convention in their prologues and epilogues.

Hostility to women playwrights expressed itself in terms of certain ideas that appeared over and over. For example, *The Female Tatler* for 8 July 1709 illustrates a widespread attitude: "Mrs. Cavil . . . asserted, that no Woman ever yet turn'd Poetess, but lost her Reputation by appearing at Rehearsals, and conversing with Imoinda, Desdemona, and a Maidenhead Amintor at my Years . . . and that the Treatment Authors meet with from the Play'rs, is too gross for a Woman to bear." These objections are mocked in the name given to the speaker, but they accurately describe the elements in theatrical life that damaged the reputation of the woman playwright. The first was the public nature of the profession. A dramatist not only attended rehearsals but also readings, performances, and benefits. There she had to deal with the "gross" treatment of the players. The Restoration and eighteenth-century theater was rough, often the scene of drunkenness and violence, backstage as well as in the pit. It was no place for a woman who wished to be respectable. Moreover, the woman playwright associated with actresses. The original actresses were professionally inexperienced and pleased primarily by sexual novelty and attraction, as Pepys's diary amply witnesses. Many were promiscuous, and some became famous courtesans, vaulting from the stage to the court, like Nell Gwynne. By the end of the Restoration, Mrs. Bracegirdle's example made it possible for a woman both to act and to preserve a reputation for chastity, but many actresses continued to exploit their sex. Women playwrights appeared at the same moment historically as actresses, in the 1660s, and some of the best known, Manley for example, flouted contemporary moral conventions as openly as actresses, while those who did not suffered nonetheless from guilt by association. Behn exploited this association by having the actress who spoke the epilogue to *Sir Patient Fancy* assert that women have more expertise at love than men: "Quickest in finding all the subtlest ways/To make your Joys, why not to make you Plays?" (4:116).

Humorous equation of the authoress and the prostitute was used in the 1695–96 season as the basis of double entendre to promote women's plays. Motteux's epilogue for *She Ventures and He Wins* compared the presentation of a first play by "Ariadne" to loss of virginity:

> Our Poetess is troubled in her Mind,
> Like some young Thing, not so discreet as kind,
> Who, Without Terms, has her dear Toy resign'd.
> ...........................................................................
> Our Authoress now is in, at your Devotion,
> Tho' she, perhaps to please you, want the Notion,
> Be gen'rous once, she'll quickly mend her Motion.

Wycherley's prologue to Trotter's *Agnes de Castro* described the author venturing "scorn"

> but to pleasure you,
> Nay, her own pleasure does for yours forego;
> And like the Pregnant of her Sex, to gain,
> But for your pleasure, more Disgrace and Pain;
> ...........................................................................
> Then be not, as Poor Women often find,
> Less kind to her, because she's more inclin'd
> At venture of her Fame, to please Mankind.

When Pix wrote a tragedy, then a comedy, the prologue to the second, *The Spanish Wives,* assured the "Gallants":

> The First Time she was grave, as well she might,
> For Women will be damn'd sullen the first Night;
> But faith, they'l quickly mend, so be n't uneasie:
> To Night she's brisk, and trys New Tricks to please ye.

A few years later, in 1700, the prologue "By a Gentleman" offered Centlivre's first play, *The Perjured Husband,* as "a Lady's Treat":

> . . . the kind Creature does her best to please ye.
> Humbly she sues, and 'tis not for your Glory
> T'insult a Lady—when she falls before ye.
> (1)

In such identification of the authoress and the whore, both of whom had to please the paying customer, violators of the Salic law of wit were presumed guilty of sexual misconduct. For example, Pope attacked Eliza Haywood in the *Dunciad* for sexual misbehavior rather than dullness.

If the woman playwright was ipso facto a whore, then ipso facto she wrote bawdy plays. Motteux's prologue to Pix's *Innocent Mistress* addressed this preconception:

> Methinks I see some here who seem to say
> Gad, e're the Curtain's drawn I'll slip away;
> No Bawdy, this can't be a Woman's Play.

So widespread was this assumption that an ugly and brutal comedy, *The Roving Husband Reclaimed* (London, 1706) was satirically published as "Writ by a Club of Ladies, in Vindication of Virtuous Plays." If a woman's play was not lewd absolutely, it was lewd relatively, that is, too lewd to be written by one of the modest sex. A moralistic contemporary of Centlivre, so moralistic as to find offence in *The*

*Wonder*, put this assumption baldly, saying in that play
"might above all others have been expected a Scheme of
good Morality, modest Characters . . . if we . . . consider,
that the Author was a Woman."[12]

An alternative and contradictory line of attack was not
that these disreputable women wrote bawdy plays but that
they passed off their lovers' works as their own. Behn's
plays were attributed to a "Friend in Bosom."[13] Manley's
prologue to *The Lost Lover* anticipated those "Who, if our
Play succeeds, will surely say,/Some private Lover helpt
her on her way." Centlivre in the dedication to *The
Platonick Lady* angrily denounced those who claimed her
good plays were "given [her] by some Gentleman." Denial
of credit for authorship, a most effective means of exclusion from Parnassus, extended even to women who
avoided scandal. In 1705 Trotter protested against the
"generality" of men, who "when any thing is written by a
woman, that they cannot deny their approbation to, are
sure to rob us of the glory of it, by concluding 'tis not her
own; or at least, that she had some assistance, which has
been said in many instances to my knowledge unjustly"
(*Works*, 2:190). Anne Killigrew wrote a poem "Upon the
saying that my Verses were made by another":

> My Laurels thus an Others Brow adorn'd,
> My Numbers they Admir'd, but Me they scorn'd:
> An others Brow, that had so rich a store
> Of Sacred Wreaths, that circled it before. . . .
> (*Poems*, p. 46)

Jane Wiseman described a similar experience in the dedication to her *Antiochus the Great*: "The Language they are
unwilling to believe my own: and have chose one of our
best Poets for my Assistant, one I had not the happiness to
know, 'till after the Play was finish'd." Mary Pix accepted
this sort of accusation as a left-handed compliment. In the

dedication to *Ibrahim* she said, "I am often told, and always pleased when I hear it, that the Works not mine." Mary Davys commented similarly in her preface to *The Northern Heiress:* "As a Child born of a common Woman, has many Fathers, so my poor Offspring has been laid at a great many Doors . . . I am proud they think it deserves a better Author."

Many of these current ideas about women playwrights are dramatized in *Three Hours After Marriage* (1717), the uproarious and scandalous farce by Pope, Gay, and Arbuthnot. The play satirizes the woman playwright in the character of Phoebe Clinket, who, as her name indicates, is a slightly mad author of ludicrous, jingling rhymes, such as "Swell'd with a Dropsy, sickly Nature lies,/And melting in a Diabetes, dies" (p. 5). Her uncle, Dr. Fossile, explains that "the poor Girl has a Procidence of the Pineal Gland, which has occasioned a Rupture in her Understanding. I took her into my House to regulate my Oeconomy; but instead of Puddings, she makes Pastorals; or when she should be raising Paste, is raising some Ghost in a new Tragedy" (pp. 3–4). Clinket's entrance demonstrates her disruption of the household. She is attended by her maid Prue, who bears "a Writing-Desk on her Back" (p. 4) so that Clinket will have writing implements and an amanuensis always at hand. Prue fears, "I shall never get my Head-Cloaths Clear-starch'd at this rate" (p. 4). Clinket upbraids her as a "Destroyer of Learning" (p. 4) for using manuscripts for household purposes: "Remember how my Lyrick Ode bound about a Tallow-Candle; thy wrapping up Snuff in an Epigram; nay, the unworthy Usage of my Hymn to Apollo, filthy Creature!" (p. 5). She is unwomanly not only in her disregard of housekeeping but in her unconcern about her appearance, "her Head-dress stain'd with Ink, and Pens stuck in her Hair" (p. 4). When her uncle in a fit of disgust throws her works into the fire, her reaction shows her lack of concern for love, money, and dress, the proper interests of women:

> Clinket. Ah! I am an undone Woman.
> Plotwell. Has he burnt any Bank-Bills, or a new Mechlen Head-Dress?
> Clinket. My Works! my Works!
> 1st Player. Has he destroy'd the Writings of an Estate, or your Billet-doux?
> Clinket. A Pindarick Ode! five Similes! and half an Epilogue!
> 2nd Player. Has he thrown a new Fan or your Pearl Necklace into the Flames?
>
> (pp. 24–25)

She is pedantic, and she is naive, oblivious to sexual intrigue and innuendo around her and disallowing in plays "the Libertinism of Lip-Embraces" (p. 17) because she "would not stand upon the brink of an Indecorum" (p. 17). She is conceited, repeating her own lines and praising her own play: "So adapted for tragical Machines! So proper to excite the Passions! Not in the least encumber'd with Episodes! The *Vray-semblance* and the *Miraculous* are linkt together with such Propriety!" (p. 15).

Her conceit enables her to endure her failure as a playwright. Year after year her works are returned as unactable by the players: "Some of those People have had the Assurance to deny almost all my Performances the Privilege of being Acted. Ah! what a *Goût de travers* rules the Understandings of the Illiterate!" (p. 15). She attempts to get a more favorable reception for her latest play, *The Universal Deluge, or the Tragedy of Deucalion and Pyrrha,* by presenting it as a man's. Mr. Plotwell's "personating the Author will infallibly introduce my Play on the Stage, and spite of their Prejudice, make the Theatre ring with Applause" (p. 17). Nonetheless, when she reads the play to two actors and a critic named Sir Tremendous, they insist the work will be damned. When Clinket reluctantly consents that they cut "some few things" (p. 23), they strike out the fable, characters, and diction—and Clinket faints.

A network of double entendre around Clinket makes the familiar equation of poetess and whore. For example, Clinket and Sir Tremendous admire each other's literary opinions in these terms:

> Clinket. I am so charm'd with your manly Penetration!
> Sir Tremendous. I with your profound Capacity!
> Clinket. That I am not able—
> Sir Tremendous. That it is impossible—
> Clinket. To conceive—
> Sir Tremendous. To express—
> Clinket. With what Delight I embrace—
> Sir Tremendous. With what Pleasure I enter into—
> Clinket. Your Ideas, most learned Sir Tremendous!
> Sir Tremendous. Your Sentiments, most divine Mrs. Clinket.
>
> (p. 20)

Again, when the players return her play, she writes Plotwell:

> Sir, The Child which you father'd is return'd back upon my Hands. . . . How unfortunate soever my Offspring is, I hope you at least will defend the Reputation of the unhappy
>
> Phoebe Clinket
> (p. 76)

This letter is intercepted by Fossile, who is horrified, exclaiming to his niece, "To what a miserable Condition has thy Poetry reduced Thee!" (p. 77). Oblivious to his assumption, she replies, "I am not in the least mortified with the Accident. I know it has happen'd to many of the most famous Daughters of Apollo, and to my self several times. . . . I have had one return'd upon my Hands every Winter for these Five Years past. I may, perhaps, be excell'd by others in Judgment and Correctness of Manners, but for Fertility and Readiness of Conception, I will yield to nobody" (p. 77).

*Three Hours After Marriage* was a sharp satire of particular persons, and the original audience identified Phoebe Clinket as the Countess of Winchilsea. Clinket was like the countess in her indifference to love intrigue, dress, and "the dull mannage of a servile house," in writing a hymn to Apollo and verses on disease, and in several smaller points. Some modern critics have argued that Clinket was a satire of Centlivre, although the only point of comparison is the resentment of actors' cuts. More recent critics correctly say that the character, while making specific hits at Lady Winchilsea, is a general satire of the woman playwright.[14] The generalized nature of the satire can be seen best, not by considering the play in isolation, as is usual, but by considering it with the two other theatrical satires of the woman dramatist, *The Female Wits* and *Bays in Petticoats*. Although *Three Hours After Marriage* is only partially a "rehearsal" play and although Clinket is not the main character, the three plays show similarities of characterization and idea. The personal satire aside, Marsilia, Phoebe Clinket, and Mrs. Hazard are fundamentally alike. They are conceited women, blind to the defects of their writing, who annoy the players with their importunity and criticism and become the laughingstock of their acquaintance. For being so unwomanly as to write plays, Marsilia alienates her one honest admirer, Phoebe will be disinherited and is thought a whore, and Hazard loses her fiancé (Surly though he is). Basically these three women are in the dramatic tradition of the *femmes savantes* satirized in plays such as Jonson's *Volpone* (1606), Thomas Wright's *The Female Vertuosos* (1693), Vanbrugh's *Aesop* (1696),

Charles Johnson's *The Generous Husband* (1711), and Cibber's *The Refusal* (1721).[15] Such plays, as well as nondramatic literature, ridiculed intellectual women—including women playwrights—as educated above their dim intelligence, conceited, overtalkative, affected, pedantic, and distasteful to men.

These are of course clichés. However, the compliments bestowed on women playwrights also fall into cliché. Their writing is regularly complimented as "manly" or "masculine," as in Cowley's verses praising Philips's work:

> 'Tis solid, and 'tis manly all,
>   Or rather, 'tis Angelical:
>     For, as in Angels, we
>     Do in thy Verses see
> Both improv'd Sexes eminently meet;
> They are than Man more strong, and more than Woman
>   sweet.[16]

Behn was similarly praised: "With all the thought and vigour of our Sex / The moving softness of your own you mix."[17] She supposedly combined "A Female Sweetness and a Manly Grace."[18] Complimentary verses equally often commend women writers for their virtue. Dryden, for example, praised Anne Killigrew as a "vestal." Trotter's stage failures were admired for their modest diction and reform intent, the role of virtuous stage reformer being appropriate to her sex. Women playwrights are often complimented for choosing an appropriately "feminine" subject. In the *Tatler* for 23 May 1709 Steele for this reason commended Centlivre's *Busy Body:*

> The Plot and Incidents of the Play are laid with that Subtilty of Spirit which is peculiar to Females of Wit, and is very seldom well performed by those of the other Sex, in whom Craft in Love is an Act of Invention, and not, as with Women, the Effect of Nature and Instinct.[19]

All these compliments sound more patronizing and invidious than they were perhaps intended to be. The standard of wit was, after all, masculine, and it was high praise to say, as did the preface to the 1667 edition of Philips's *Poems*, "Some of them would be no disgrace to the name of any Man" (sig. a1ᵛ). Further, women writers were praised for their virtue because women were praised for their virtue, and the assumption that there was a natural feminine talent for reform tragedy or intrigue comedy, although patently absurd, reflects traditional views of women.

The absence of other terms in which to describe women writers is illustrated in a commendatory poem to Philips written by a woman critic calling herself Philo-Philippa. Her attitudes are feminist:

> Ask me not then, why jealous men debar
> Our Sex from Books in Peace, from Arms in War;
> It is because our Parts will soon demand
> Tribunals for our Persons, and Command.
>   Shall it be our reproach, that we are weak,
> And cannot fight, nor as the School-men speak?
> Even men themselves are neither strong nor wise,
> If Limbs and Parts they do not exercise.[20]

But her terms of praise are precisely those of the male critics:

> If Souls no Sexes have, as 'tis confest,
> 'Tis not the he or she makes Poems best:
> Nor can men call these Verses Feminine,
> Be the sence vigorous and Masculine.[21]

Women writers were occasionally compared with Sappho, but otherwise compliments monotonously praise them on the grounds of virtue or "masculine" ability. These compliments had far-reaching effects on women playwrights.

# [ 7 ]

# Astrea and Orinda

Our Sex . . . are Guilty of Writing so little. I wish they
would . . . let the noble examples of the deservedly
celebrated Mrs. Philips, and the incomparable Mrs.
Behn rouse their Courages, and shew Mankind the
great injustice of their Contempt.

*An Essay In Defence of the Female Sex,* 1696

"*The* incomparable Astrea" and "the matchless Orinda"
first appeared in print within a few years of each other,
and the wide praise they won from distinguished contemporary wits was preserved in the commendatory verses
published with their works. Their success had an enormous impact on women. For example, *Female Poems on
Several Occasions* (1679) is prefaced with an engraving of
the author's portrait labeled with her pen name Ephelia,
just as Katherine Philips's *Poems* (1667) was prefaced with
her portrait labeled Orinda. Ephelia not only wished for
"sweet Orinda's happy Strain" (p. 87) but also wrote a
poem "To Madam Bhen" [*sic*] expressing her "Wonder
and Amazement . . . To see such things flow from a
Womans Pen,/ As might be Envy'd by the Wittiest Men" (p.
72). Behn's example presumably spurred Ephelia to write
her comedy, *Pair Royal of Coxcombs.*

To say that a woman writer had excelled both Astrea and Orinda became a convention of compliment:

> The fam'd Orinda's and Astrea's Lays,
> With never dying Wit, bless'd Charles's Days,
> And we suppos'd Wit cou'd no higher rise,
> Till you succeeding, Tear from them the Prize. . . .

These verses in praise of Trotter's *Fatal Friendship* typify the equation usually made between Behn and Philips on the basis of talent. A sharp distinction between them, however, was always made on the basis of their lives. Sarah Piers in commendatory verses to Trotter's *Unhappy Penitent* put the distinction precisely:

> . . . like the Morning Star Orinda rose
> A Champion for her Sex, and wisely chose,
> Conscious of Female weakness, humble ways
> T' insinuate for applause, not storm the Bays.
> Next gay Astrea briskly won the Prize,
> Yet left a spacious room to Criticize.

Women playwrights chose to imitate either Behn or Philips and, in doing so, chose between antithetical responses to the Salic law of wit. That choice determined the kinds of plays they wrote, their presentation of themselves and their works, and, to a great extent, the nature of their successes and failures.

### Orinda

Katherine Philips achieved her immediate, enormous, almost legendary fame by adopting a superfeminine persona and avoiding competition with men. She chose a nonmasculine subject, female friendship, for her poems, which she wrote in modest, inoffensive language. The performance of *Pompey* was arranged for her by male patrons. Once she inadvertently encroached upon male territory. While working on *Pompey*, she learned that Waller and a group of the prestigious court wits were translating the same play. Orrery had to insist that she continue her own version. She wrote Poliarchus: "You will wonder at my Lord's Obstinacy in this Desire to have me translate *Pompey*, as well because of my Incapacity to perform it, as that so many others have undertaken it."[1] Declining to compete with men for money and fame, she allowed her poems to circulate only in manuscript, carefully maintaining an amateur status. Her exaggerated response to the surreptitious edition of her works, preserved in a letter to Poliarchus, was a prominent part of the preface to the later, posthumous editions of her works. In her letter, she herself called attention to the inappropriateness of authorship for women:

> This is a most cruel accident, and hath made so proportionate an impression upon me, that really it hath cost me a sharp fit of sickness since I heard it. . . . I am so far from expecting applause for any thing I scribble, that I can hardly expect pardon; and sometimes I think that employment so far above my reach, and unfit for my sex, that I am going to resolve against it for ever. . . . The truth is, I have an incorrigible inclination to that humour, only for my own amusement in a retir'd life; I did not so much resist it as a wiser woman would have done. . . .
>
> (*Poems*, sigs. A1$^r$–A2$^v$)

Her lifelong deference to men was rewarded with praise "for her Verses and her Vertues both."[2] Every commendatory poem included in her posthumous collected works praises her virtue and humility. Cowley describes her this way:

They talk of Sappho, but, alas! the shame
Ill Manners soil the lustre of her fame.
Orinda's inward Vertue is so bright,
That, like a Lantern's fair enclosed light,
It through the Paper shines where she doth write.
                                        (*Poems,* sig. c1$^r$)

Again: "Orinda does our boasting Sex out-do,/Not in wit
only, but in virtue too" (*Poems,* sig. g1$^r$). It is impossible to
do her justice, "Whether her Vertue, or her Wit/We chuse
for our eternal Theme" (*Poems,* sig. e1$^r$). Even Philo-
Philippa concludes with the couplet, "Flying above the
praise you shun, we see/Wit is still higher by humility"
(*Poems,* sig. d2$^v$).

In the middle of the eighteenth century she was still
praised as the most respected type of female poet. Sir
Charles Grandison, arbiter of propriety, warns his ward
Emily against the "titles of Wit, and Poetess" although he
concedes, "The easy productions of a fine fancy, not made
the business of life, or its boast, confer no denomination
that is disgraceful, but very much contrary." The conversation then turns to "the Orinda's" who do the female sex
honor, and Emily is reassured that "Your diffidence and
sweet humility . . . would, in you, make the most envied
accomplishments amiable."[3] For a hundred years men
praised Katherine Philips more for her humility than for
her poetry.

Orinda was Philips's most successful creation. She found
the model for her persona in the most respected women
authors before her, the noblewomen of the Renaissance.
This middle-class woman assumed the role of the aristocratic amateur. When she began to write plays, she translated from the French, like the Countess of Pembroke, and
like her chose a type of tragedy fashionable in aristocratic
circles. Although her life of country retirement with her

husband was analogous to the lives of the noblewomen she imitated, she could not, as they did, command respect by rank or fortune. She had to earn acceptance, and she did this by being properly feminine. In effect, the Orinda persona transformed nobility into gentility, a stance more appropriate to Philips's class, a stance that grew in popularity, even among the upper classes, with the growing dominance of bourgeois morality. In two senses, then, Philips was ladylike.

Philips, like the noblewomen she imitated, had a paradoxical influence: her example made it permissible for women to write, but at the same time it worked against self-assertion, a quality indispensable in a stage playwright. Her numerous imitators modestly confined themselves to manuscript circulation of poetry and closet drama. Anne Killigrew, for example, admired "Orinda, (Albions and her Sexes Grace)," who "Ow'd not her Glory to a Beauteous Face" but to "her Radiant Soul" (*Poems*, p. 46). Killigrew left her work in manuscript, and her epitaph commended her "modesty" because she "fled, as she deserv'd, the bays" (*Poems*, unpaged). When Killigrew, like Philips, died of smallpox, Dryden made the coincidence the occasion for compliment: "As equal were their Souls, so equal was their Fate" (*Poems*, unpaged). Killigrew's fate was indeed like Orinda's: her virtues were remembered longer than her verses. Similarly, Mary Leapor's works, including her unperformed play, were published only posthumously, with a preface recommending them because "her Conduct and Behaviour entirely corresponded with those virtuous and pious Sentiments which are conspicuous in her Poems" (*Poems*, unpaged).

The Countess of Winchilsea was highly articulate about her use of Philips as a model. Lady Winchilsea's preface to her manuscript volume is an extended paraphrase of Orinda's letter about the surreptitious edition of her

works. In the same tone of self-deprecation, the countess
apologizes for writing:

> I have writt, and expos'd my uncorrect Rimes, and
> immediately repented; and yett have writt again, and
> again suffer'd them to be seen; tho' att the expence of
> more uneasy reflections. . . . had nott an utter change in
> my Condition, and Circumstances, remov'd me into the
> solitude, & security of the Country . . . I think I might
> have stopp'd ere it was too late . . . having pleaded an
> irresistable impulse, as my excuse for writing . . . I must
> also expresse my hopes of excaping all suspition of
> vanity, or affectation of applause from itt. . . .
>
> $\qquad\qquad\qquad\qquad$ (*Poems*, pp. 7–9)

Urged by her friends to publish, she explained that her
refusal was based "upon recalling to my memory, some of
the first lines I ever writt, which were part of an invocation
of Apollo, whose wise and limitted answer to me, I did
there suppose to be

> I grant thee no pretence to Bays,
>   Nor in bold print do thou appear;
> Nor shalt thou reatch Orinda's prayse,
>   Tho' all thy aim, be fixt on Her.
>
> $\qquad\qquad\qquad$ (*Poems*, p. 7)

While the countess followed Orinda in her self-
deprecating refusal to publish, she also used her example
as a justification for writing drama: "Plays, were translated
by our most vertuous Orinda; and mine, tho' originals, I
hope are not lesse reserv'd" (*Poems*, p. 11). "The great
reservedness of Mrs. Philips" the countess noticed particularly in her treatment of love:

> the prayses I have heard given her upon that account,
> together with my desire not to give scandal to the most
> severe, has often discourag'd me from making use of itt,

and given me some regrett for what I had writt of that kind, and wholy prevented me from putting the Aminta of Tasso into English verse . . . after I had finish'd the first act extreamly to my satisfaction . . . but there being nothing mixt with itt, of a serious morality, or usefullnesse, I sacrafis'd the pleasure I took in itt.

(*Poems*, p. 10)

Like Phoebe Clinket, the countess feared even "the brink of an Indecorum." Consequently, she limited her genres to tragedy and tragicomedy, and her subject matter to the appropriately feminine, the love and innocence indicated in the title of her first play. She is a typical member of the Orinda school of women writers not only in using modest language but also in avoiding explicit treatment of sex. Orindas write about love as romance.

In effect, Orinda was the model for the authoress as the graceful amateur. Her response to the Salic law was appeasement. She apologized for writing and for women writers; she restricted herself in language and subject. She deferred, in Mary Leapor's words, to "The threat'ning Critic with his dreadful Rules" (*Poems*, 1: 268), rules of feminine propriety as well as rules of composition. Sensitive about the inferior education of women, the Orindas greatly respected the dramatic unities insisted upon by the learned. Philips translated neoclassical plays that adhered to these unities. The Countess of Winchilsea pointed out that "Poetry has been of late so explain'd, the laws of itt being putt into familiar languages, that even those of my sex, (if they will be so presumptuous as to write) are very accountable for their transgressions against them" (*Poems*, p. 9). The Orinda playwright often achieved only turgid dullness in pursuit of an imaginary correctness.

The Orinda persona disarmed criticism, but often at the price of mental distress. The Countess of Winchilsea, for example, was too good a poet not to perceive Behn's

excellence—"amongst Femens was not on the earth/Her
superiour in fancy, in language, or witt"—but she agreed
with those who said "that a little too loosly she writt"
(*Poems*, p. 92). So she chose Orinda as a model and urged
her own muse to fly "with contracted wing" (*Poems*, p. 6)
because of her sensitivity to criticism: "The hopes to thrive,
can ne're outweigh the fears" (*Poems*, p. 6). The countess
praised a woman who had "The Skill to write, the Modesty
to hide" (*Poems*, p. 57). There was no reason, she said, for a
poetess to be "a comon jest" unless she had "publickly the
skill professt" or made "that gift her pride" (*Poems*, p. 44).
Her obsession with this idea was in perpetual conflict with
her need to use her talent, and the result was mental
disorder. Philips's "sharp fit of sickness" because of the
surreptitious publication of her works may or may not
have been a pose, but the countess's spleen was real. A
hundred years earlier, Elizabeth Cary's more severe sup-
pression of her talents had led to more severe mental
illness. The self-effacing reduction of talent to an amateur
pastime sometimes produced mental anguish in women of
real literary ability.

### Astrea

Aphra Behn was the model for the commercial woman
writer outside the circle of propriety. She lived and wrote,
not like her female predecessors, but like her male contemporaries. As a colonial traveler and spy, Behn had
already lived for years as freely as a man before she began
writing plays. Entering the playhouse at a time when the
profession of the woman playwright was synonymous with
that of the whore, she acquired a reputation for sexual
exploits, which she did not bother to comment on. She
ignored the social conventions in her life and flouted the

Salic law of wit in her career, competing vigorously with men for money and fame. Instead of restricting herself to elevated tragedy, she intruded into the profitable masculine domain of bawdy comedy and wrote freely about sex, using erotic imagery and double entendre. She also expressed herself vigorously in the masculine arena of politics. She was unimpressed with "the most of that which bears the name of Learning, and which . . . continually employs so many ignorant, unhappy souls for ten, twelve, twenty years in the University (who yet poor wretches think they are doing something all the while)" (1: 221). And so she was unintimidated by her own lack of formal education: "Plays have no great room for that which is men's great advantage over women, that is Learning; We all well know that the immortal Shakespeare's Plays (who was not guilty of much more of this than often falls to women's share) have better pleas'd the World than Johnson's works" (1: 224). She ridiculed the rules of the drama as the "learned Cant of Action, Time and Place" (4: 116): "I think a Play the best divertisement that wise men have: but I do also think them nothing so who do discourse as formallie about the rules of it, as if 'twere the grand affair of humane life. . . . for their musty rules of Unity, and God knows what besides, if they meant anything, they are enough intelligible and as practible by a woman" (1: 223–24). Instead of accepting criticism humbly, she was hot-tempered, quick to defend herself, openly contemptuous of the "half Wits" and poetasters of the age. In the epilogue to *The Lucky Chance* she demanded "a Trial by her Peers" (3: 278), the true wits of the day.

Astrea demanded recognition for her works, not her life. When personal hostility to her threatened the fate of her plays, she brought them out anonymously as the work of a man and thus secured their success. She sought to evade the Salic law, not by humility, but by energy and wit.

She was self-sufficient and published prolifically in other mediums—the novel, poetry, translation—to maintain her economic independence. If Orinda was the first modern lady writer, earning that honorific by gentility rather than rank, Astrea was the first modern woman of letters. Her followers dared an unorthodoxly public life to seek popular and commercial success.

Delariviere Manley signaled her literary allegiance to Astrea in her first play, *The Lost Lover,* by including among the dramatis personae "Orinda, an Affected Poetess." Manley was even more bold than Behn in the assertiveness and feminism of her life and works. Having been socially ostracized by the double standard, she proceeded to attack it in her work and flaunt it in her life. In her fiction she repeatedly used her own seduction as an example to criticize sociosexual injustices to women. She avowed for herself a standard of sexual independence—"she must first be in Love with a Man before she thought fit to reside with him" (*Rivella,* p. 41)—a standard possible only for the woman economically independent. She made erotic treatment of sex the cornerstone of her commercial success, and, like Behn, she defended her erotic language on the grounds that male playwrights wrote the same way. Manley was like Behn in a number of other ways: she thought of herself as a wit, she defended her works and attacked her critics with spirit, she created a feminist character in Almyna, she expressed strong political opinions. She wrote for money and turned her major energies to journalism and more lucrative scandal novels when personal attack on her in *The Female Wits* damaged her career as a playwright.

Eliza Haywood's career was similar. She abandoned husband and respectability and wrote to support herself. Like Behn, she did not comment on her private life, but she did assert herself as a writer, challenging the critics, as in the prologue to *A Wife to Be Let:*

> Criticks! be dumb to-night—no Skill display;
> A dangerous Woman-Poet wrote the Play:
> One, who not fears your Fury, tho' prevailing,
> More than your Match, in every thing, but Railing.
> Give her fair Quarter, and whene'er she tries ye,
> Safe in superior Spirit, she defies ye. . . .

Like Manley, Haywood found the erotic novel more re-
munerative than the stage. She was in the Astrea tradition,
and her contemporaries recognized this. James Sterling,
for example, in commendatory verses to Haywood addressed "envious Man":

> Read, proud Usurper, read with conscious Shame,
> Pathetic Behn, or Manley's greater Name;
> Forget their Sex, and own when Haywood writ,
> She clos'd the fair Triumvirate of Wit. . . .[4]

The Astreas were characteristically assertive. Hoper, who
acted in her own *Queen Tragedy Restored* in spite of her
scandalized friends, in the prologue aspired "to be rank'd
with Sappho, Phillips, Behn,—/And prove that Women
write as well as Men." Davys published her plays and
novels in spite of criticism that this was improper for a
clergyman's widow.

The Astrea persona, the stance of the first modern
women, like the Orinda persona, posed some problems.
On a practical level, the woman playwright who earned
her own living and at the same time found herself at a
disadvantage in the theater often of necessity turned to
other literary forms, such as the novel, journalism, and
literary hackwork. A number of early eighteenth-century
women dramatists also acted occasionally—Haywood,
Hoper, Cooper, and perhaps Centlivre. Into other professions they diverted energy that might have gone into
playwrighting. In addition to this practical difficulty, As-

treas had the emotional problem of coping with the antagonism aroused by their success, an antagonism that often masked itself in vicious personal attack for real or supposed violations of prevailing sexual mores. If the Orindas often felt guilty about adventuring in print, the Astreas often felt guilty about adventuring in life. This guilt could also produce mental disorder. The inconsistencies, evasions, and occasional incoherencies in the autobiographies of both Letitia Pilkington and Charlotte Charke indicate emotional suffering.

Imitation of Astrea and Orinda, then, generated personae—later stereotypes—of the "lady writer" and the "female adventuress," neither of which was fully satisfactory. Few women, especially in the changing moral climate after the Revolution of 1688, could, like Manley or Haywood, risk Astrea's disregard of social conventions. A woman who needed to earn money, and most women playwrights did, could not, like the Countess of Winchilsea, afford to be as reticent about publication as Orinda. For these reasons, many women tried to effect some compromise between these two roles. Their attempts to reconcile antithetical personae account for some of the anomalies in their careers. A case in point is the career of Catherine Trotter. She wrote for money because of economic distress, and based her first play, *Agnes de Castro*, on Aphra Behn's novel of that name. At the same time that she set up as a feminist and wit, she also published anonymously, explaining in the dedication to *Agnes* that she concealed her name "to shun that of Poetess." She modestly submitted *The Revolution of Sweden* to Congreve's approval before finishing it, but in spite of his advice persisted in making the heroines feminist. To maintain her respectability she wrote such heavily moralized plays that she failed commercially, thus losing the income for which she had originally turned to the stage. Similar anomalies are evident in the career of Mary Pix. She strenuously protested her modesty and humility at the same time that she wrote feminist commendatory poems for her friends. Such contradictory behavior shows a strong desire to have both Astrea's success and Orinda's respectability.

Eighteenth-century gentility increasingly pulled women toward the Orinda mode. Susanna Centlivre was the most striking example because in so many ways her life and career resembled Behn's. Each was the most successful and prolific woman playwright of her age. Each specialized in intrigue comedy; and Centlivre's critical opinions, like Behn's, were uncomplicated by reform intent: "I think the main design of Comedy is to make us laugh" (*Letters of Wit*, p. 362). Both were women of strong political loyalties. The similarities were not lost on Centlivre's contemporaries, who saw "the inimitable Mrs. Bhen [*sic*] so nearly reviv'd in Mrs. Centlivre" (*Female Tatler*, 12 December 1709). Centlivre deliberately imitated Behn at the beginning of her career, signing her first published works, the 1700 letters, with Behn's pen name, Astrea. (One of them, her epistolary "Journey to Exon" is an imitation of Manley's epistolary "Journey to Exeter.")[5] Centlivre called attention to Behn as the model for the comic subplot of her first play, *The Perjured Husband*, by alluding in it to two of Behn's translations, *The Lover's Watch* (1: 19) and *The Voyage to the Island of Love* (1: 35).

At the same time, however, Centlivre was also thinking of Orinda. In the summer of 1700 she wrote to Abel Boyer, who was negotiating in London for the performance of her first play, "I wish for the Genius of Behn or Philips" (*Letters of Wit*, p. 361). The play is a hybrid of both. Alongside the prose intrigue subplot in the Astrea manner, Centlivre placed an unrelated main plot of blank verse tragedy, the respectable Orinda genre. While

Centlivre generally shared Behn's iconoclastic opinions,
she showed an Orinda-like deference in the expression of
them. Sometimes this had ludicrous results. For example,
in the preface to *Love's Contrivance*, she rejects the dramatic
rules, but her argument seesaws in an effort not to offend:

> The Criticks cavil most about Decorums, and cry up
> Aristotle's Rules as the most essential part of the Play. I
> own they are in the right of it; yet I dare venture a
> Wager they'll never persuade the Town to be of their
> Opinion, which relishes nothing so well as Humour
> lightly tost up with Wit. . . . I do not say this by way of
> condemning the Unity of Time, Place, and Action; quite
> contrary, for I think them the greatest Beauties of a
> Dramatick Poem; but since the other way of writing
> pleases full as well, and gives the Poet a larger Scope of
> Fancy, and with less Trouble, Care, and Pains, serves his
> and the Player's End, why should a Man torture, and
> wrack his Brain for what will be no Advantage to him.
> (2)

Centlivre similarly acknowledged the proprieties in her
private life, making a respectable marriage and avoiding
scandal. Her personal reputation among her own contemporaries was apparently bourgeois and domestic. Indeed,
near the end of her life, Nicholas Amhurst wrote a poem
addressing her as Orinda (*Poems on Several Occasions*, p.
95).

In her plays Centlivre eventually found a successful
compromise between the Orinda and Astrea modes. Behn
wrote comedy of witty sex intrigue; Centlivre moved to
"laughing comedy with an improved moral tone."[6] A comparison of Behn's *Rover* with any of Centlivre's three most
popular comedies shows the distance between the two
playwrights. The difference was crucial to Centlivre's
reputation in the eighteenth and nineteenth centuries.
One of the striking things about Centlivre's career is that

her commercial success was accompanied by remarkably few personal attacks on her. Those criticisms of her during her lifetime are usually directed at her work. Typical is this reference in *A Satyr upon the Present Times* (London, 1717):

> . . . Females in the awful Buskin tread,
> And scribble Plays when they can hardly read;
> The *Cruel Gift* has won the Town's Applause,
> But we are always pleas'd without a Cause. . . .
> (p. 16)

Personal attacks against Centlivre for lewdness of life or works did not come until after her death. By mid-century this sort of allusion was typical:

> The modest Muse a veil with pity throws
> O'er Vice's friends and Virtue's female foes;
> Abash'd she views the bold unblushing mien
> Of modern Manley, Centlivre, and Behn. . . .[7]

In spite of her compromise between Astrea and Orinda, Centlivre was nonetheless sometimes labeled a bawdy playwright by analogy with Behn because she was equally successful.

The increasing verbal prudery of the next century increased the split between Astrea and Orinda, and the split was written into literary history. When John Pearson published a reprint of Behn's plays in 1871, there was such a storm of protest that the next year he issued a pamphlet called *Two Centuries of Testimony in Favour of Mrs. Aphra Behn,* in which he pointed out that Behn, no more or less immoral than other Restoration playwrights, had been made a scapegoat for them. Pearson felt it necessary, however, to fall back on another, less than wholehearted defense: "My reprint was expressly made for the use of historical students and antiquarians, and to complete the dramatic collections of amateurs. Only a limited number of copies were struck off, and the form and price of the work show evidently that it was never designed for general and promiscuous reading" (p. 17). A. W. Ward in his *History of English Dramatic Literature to the Death of Queen Anne* (1899) recognized Behn's talent but declined to discuss (or even to name) her plays because of their supposed licentiousness. Vilification of Behn assumed ludicrous proportions in John Doran's comment that "she was a mere harlot, who danced through uncleanness."[8] Less pathological but equally ludicrous was Ernest A. Baker's introduction to the 1905 reprint of Behn's novels; he devoted twelve of the twenty pages of his commentary to a diatribe against her plays. While Astrea's reputation declined, Orinda's virtues were still the best publicity for her verses. In 1883 Edmund Gosse placed Katherine Philips first among seventeenth-century women writers "not exactly by merit . . . but by the moral eminence which she attained. . . . her muse was uniformly pure. . . ."[9]

The literary history of women playwrights, then, embodies the Salic law of wit. Double-standard moral judgments were made the basis of double-standard literary judgments. The Salic law of wit, the critical double standard, judged women not on aesthetic grounds but on the relative "modesty" or "immodesty" of their works. Moreover, when women assumed the Astrea and Orinda personae, they reinforced rather than evaded the Salic law. This was inevitable: women were imitating the two women who had received the most praise from their male contemporaries, and that praise reflected masculine values. Indeed, the compliments to women playwrights were in this way more invidious than the abuse. The virtuous amateur won praise when she confined herself to appropriate subjects and genres, employed modest language, and avoided fame. Alternatively, a woman could win approval if she wrote with "manly" strength, so exceptionally that she was not like other women. These terms were impossible to fulfill. If a woman espoused modesty and shunned publicity, she could not live the life of a working playwright. If she was a "phoenix" who wrote like a man, she was in effect no longer a woman. Neither persona permitted dramatization of peculiarly feminine perceptions: Orindas wrote as men thought they should, and Astreas wrote as men.

Thus both personae confirmed traditional attitudes. The Orindas acquiesced in the belief that love and intrigue were subjects suited to the female mind: "Love seems the only proper Theme (if any can be so) for a Woman's Pen."[10] The Astreas exploited the restriction, as in the prologue to Centlivre's *Cruel Gift:*

. . . here's Intrigue, and Plot, and Love enough.
The Devil's in it, if the Sex can't write
Those things in which They take the most Delight. . . .
(2)

When women wrote like men, they expressed male prejudices. Painful examples of this are Behn's satire of the scholarly woman as an affected pedant in Lady Knowell in *Sir Patient Fancy* and Centlivre's satire of the scientifically-inclined woman in Valeria in *The Basset Table,* a satire that also slyly mocks Mary Astell and her hopes for women's education. In the context of traditional dramatic satire of *femmes savantes,* the portraits of Lady Knowell and Valeria are relatively gentle,[11] but one wishes they had not been written at all. Both roles confirmed a belief in innate female inferiority in that neither allowed a woman to produce a fine comedy of manners in the great age of that genre. While the closet dramatists confined themselves to tragedy and tragicomedy, the working woman playwright, by definition socially disreputable, was excluded from introduction to that level of society that would have allowed her to observe and write with assurance about upper-class manners.[12] The indirect presentation of their works by both types of women writers also tended to reinforce ideas of feminine inferiority. When Orindas left their plays in manuscript, they consigned themselves to oblivion, or at best scholarly resuscitation. Their work was unknown, and this confirmed the belief that women writers were anomalous. Similarly, when Astreas presented their plays anonymously with prologues and epilogues implying male authorship, the initial anonymous production reinforced the same belief. Moreover, both the Astrea and Orinda personae seemed to confirm the idea that women are intellectually inferior because both limited originality. A writer whose primary purpose is to appease hostility risks greatly by saying anything original, while the writer whose primary purpose is to succeed commercially imitates previous commercial successes and often caters to the sensational and the ephemeral. The limited originality of women playwrights was encouraged by the declining originality of the traditional drama. The period when women began to enter the theater in numbers was a period of great actors and actresses rather than of great playwrights, men or women.

The embodiment of the Salic law of wit in literary criticism and in the Astrea and Orinda responses to it presents problems in revaluation today of the work of England's early women playwrights. While the quality of Behn and Centlivre's work has always elicited interest and while they have begun to receive proper appreciation since the middle of this century, their plays are not included in the standard anthologies of Restoration and eighteenth-century drama, and so remain largely inaccessible to students. Moreover, the stereotypes of the "female adventuress" and the "lady writer" still persist in criticism, and these stereotypes not only blur the real differences among the women playwrights but also obscure important similarities that were factors in their theatrical success. For example, sex was least a barrier to writing for the stage for those women who were single, childless, and economically autonomous. By and large, the women playwrights were a good deal more like Behn than like Philips, even when, bowing to social propriety, they assumed the persona of Orinda. The overwhelming impression given by all these women is one of energy. As pioneers, they opened the theater to women dramatists, and in the process produced some colorful episodes in theatrical history. As playwrights, two of them, Behn and Centlivre, wrote plays that provided pleasure for generations and earned a permanent position in dramatic literature. Attempting a public profession at variance with traditional demands of feminine propriety, England's early women playwrights achieved some remarkable successes in spite of the Salic law of wit.

# Notes

## Chapter 1

1. Katherine of Sutton's plays are preserved in the Barking ordinarium. Sibille Felton, abbess of Barking from 1394 to 1419, caused this to be written and presented it to the convent in 1404. Karl Young was the first to publish the Barking plays, in "The Harrowing of Hell in Liturgical Drama," *Transactions of the Wisconsin Academy of Sciences, Arts, and Letters* 16 (1910): 888–947. Young later included the plays in his *Drama of the Medieval Church*, 2 vols. (Oxford: Clarendon Press, 1933), 1: 164–66, 381–84. Meanwhile, the entire ordinale had been edited by J. B. L. Tolhurst and printed in two volumes of the Henry Bradshaw Society Publications in 1927–28. The Latin quotations are from Young, *Drama*, 1: 165.

2. Although English women did not act on the public stage until almost exactly three hundred years later, they participated more widely in English medieval drama than is generally realized. Women belonged to religious gilds responsible for plays—for example, the York Pater Noster Gild and the Norwich St. Luke's Gild—and participated to some extent in the trade gilds. See Karl Young, "The Records of the York Play of the *Pater Noster*," *Speculum* 7 (1932): 544; Lucy Toulmin Smith, ed., *York Plays* (Oxford: At the Clarendon Press, 1885), pp. xxviii–xxxix; Harold C. Gardiner, *Mysteries' End*, Yale Studies in English, Vol. 103 (New Haven, Conn.: Yale University Press, 1946), p. 42; Eileen Power, *Medieval Women* (Cambridge: At the University Press, 1975), pp. 55–69. At Chester the "wurshipffull wyffys" of the town bound themselves to bring forth the pageant of the Assumption of the Virgin. This pageant was a regular part of the Chester cycle until it was excised at the Reformation. The wives acted their play separately until it was excised at the Reformation. The wives acted their play separately until 1488 before Lord Strange and again in 1515. See W. W. Greg, ed., *The Trial and Flagellation with Other Studies in the Chester Cycle*, The Malone Society Studies (Oxford: Oxford University Press, 1935), pp. 137, 170–71; F. M. Salter, *Mediaeval Drama in Chester* (Toronto: University of Toronto Press, 1955), pp. 50, 70–71. Women also participated in church *ludi*. There are records of an Abbess of Fools or Girl Abbess elected from the novices on Holy Innocents' Day at the nunneries of Godstow and Barking in the thirteenth century. See Eileen Power, *Medieval English Nunneries c. 1275–1535* (Cambridge: At the University Press, 1922), p. 312.

3. Barking was an abbey holding of the king in chief; as tenant in chief,

Katherine of Sutton was a baroness in her own right. She was almost certainly a noblewoman by birth also. In the later Middle Ages Barking accepted novitiates only from the aristocracy and the wealthiest bourgeois class; moreover, the nun of highest social rank usually became abbess. See Power, *Medieval English Nunneries*, pp. 4–13, 42.

4. Information about Lady Lumley is taken from the introduction to *Iphigeneia at Aulis*, edited by Harold H. Child for the Malone Society Reprints (London: Chiswick Press, 1909). Myra Reynolds, *The Learned Lady in England 1650–1760* (Boston: Houghton Mifflin, 1920), pp. 13–14, also discusses Lady Lumley.

5. In *The Poems of Elizabeth I*, ed. Leicester Bradner (Providence, R.I.: Brown University Press, 1964).

6. Biographical information is taken from Frances Berkeley Young, *Mary Sidney Countess of Pembroke* (London: David Nutt, 1912) and Mona Wilson, *Sir Philip Sidney* (London: Duckworth, 1931). *Antonie* has been edited by Alice Luce (Weimer: E. Felber, 1897) and by Geoffrey Bullough in *Narrative and Dramatic Sources of Shakespeare*, 8 vols. (New York: Columbia University Press, 1957–75), 5:358–406. The translation of the psalms by the Countess of Pembroke and Sir Philip Sidney has been edited by J. C. A. Rathmell (Garden City, N.Y.: Doubleday, 1963). This volume is supplemented by G. F. Waller, "*The Triumph of Death*" *and Other Unpublished Poems by Mary Sidney, Countess of Pembroke* (Salzburg: Institut für Englische Sprache und Literatur, 1977). The Pembroke circle of Senecan writers is discussed by John W. Cunliffe, *The Influence of Seneca on Elizabethan Tragedy* (London: Macmillan, 1893); Joan Rees, *Samuel Daniel* (Liverpool: Liverpool University Press, 1964); Cecil Seronsy, *Samuel Daniel* (New York: Twayne, 1967). T. S. Eliot discusses the influence of the Pembroke circle in "Apology for the Countess of Pembroke," *The Use of Poetry and the Use of Criticism* (London: Faber and Faber, 1933). Mary Herbert is memorialized beautifully but stereotypically in "On the Countesse Dowager of Pembroke," long ascribed to Ben Jonson but written by William Browne of Tavistock, in *Ben Jonson*, ed. C. H. Herford and Percy and Evelyn Simpson (Oxford: Clarendon Press, 1925–52), 8: 433.

7. *The Complete Works of Sir Philip Sidney*, ed. Albert Feuillerat (Cambridge: Cambridge University Press, 1912–26), 3:38.

8. *The Countess of Pembroke's "Antonie,"* ed. Luce, p. 97.

9. A. W. Pollard and G. R. Redgrave, *A Short-Title Catalogue of Books Printed in England, Scotland, and Ireland 1475–1640* (London: The Bibliographical Society, 1926), pp. 255, 412.

10. *A Poetical Rhapsody*, ed. Hyder Rollins (Cambridge, Mass.: Harvard University Press, 1931), 1: 17.

11. This was edited and published in 1861 by Richard Simpson as *The Lady Falkland: Her Life* (London: Catholic Publishing Company). In-text citations refer to this volume. Two biographies based on the *Life* are Lady Georgiana Fullerton, *The Life of Elisabeth Lady Falkland* (London: Burns and Oates, 1883) and Kenneth B. Murdock, *The Sun at Noon* (New York: MacMillan, 1939), pp. 6–38. Both are concerned with Cary as a Catholic convert; neither is aware of her

unique position in the history of English drama. *Mariam* was edited for the Malone Society Reprints by A. C. Dunstan and W. W. Greg (Oxford: Oxford University Press, 1914). In-text citations refer to this edition; I have modernized the u/v and i/j conventions and discarded nonfunctional italics. *Mariam* is discussed at length by A. C. Dunstan in *Examination of Two English Dramas* (Königsberg: Hartungsche Buchdruckerei, 1908). Dunstan also discusses Cary's use of source material in the introduction to the Malone Society edition of the play. *Mariam* is briefly discussed by Alexander Witherspoon, *The Influence of Robert Garnier on Elizabethan Drama* (New Haven, Conn.: Yale University Press, 1924), pp. 150–55, and Maurice J. Valency, *The Tragedies of Herod and Mariamne* (New York: Columbia University Press, 1940), pp. 87–91. Valency points out that Cary's *Mariam* is the first of many English plays written about Herod and Mariamne. Donald A. Stauffer, "A Deep and Sad Passion," *The Parrott Presentation Volume*, ed. Hardin Craig (1935; reprint ed., New York: Russell and Russell, 1967), pp. 289–314, shows that Elizabeth Cary wrote *The History of Edward II*, formerly ascribed to Henry Cary.

12. Introduction to the Malone Society edition, p. ix.

13. Quoted by Fullerton, *Life of Lady Falkland*, p. 120.

14. *The Complete Works of John Davies of Hereford*, ed. Alexander Grosart (Edinburgh: Edinburgh University Press, 1878), 2: 4–5.

15. Biographical information is taken from Carola Oman, *Henrietta Maria* (London: Hodder and Stoughton, 1936). Henrietta Maria's pervasive influence on theatrical history is discussed in detail by Alfred Harbage, *Cavalier Drama* (1936; reprint ed., New York: Russell and Russell, 1964), which suggests the queen as the author of *Florimene;* and by Kathleen M. Lynch, *The Social Mode of Restoration Comedy* (New York: MacMillan, 1926).

16. Quotations are from Gerald Eades Bentley, *The Jacobean and Caroline Stage* (Oxford: At the Clarendon Press, 1941–68), 4:548–49.

17. Quoted by Harbage, *Cavalier Drama*, pp. 14–15.

18. Except for my inferences about the effect of Newcastle's dramatic activities on his daughters, biographical information on the Cavendish sisters is taken from the DNB and from Nathan Comfort Starr's introduction to his edition of *The Concealed Fansyes* in *PMLA* 46 (1931): 802–38. Page references in the text refer to Starr's edition. Harbage, *Cavalier Drama*, pp. 228–29, describes the plays of the Cavendish sisters.

19. I have drawn on a number of sources for biographical information. Standard and useful are Douglas Grant, *Margaret the First* (Toronto: University of Toronto Press, 1957) and Henry Ten Eyck Perry, *The First Duchess of Newcastle and Her Husband as Figures in Literary History* (Boston: Ginn, 1918). Of the numerous biographical essays, the finest is Virginia Woolf's in *The Common Reader* (New York: Harcourt, Brace and Co., 1925), pp. 101–12. The best source of biographical material is the duchess herself, particularly in the introductions, dedications, and letters in her various works. Her autobiography, "A True Relation of my Birth, Breeding, and Life," originally the last section of *Natures Pictures* (1656), is included by C. H. Firth in his edition of the duchess's *Life of William Cavendish, Duke of Newcastle* (London: John C. Nimmo, 1886). These two

works of the duchess are available in several editions. Firth also prints the duchess's letter "To the Two Most Famous Universities of England," a moving appeal for education for women.

20. "A True Relation," ed. Firth, pp. 157–58.

21. Ibid., p. 177.

22. My interpretation draws upon Jean Gagen, "Honor and Fame in the Works of the Duchess of Newcastle," *Studies in Philology* 56 (1959): 519–38.

23. Jean Gagen focuses on this type of character, which she calls "the oratorical lady," in her excellent discussion of the duchess's plays in "A Champion of the Learned Lady," chap. 2 in *The New Woman: Her Emergence in English Drama 1600–1730* (New York: Twayne, 1954). Gagen's discussion led me to examine the pervasive feminism in the duchess's plays.

24. Francis Needham, ed., *Welbeck Miscellany*, 1 (1933) from a fair copy in the duke's handwriting.

25. *Pepys on the Restoration Stage*, ed. Helen McAfee (New Haven, Conn.: Yale University Press, 1916), pp. 171–72.

26. *The London Stage, 1600–1700*, ed. William Van Lennep (Carbondale, Ill.: Southern Illinois University Press, 1965), p. 108. Harbage, *Cavalier Drama*, pp. 232–33, suggests that the duchess wrote at least the first draft of *Lady Alimony*, performed at the Cockpit in 1659. While the play is structurally odd and schematic enough to be hers, its anonymity is conclusive proof against her authorship.

27. Biographical information is taken from Philip Webster Souers, *The Matchless Orinda* (1931; reprint. ed., New York: Johnson, 1968). Edmund Gosse's essay "The Matchless Orinda" appears in his *Seventeenth Century Studies* (1883; reprint ed., New York: Dodd, Mead, 1897), pp. 229–58.

28. John Aubrey, *Brief Lives*, ed. Andrew Clark (Oxford: At the Clarendon Press, 1898), 2:154.

29. Ibid., p. 153.

30. *Poems By the most deservedly Admired Mrs. Katherine Philips The matchless Orinda. To which is added Monsieur Corneille's Pompey & Horace, Tragedies. With several other Translations out of French* (London: for H. Herringman, 1667), sig. Ggg1$^{r-v}$. In-text citations refer to this edition; the two plays are paged separately from the poems. Philips's poems and the songs from *Pompey* are available in *Minor Poets of the Caroline Period*, ed. George Saintsbury (Oxford: At the Clarendon Press, 1905), 1:485–612.

31. See the discussion by Dorothea Canfield Fisher, *Corneille and Racine in English* (New York: Columbia University Press, 1904), pp. 28–50.

32. *The Diary of John Evelyn*, ed. E. S. de Beer (Oxford: At the Clarendon Press, 1955), 3:505.

33. Van Lennep, *London Stage*, 1:128–29.

34. Ibid., p. 153; McAfee, *Pepys*, pp. 199–200.

## Chapter 2

1. All in-text citations of Behn's works refer to *The Works of Aphra Behn,* ed. Montague Summers, 6 vols. (London: William Heinemann, 1915). For the convenience of the reader, citations of plays include the act and scene numbers followed, after a semicolon, by the volume and page numbers. Other citations refer to volume and page numbers only. I have used the Summers edition, in spite of its occasional inaccuracies, because it is the only easily accessible modern edition of Behn's works. A few individual plays are available in good modern editions. *The Rover* has been edited by Frederick M. Link for the Regents Restoration Drama Series (Lincoln, Neb.: University of Nebraska Press, 1967). *The Emperor of the Moon* is included in *Ten English Farces,* ed. Leo Hughes and A. H. Scouten (Austin, Texas: University of Texas Press, 1948).

2. The most recent biography is Maureen Duffy, *The Passionate Shepherdess: Aphra Behn 1640–89* (London: Jonathan Cape, 1977). Frederick Link, *Aphra Behn* (New York: Twayne, 1968) includes a useful annotated bibliography of the extensive literature on Behn. The authority on Behn's years in Surinam and Antwerp is W. J. Cameron, *New Light on Aphra Behn* (Auckland: University of Auckland Press, 1961). Two readable general biographies are George Woodcock, *The Incomparable Aphra* (London: Boardman, 1948) and Victoria Sackville-West, *Aphra Behn* (New York: Viking, 1928). Emily Hahn has written a pleasant fictional biography, *Purple Passage* (Garden City, N. Y.: Doubleday, 1950), covering the obscure years of Behn's life up through the successful production of her first play. Gerald Duchovnay, "Aphra Behn's Religion," *Notes and Queries,* n.s. 23 (1976): 235–37, offers documentary evidence that Behn was a Roman Catholic in the last years of her life.

3. Robert Adams Day, "Aphra Behn's First Biography," *Studies in Bibliography* 22 (1969): 227–40, carefully analyzes the relationship between the 1696 "Memoirs" and the expanded versions of 1698 and 1705. The 1705 version of the "Memoirs" is included in Vol. 5 of the Pearson reprint of *The Plays, Histories, and Novels of Aphra Behn,* 6 vols. (London: Pearson, 1871).

4. These are reprinted in full in Cameron, *New Light,* pp. 34–86.

5. Quoted from Woodcock, *The Incomparable Aphra,* p. 43.

6. Charles Gildon, "The Epistle Dedicatory" to Behn's novels, Pearson reprint, 5:xi.

7. Ibid.

8. Woodcock, *Incomparable Aphra,* p. 49; Link, *Behn,* p. 22.

9. There is an excellent discussion of Behn's use of the "Spanish plot" and Spanish sources in John Loftis, *The Spanish Plays of Neoclassical England* (New Haven, Conn.: Yale University Press, 1973), pp. 133–50. Loftis examines in detail *The Rover* Parts I and II, *The Young King, The False Count,* and *The Dutch Lover.*

10. See, for example, Link, *Behn,* p. 157.

11. John Downes, in *Roscius Anglicanus* (1708), reports that in this play "Mr. Otway the Poet having an Inclination to turn Actor; Mrs. Bhen gave him the

King in the Play, for a Probation Part, but he being not us'd to the Stage; the full House put him to such a Sweat and Tremendous, Agony, being dash't, spoilt him for an Actor." This story is frequently quoted to show Otway's youthful desire to be an actor and/or his early acquaintance with Behn. It also shows, however, that Behn's first play opened to a full house. The quotation is taken from the facsimile edition prefaced by Joseph Knight (London: J. W. Jarvis, 1886), p. 34.

12. Quoted by Woodcock, *Incomparable Aphra*, p. 92.

13. *The Works of Mr. Thomas Brown*, 9th ed. (London: for Al. Wilde, 1760), 2:154–55.

14. Quoted by Woodcock, *Incomparable Aphra*, p. 117.

15. Quoted, ibid., p. 102.

16. Robert Gould, "The Play-House. A Satyr," *Poems Chiefly consisting of Satyrs and Satyrical Epistles* (London, 1689), p. 174.

17. Ibid., p. 173.

18. Quoted by Woodcock, *Incomparable Aphra*, p. 193.

19. Quoted, ibid., p. 211.

20. The elegy is printed in G. Thorn-Drury, *A Little Ark containing Sundry Pieces of Seventeenth-Century Verse* (London: P. J. and A. E. Dobell, 1921), pp. 53–57. The quoted lines are on p. 56.

# Chapter 3

1. Biographical information is taken from Thomas Birch's "Account of the Life of the Author," prefixed to his edition of *The Works of Mrs. Catharine Cockburn, Theological, Moral, Dramatic, and Poetical*, 2 vols. (London: for J. and P. Knapton, 1751). Birch's biography is cited in the text as *Life*. There is also an essay by Edmund Gosse, "Catherine Trotter, the Precursor of the Bluestockings," *Transactions of the Royal Society of Literature*, 2d ser. 34 (1916): 87–118. Alison Fleming wrote a biographical sketch, "Catherine Trotter—the Scots Sappho," *The Scots Magazine* 33 (July 1940): 305–14. Gosse and Fleming are unacquainted with Trotter's novel, and Birch does not mention it. Birch's edition of the *Works* is incomplete, containing primarily theological writings and letters; only one play, *Fatal Friendship*, is included.

2. Robert Adams Day, introduction to *Olinda's Adventures*, The Augustan Reprint Society, No. 138 (Los Angeles, Calif.: William Andrews Clark Memorial Library, University of California, 1969).

3. Biographical information is taken from a number of sources. Most useful is Paul Bunyan Anderson, "Mistress Delariviere Manley's Biography," *Modern Philology* 33 (1936): 261–78. Anderson shows that Manley was known to her contemporaries as Delariviere, although most modern commentators refer to her as Mary de la Rivière Manley; apparently her name was confused with that of her older sister, Mary Elizabeth. Information is also taken from Manley's autobiography, *The Adventures of Rivella* (London, 1714), cited in the text as *Rivella*. Gwendolyn B. Needham has two useful essays: "Mary de la Rivière

Manley, Tory Defender," *The Huntington Library Quarterly* 12 (May 1949): 253–88; and "Mrs. Manley: An Eighteenth-Century Wife of Bath," *The Huntington Library Quarterly* 14 (May 1951): 259–84. A further biographical note is provided by Richard B. Kline, "Anne Oldfield and Mary de la Rivière Manley: The Unnoticed Reconciliation," *Restoration and Eighteenth Century Theatre Research* 14 (November 1975): 53–58. Manley is the subject of Swift's "Corinna"; see Swift's *Poems*, ed. Harold Williams, 2d ed. (Oxford: Clarendon Press, 1958), 1:148–50.

4. Delariviere Manley, *Secret Memoirs and Manners of Several Persons of Quality of Both Sexes. From the New Atalantis, an Island in the Mediterranean*, 7th ed. 4 vols. (London: J. Watson, 1736), 2:188. In-text citations of the *Atalantis* refer to this edition.

5. Manley must have been a few years older than thirteen at the time of her marriage. She habitually lowered her age in her autobiographical fictions.

6. According to *A Comparison Between the Two Stages* (London, 1702), p. 31, *The Royal Mischief* "made a shift to live half a dozen Days."

7. The scattered comments of Pix's contemporaries, her few references to herself in her writings, and the DNB are the only sources of biographical information about her.

8. An advertisement for the novel is appended to *Ibrahim*. In 1704 Pix published another nondramatic work, *Violenta, or the Rewards of Virtue: turn'd from Boccace into verse*, an adaptation of the eighth novel of the second day of the *Decameron*.

9. Charles Gildon's continuation of Langbaine's *Lives and Characters of the English Dramatick Poets* (London: for Nich. Cox and William Turner, 1699), p. 111.

10. James M. Edmunds, "An Example of Early Sentimentalism," *MLN* 48 (1933): 94–97, discusses *The Spanish Wives* as an early sentimental play.

11. Gildon's Langbaine, p. 112. Fredson Bowers, "Underprinting in Mary Pix, *The Spanish Wives* (1696)," *Library*, 5th ser. 9 (1954): 248–54, speculates that short printing was used to provide early copies for sale.

12. Cf. Olinda, the autobiographical character in Trotter's *Olinda's Adventures:* "I involv'd the whole Sex in her Faults, and with Aristotle (I hope one may condemn ones self with Aristotle) Repented that I had ever Trusted a Woman" (p. 150). Perhaps Trotter's authorship of the novel was as open a secret as her authorship of *Agnes de Castro*.

13. Publication may also have been squelched, for *The Female Wits* was not printed until 1704. See the discussion by Lucyle Hook in her introduction to *The Female Wits*, The Augustan Reprint Society, No. 124 (Los Angeles, Calif.: William Andrews Clark Memorial Library, University of California, 1967). Dane Farnsworth Smith also discusses the play in *Plays about the Theatre in England* (London: Oxford University Press, 1936), pp. 71–78.

14. See, for example, the prologue to *The French Beau*, pointed out by G. Thorn-Drury, "An Unrecorded Play-Title," *Review of English Studies* 6 (July 1930): 316–18.

15. Steele's letters to Manley are printed in *The Correspondence of Richard Steele*,

ed. Rae Blanchard (Oxford: Oxford University Press, 1941). Much information about Manley, including the details of the Steele-Manley quarrel, is found in G. A. Aitken, *The Life of Richard Steele*, 2 vols. (1889; reprint ed., New York: Greenwood, 1968) and Willard Connely, *Sir Richard Steele* (1934; reprint ed., Port Washington, N.Y.: Kennikat, 1967). See also Calhoun Winton, "Steele, Mrs. Manley, and John Lacy," *Philological Quarterly* 42 (April 1963): 272–75.

16. Pointed out by Anderson, "Manley's Biography," p. 272.

17. Allardyce Nicoll, *A History of English Drama 1660–1900*, 3d ed. (Cambridge: Cambridge University Press, 1969), 2:79.

18. Needham, "Mrs. Manley," p. 259, is misleading when she says that Manley was the first woman in England to be "jailed for her writings." Behn (see above, chap. 2) had been arrested for her attack on the Duke of Monmouth.

19. Needham, "Mrs. Manley," p. 268. Joyce M. Horner, "The English Women Novelists and their Connection with the Feminist Movement (1688–1797)," *Smith College Studies in Modern Languages*, Vol. 11, nos. 1–3 (1930), discusses the sensational popularity of the *Atalantis* and compiles numerous allusions to the novel by Manley's contemporaries, the most famous being Pope's "As long as *Atalantis* shall be read" in *The Rape of the Lock*. Manley's novels are available in the Scholars' Facsimiles series and the Foundation of the Novel series.

20. According to *An Impartial History of the Life, Character, Amours, Travels, and Transactions of Mr. John Barber, City-Printer, Common-Councilman, Alderman, and Lord Mayor of London* (London: for E. Curll, 1741), p. 24, it was through Manley that Barber met "those Persons who contributed to make his Fortune . . . besides the large Sums he acquired from her Writings: The Atalantis, her Novels, Play of Lucius, with many Political Pamphlets."

21. This transaction is discussed by Ralph Strauss, *The Unspeakable Curll* (London: Chapman and Hall, 1927), pp. 44–47.

22. Steele aided the revival with a puff by printing the prologue in the *Theatre*. See John Loftis, *Steele at Drury Lane* (Berkeley, Calif.: University of California Press, 1952), p. 70.

23. Daniel Hipwell, "Mary de la Rivière Manley," *Notes and Queries*, 7th ser. 8 (1889): 157.

24. Both her poem and Congreve's letter are included in Birch's edition of Trotter's *Works*.

25. Staring B. Wells, ed., *A Comparison Between the Two Stages* (Princeton, N.J.: Princeton University Press, 1942), p. 130.

26. "A Poem, Occasioned by the Busts Set Up in the Queen's Hermitage," Trotter, *Works*, 2:573.

27. Gildon's Langbaine, p. 111.

28. Information about Powell is taken from the DNB.

29. *The Czar of Muscovy* is omitted from the microprint collection *Three Centuries of English and American Plays*.

30. John Downes, *Roscius Anglicanus* (London: J. W. Jarvis, 1886), p. 48.

## Chapter 4

1. J. E. Norton in a two-part article, "Some Uncollected Authors: XIV," *The Book Collector* 6, lists and describes the eighteenth-century editions of Centlivre's works. The Summer 1957 issue, pp. 172–78, lists first editions of the plays; the Autumn 1957 issue, pp. 280–85, catalogues the poems, prose writings, and collected works. Supplements to Norton's bibliography are provided in the following: Alan D. McKillop, "Mrs. Centlivre's *The Wonder:*—A Variant Imprint," *The Book Collector* 7 (Spring 1958): 79–80; D. G. Neill, "A Poem by Mrs. Centlivre," *The Book Collector* 7 (Summer 1958): 189–90; Jacqueline Faure, "Two Poems by Susanna Centlivre," *The Book Collector* 10 (Spring 1961): 68–69.

2. The four primary accounts of Centlivre's life are these:
Giles Jacob, *The Poetical Register; or, The Lives and Characters of all the English Poets. With an Account of their Writings,* 2 vols. (London: A. Bettesworth, W. Taylor, and J. Batley, 1719); Jacob asserts in his preface that most of the accounts of living authors "came from their own Hands."

Abel Boyer's obituary notice in *The Political State of Great Britain* 27 (December 1723): 670–71; Boyer and Centlivre were correspondents in 1700.

*Scanderbeg, or Love and Liberty. A Tragedy. Written by the late Thomas Whincop, Esq. To which are added a List of all the Dramatic Authors, with some Account of their Lives* (London: for W. Reeve, 1747); this account provides most of the popular romantic embroidery of Centlivre's life and is the original source of the Hammond tale. John Mottley, usually assumed to be the author of the *Scanderbeg* list, was twenty years Centlivre's junior and author of several plays a few years before she left the theater.

W. R. Chetwood, *The British Theatre* (Dublin, 1750); Chetwood, author of two plays in 1720, was prompter at Drury Lane during the latter years of Centlivre's career. Quotations are taken from the London edition of 1752 for R. Baldwin.

3. *Scanderbeg* list, p. 187.

4. Two modern scholars have added considerably to the knowledge of Centlivre's life: James R. Sutherland, "The Progress of Error: Mrs. Centlivre and the Biographers," *Review of English Studies* 18 (April 1942): 167–82; and John Wilson Bowyer, *The Celebrated Mrs. Centlivre* (1952; reprint ed., New York: Greenwood, 1968), the only full-length biography. These studies, however, have been unable to ascertain the facts about Centlivre's life before 1700. In fact, they compound the confusion. Sutherland further complicates the question of Centlivre's maiden name with the unsubstantiated hypothesis that she was perhaps Freeman's illegitimate daughter and "Rawkins and his wife—people of 'mean parentage'—the couple to whom she was farmed out in her infancy" (p. 169). Bowyer's eagerness to harmonize every account of Centlivre's early life leads him to equally unprovable speculations, e.g., that she had both a stepmother and a stepfather, that Rawkins was an alias for Carroll. John H. MacKenzie, "Susan Centlivre," *Notes and Queries* 198 (September, 1953): 386–90, asserts positively that he has located the playwright's baptismal record and so

settled the questions of her birthdate, birthplace, and father's name. MacKenzie ignores the fact that Freeman was such a common name that records of several Susanna Freemans have been located (see Bowyer, pp. 4–5).

5. Quoted by Sutherland, "Progress of Error," p. 174, n. 4.

6. John Wilson Bowyer, "Susanna Freeman Centlivre," *MLN* 43 (February, 1928): 78–80, established this definite connection between the playwright and Holbeach on the basis of two of Centlivre's previously undiscovered poems. Sutherland, "Progress of Error," p. 169, n. 3, quotes the *Flying Post's* description of a party Centlivre gave in Holbeach on George I's birthday in 1716.

7. Sutherland, "Progress of Error," p. 177.

8. Chetwood, *British Theatre*, p. 141.

9. The authorship of the Celadon letters is uncertain, whether or not they express a genuine as opposed to a literary emotion. Charles Stonehill includes all the Celadon letters and a number of Centlivre's letters in his edition of *The Complete Works of George Farquhar*, 2 vols. (London: Nonsuch Press, 1930), 2: 216–69. Norton, "Some Uncollected Authors," p. 283, mistakenly assigns the Celadon letters to Boyer. The Celadon letters in *Letters of Wit, Politicks and Morality* are probably by Ayloffe, as suggested by Robert Adams Day, *Told in Letters: Epistolary Fiction Before Richardson* (Ann Arbor, Mich.: University of Michigan Press, 1966), p. 262.

10. Bowyer, *Celebrated Centlivre*, pp. 31–33, ascribes the ninth poem, "Polimnia: Of Rhetorick," to Centlivre on the basis of a passage in *A Letter from the Dead Thomas Brown to the Living Heraclitus* (1704).

11. *Scanderbeg* list, p. 188.

12. Bowyer, in *Celebrated Centlivre*, quotes the marriage license, pp. 92–93; examines the tax records for the Buckingham Court residence, p. 149; and summarizes the provisions of Joseph Centlivre's will, p. 254, n. 6.

13. William Egerton, *Faithful Memoirs of the Life, Amours and Performances, of That justly Celebrated, and most Eminent Actress of her Time, Mrs. Anne Oldfield* (London, 1731), pp. 58–59.

14. *Original and Genuine Letters Sent to the Tatler and Spectator* (London: for R. Harbin, 1725), 2:34.

15. Bowyer, *Celebrated Centlivre*, pp. 229–31.

16. Ibid., p. 232.

17. The poem is printed in *A New Miscellany of Original Poems, Translations and Imitations By the most eminent Hands*, ed. Anthony Hammond (London: for T. Jauncy, 1720), pp. 326–30. The quotation is from p. 330. The same anthology, pp. 331–34, reprints Amhurst's two poems to Centlivre.

18. These were included in *The Miscellaneous Works of Nicholas Rowe*. Centlivre's pastoral is on pp. 83–88 of the third edition (London: W. Feales, 1733).

19. Citation of Centlivre's works presents numerous problems. There is no edition of her complete works. In-text citations refer to the 1872 Pearson reprint, *The Dramatic Works of the Celebrated Mrs. Centlivre*, 3 vols., of the original edition of the *Works* published in London, 1761. (The Pearson reprint was reprinted again in 1968 by the AMS Press of New York.) Citations give the

volume number and the page number for paginated material. Prologues, epilogues, prefaces, and dedications are not paginated. Scene division in the plays is erratic, and there are no line numbers. A further problem is that prefaces and dedications are frequently omitted. The anonymous introduction to the 1761 *Works* states incorrectly that Centlivre "sent her Performances, like Orphans, into the World, without so much as a Nobleman to protect them" (1:viii). The 1761 editor apparently used editions of single plays from which the prefatory material was often missing. When there is no in-text citation for such materials, I am quoting from first editions. The *Works* are also a problem in that they include a truncated version of Part II of *The Busy Body*. There are only two satisfactory modern editions of single plays. Jess Byrd prepared a facsimile of the 1709 edition of *The Busy Body* for the Augustan Reprint Society, No. 19 (Los Angeles, Calif.: William Andrews Clark Memorial Library, University of California, 1949); Thalia Stathas's excellent edition of *A Bold Stroke for a Wife* is available in the Regents Restoration Drama Series (Lincoln, Neb.: University of Nebraska Press, 1968).

20. Susanna Centlivre, *A Woman's Case: in an Epistle to Charles Joye, Esq.; Deputy-Governor of the South-Sea* (London: for E. Curll, 1720), pp. 2–4.

21. See Bowyer, *Celebrated Centlivre*, p. 154.

22. Centlivre, *A Woman's Case*, p. 4.

23. Alexander Pope, *A Further Account of the most Deplorable Condition of Mr. Edmund Curll* (1716) in *The Prose Works*, ed. Norman Ault (Oxford: B. Blackwell, 1936), 1:279. Pope maliciously places Centlivre among Curll's hacks; actually Curll paid Centlivre handsomely for the few plays of hers that he printed (see Bowyer, *Celebrated Centlivre*, pp. 191–93). It is interesting that Pope, whose barbs were so often personal, never alludes to any scandal about Centlivre. This tends to confirm my belief that Centlivre's reputation as an adventuress was posthumous.

24. Bowyer, *Celebrated Centlivre*, pp. 244–45.

25. Centlivre, *A Woman's Case*, p. 7.

26. *Scanderbeg* list, pp. 189–92.

27. The episode of Ogle's sudden penchant for fighting may have been suggested by Massinger and Fletcher's *Little French Lawyer*.

28. Gravello's false advertisement of Lucasia as an heiress is reminiscent of *Volpone*.

29. Arthur Bedford, an inferior Collier, is more right than wrong in his description of the play: "The Epilogue of the *Gamester*, speaks against this particular Vice; but the Design of the Play, and the Conduct of Valere the Gamester seems rather to infer, that *It is good to have Two Strings to our Bow*. If we Game and succeed therein we are provided for; if that fails we shall pass for Gentlemen, and may marry Rich Fortunes; and tho' we break our Oaths and Promises which we made at first, yet the Ladies will soon believe us at another Time." *The Evil and Danger of Stage Plays* (London: W. Bonny and Henry Mortlock, 1706), p. 128. Arthur Sherbo, *English Sentimental Drama* (East Lansing, Mich.: Michigan State University Press, 1957), pp. 113–15, analyzes the lack of seriousness of the action.

30. The relationship between *The Double Gallant* and *Love at a Venture* is discussed by Bowyer, pp. 80–83; Richard Hindry Barker, *Mr. Cibber of Drury Lane* (1939; reprint ed., New York: AMS Press, 1966), pp. 68–70; F. W. Bateson, "The Double Gallant of Colley Cibber," *Review of English Studies* 1 (July 1925): 343–46; F. E. Budd, ed., *The Dramatic Works of William Burnaby* (London: Scholartis Press, 1931), pp. 91–92. Leonard Ashley, *Colley Cibber* (New York: Twayne, 1965), pp. 60–61, describes *The Double Gallant* as a partisan of Cibber.

31. Bateson, "*Double Gallant*," p. 346.

32. *An Apology for the Life of Colley Cibber Written by Himself*, ed. B. R. S. Fone (Ann Arbor, Mich.: University of Michigan Press, 1968), pp. 182–83.

33. Cibber, *Apology*, p. 346.

34. In the 1734 version of Fielding's *The Author's Farce*, Marplay, Sr. (Cibber) instructs Marplay, Jr. (Theophilus Cibber): "The art of writing, boy, is the art of stealing old plays by changing the name of the play, and new ones by changing the name of the author." Quoted from the edition by Charles B. Woods for the Regents Restoration Drama Series (Lincoln, Neb.: University of Nebraska Press, 1966), p. 90.

35. Sarah Fyge Egerton, *Poems on Several Occasions, Together with a Pastoral* (London: J. Nutt, 1706), unpaged.

36. *Scanderbeg* list, p. 189.

37. *Scanderbeg* list, p. 189. Steele commented on the prejudgment in the *Tatler* (13 May 1709): "In old Times, we us'd to sit upon a Play here after it was acted; but now the Entertainment is turn'd another Way." *The Lucubrations of Isaac Bickerstaff Esq.* 4 vols. (London: Charles Lillie and John Morphew, 1713), 1:136.

38. *Scanderbeg* list, p. 190.

39. There are many appreciative discussions of *The Busy Body*, beginning with Steele's in the *Tatler* for 23 May 1709: "The Plot and Incidents of the Play are laid with . . . Subtilty of Spirit" (*Lucubrations*, 1:167). The deftness of the play is often discussed. See, for example, Frederick S. Boas, *An Introduction to Eighteenth-Century Drama 1700–1780* (1953; reprint ed., Oxford: At the Clarendon Press, 1965), pp. 101–5; F. W. Bateson, *English Comic Drama 1700–1750* (Oxford, 1929; reprint ed., New York: Russell and Russell, 1963), pp. 70–71; Robert D. Hume, *The Development of English Drama in the Late Seventeenth Century* (Oxford: Oxford University Press, 1976), pp. 116–121.

40. The authorship of the *Female Tatler* is disputed, and it has been argued that Centlivre did indeed write the article. See Bowyer, *Celebrated Centlivre*, pp. 120–27, and Paul Bunyan Anderson, "Innocence and Artifice: or, Mrs. Centlivre and *The Female Tatler*," *Philological Quarterly* 16 (1937): 358–75. Centlivre's authorship is nevertheless unlikely for the very reasons she gives. Moreover, Bowyer argues from the untenable assumption that Manley and Centlivre were still friends in 1709. Manley had virulently attacked the Marlboroughs as early as 1705 in *Queen Zarah*, while the prologue to Centlivre's *Platonick Lady* had praised the Battle of Ramillies in 1706. Bowyer may be right, however, in his hypothesis that Centlivre's pique found its way into the paper through her old friend Thomas Baker.

41. *The Ghost* is printed in Vol. 6 of *A Collection of the Most Esteemed Farces and*

*Entertainments on the British Stage* (Edinburgh: S. Doig, 1792). Other adaptations of *The Man's Bewitched* are listed by Bowyer, *Celebrated Centlivre*, pp. 131–32.
Faithful's pretense that Sir David Watchum's house is an inn has been suggested as a source for Goldsmith's *She Stoops to Conquer* by Walter and Clare Jerrold, *Five Queer Women* (London: Brentano's, 1929), pp. 168–69, and by Mark Schorer, "*She Stoops to Conquer:* A Parallel," *MLN* 48 (February, 1933): 91–94, 486.

42. This was pointed out by F. T. Wood, "*The Disappointment,*" *Review of English Studies* 5 (January, 1929): 66–69.

43. Her political sentiments certainly affected her choice of setting. Three of her plays of Spanish plot *(The Wonder, A Wife Well Managed, Marplot)*, a type of play traditionally set in Spain or Spanish possessions in Italy, are set instead in Portugal, an ally of England in the War of the Spanish Succession.

44. Bateson, *English Comic Drama*, p. 64.

45. Stathas demonstrates this in the excellent introduction to her edition of *A Bold Stroke*.

46. In the accounts of Chetwood and the *Scanderbeg* list.

47. William Hazlitt, *A View of the English Stage; or, A Series of Dramatic Criticisms* (London: Robert Stodart, 1818), p. 352.

48. *Two Old Comedies The Belle's Stratagem and The Wonder Reduced and Rearranged by Augustin Daly For Production at Daly's Theatre During the Season 1893–94* (New York, 1893), pp. 4–5.

49. *The Works of Susan Ferrier,* Holyrood Edition (London: Eveleigh Nash and Grayson, 1929), 2:634. Ferrier may be alluding to a source of her novel. Lady Rossville, like Centlivre's Anne Lovely, has four guardians of four differing temperaments, although this is not central to the plot.

50. *Times* (London), 8 June 1954, p. 11, col. 3; 14 June 1954, p. 5, col. 6.

51. *Times* (London), 18 August 1954, p. 5, col. 3.

## Chapter 5

1. *The Frolicks*, mentioned by James O. Halliwell, *A Dictionary of Old English Plays* (London: J. R. Smith, 1860), p. 105, was long believed lost. It was recently discovered in the Cornell University library and edited by Judith Milhous and Robert D. Hume (Ithaca, N.Y.: Cornell University Press, 1977). The editors describe *The Faithful Virgins*, which remains in manuscript, and argue persuasively for a date of 1670 for the tragedy, dated 1661–63 by Alfred Harbage, *Annals of English Drama 975–1700*, 2d ed., rev. by Samuel Schoenbaum (Philadelphia: University of Pennsylvania Press, 1964). Milhous and Hume have located an Elizabeth Polwhele (c. 1651–91) but are not satisfied that she is the playwright because both her father and her husband were nonconforming clergymen. The dedication of *The Frolicks* is quoted from the Milhous and Hume edition, pp. 57–58.

2. Edmund Gosse, *Seventeenth Century Studies* (New York: Dodd, Mead, 1897), p. 255, identified Ephelia as Joan Philips and suggested that she was Katherine

Philips's daughter. In 1921 G. Thorn-Drury, in *A Little Ark* (London: P. J. and A. E. Dobell), p. 29, pointed out that Orinda's daughter was named Katherine and that Gosse gave no evidence for ascription to an unknown Joan Philips. Nonetheless, she is listed as the author of Ephelia's play in Alfred Harbage's *Annals of English Drama* and of her poems in Myra Reynolds, *The Learned Lady in England* (Boston: Houghton-Mifflin, 1920), pp. 138–39.

3. Information about Wharton is taken from the DNB; Reynolds, *Learned Lady*, p. 144; and George Ballard, *Memoirs of Several Ladies of Great Britain* (Oxford: W. Jackson, 1752), pp. 297–98.

4. Biographical information about Killigrew is taken from the DNB and from Richard Morton's introduction to the facsimile edition of her *Poems* (Gainesville, Fla.: Scholars' Facsimiles, 1967). In-text citations refer to this edition.

5. Biographical information is taken from Myra Reynolds's introduction to her edition of *The Poems of Anne Countess of Winchilsea* (Chicago: University of Chicago Press, 1903). In-text citations of the poems refer to this edition. Reynolds discusses Winchilsea's plays, pp. xcvi–ciii. For discussion of the poems, see, in addition to Reynolds, Edmund Gosse, *Gossip in a Library* (London: W. Heinemann, 1891), pp. 119–32; Edward Dowden, *Essays Modern and Elizabethan* (1910; reprint ed., Freeport, N.Y.: Books for Libraries Press, 1970), pp. 234–49; Helen Sard Hughes, "Lady Winchilsea and Her Friends," *London Mercury* 19 (April 1929): 624–35; Paul Bunyan Anderson, "Mrs. Manley's Texts of Three of Lady Winchilsea's Poems," *MLN* 45 (February 1930): 95–99; Reuben A. Brower, "Lady Winchilsea and the Poetic Tradition of the Seventeenth Century," *Studies in Philology* 42 (1945): 61–80. Brower's comment about her poetry is equally applicable to her plays: "We should look for her social and literary forebears among aristocratic ladies such as the Countess of Pembroke and Elizabeth Cary, Viscountess Falkland, ladies who also cultivated piety and poetry and learning" (p. 63). The countess's poetry has recently been anthologized in *The World Split Open: Four Centuries of Women Poets in England and America, 1552–1950*, ed. Louise Bernikow (New York: Random House, Vintage Books, 1974) and in *By a Woman Writt: Literature from Six Centuries by and about Women*, ed. Joan Goulianos (Indianapolis, Ind.: Bobbs-Merrill, 1973). The title of the latter is taken from one of the countess's poems. Lady Winchilsea is the subject of Dilys Laing's "Sonnet to a Sister in Error."

6. "Apollo Outwitted," *The Poems of Jonathan Swift*, ed. Harold Williams, 3 vols. (Oxford: Clarendon Press, 1958), 1: 121.

7. Biographical information is taken from William H. McBurney, "Mrs. Mary Davys: Forerunner of Fielding," *PMLA* 74 (1959): 348–55; Jonathan Swift, *Journal to Stella*, ed. Harold Williams, 2 vols. (Oxford: Clarendon Press, 1948), 1: 264, 2: 625; and from her own comments in *The Northern Heiress* and in her collected *Works*, 2 vols. (London: H. Woodfall, 1725). In-text citations refer to volume and page number in the *Works*. McBurney discusses Davys's anticipation of Fielding in her transference of stage conventions to the novel and her vignettes of comic country types. Her *Familiar Letters Betwixt a Gentleman and a Lady*, a highly developed pre-Richardsonian epistolary novel, is available in a facsimile edition, with an introduction by Robert A. Day, published by the

Augustan Reprint Society, No. 54 (Los Angeles, Calif.: William Andrews Clark Memorial Library, University of California, 1955). Day discusses this novel further in *Told in Letters* (Ann Arbor, Mich.: University of Michigan Press, 1966), pp. 187–90.

8. Biographical information is from William H. McBurney, "Mrs. Penelope Aubin and the Early Eighteenth-Century English Novel," *The Huntington Library Quarterly* 20 (May 1957): 245–67. Aubin's play is omitted from the microprint collection *Three Centuries of English and American Plays*. Quotations are taken from the third edition (1734), printed under the altered title *The Masquerade*. Three of Aubin's novels have been reprinted with introductions by Josephine Greider in the Foundations of the Novel series, Nos. 36 and 43 (New York: Garland, 1973).

9. The principal source of biographical information is G. F. Whicher, *The Life and Romances of Mrs. Eliza Haywood* (New York: Columbia University Press, 1915). Haywood's appearances as an actress are traced by John R. Elwood, "The Stage Career of Eliza Haywood," *Theatre Survey* 5 (November 1964): 107–16. Elwood, "Swift's 'Corinna'," *Notes and Queries* 200 (December 1955): 529–30, argues that Haywood rather than Manley is the subject of that poem. The connection between Haywood and Andrew Yeatman was discovered by C. A. Moore, "A Note of the Biography of Mrs. Eliza Haywood," *MLN* 33 (1918): 248–50. Selections from Haywood's periodical essays were published as *The Female Spectator*, ed. Mary Priestley (London: John Lane, 1929). Walter and Clare Jerrold include a biographical essay in *Five Queer Women* (London: Brentano's, 1929), pp. 200–75. See also Reynolds, *Learned Lady*, pp. 212–16, and Joyce M. Horner, "English Women Novelists," pp. 18–24.

10. Quoted by Whicher, *Life and Romances*, p. 10.

11. Alexander Pope, *The Dunciad*, ed. James Sutherland, 3d ed., rev. (London: Methuen, 1963), p. 119.

12. Ibid., p. 120.

13. The DNB and Reynolds, *Learned Lady*, pp. 188–93, discuss Elizabeth Cooper. Details in both need correction by the information in Emmett L. Avery et al., *The London Stage 1660–1800*, 5 pts. in 11 vols. (Carbondale, Ill.: Southern Illinois University Press, 1960–68).

14. Biographical information is taken from the DNB and from Leapor's *Poems on Several Occasions*, 2 vols. (London: J. Roberts, 1748–51), cited in the text as *Poems*. Reynolds, *Learned Lady*, discusses Leapor, pp. 246–47.

15. Biographical information is taken principally from the *Memoirs of Mrs. Letitia Pilkington*, with an introduction by Iris Barry (London: G. Routledge, 1928); this is reprinted from the first edition of 1748–54. In-text citations refer to this edition. The *Memoirs* are supplemented by the DNB articles on Letitia Pilkington, Matthew Pilkington, and James Worsdale. The Jerrolds, *Five Queer Women*, pp. 276–346, give a lively version of Pilkington's life. Richard H. Barker, *Mr. Cibber of Drury Lane* (1939; reprint ed., New York: AMS Press, 1966), pp. 241–50, discusses Pilkington's relationship with the laureate.

16. W. R. Chetwood, *The British Theatre* (London: for R. Baldwin, 1752), p. 193.

17. Biographical information is taken from the *Narrative*, supplemented by

Avery et al., *The London Stage;* Leonard Ashley, *Colley Cibber* (New York: Twayne, 1965), pp. 151, 156–61; Barker, *Cibber,* pp. 178–80; and Helen Waddell, "Eccentric Englishwomen: VIII. Mrs. Charke," *The Spectator,* 4 June 1937, pp. 1047–48. The *Narrative* is examined in detail by Charles D. Peavy, "The Chimerical Career of Charlotte Charke," *Restoration and Eighteenth Century Theatre Research* 8 (May 1969): 1–12, and Sally Minter Strange, "Charlotte Charke: Transvestite or Conjuror?" *Restoration and Eighteenth Century Theatre Research* 15 (November 1976): 54–59. Strange doubts that Charke was a lesbian. George Graveley [Edwards], *The Wild Girl* (St. Albans, Herts.: W. Cartmel, 1949), is a play based upon Charke's autobiography.

18. The *General Advertiser* on 3 June 1746 referred to her as "Mrs. Sacheverel, late Mrs. Charke." Quoted by Avery et al., *The London Stage,* 3: cxxxii, n. 192. Charke's silence on this point in the *Narrative* makes it impossible to tell if Sacheverel was the name of the mysterious second husband. She continued to use the name Charke until her death.

19. The play is discussed in detail by Dane F. Smith, *Plays About the Theatre in England* (London: Oxford University Press, 1936), pp. 170–75.

20. Quoted by Avery et al., *The London Stage,* 3: 573.

21. Biographical information is taken from Percy Fitzgerald, *Mrs. Catherine Clive* (London: A. Reader, 1888). Clive's plays are discussed by Richard C. Frushell in "The Textual Relationship and Biographical Significance of Two Petite Pièces by Mrs. Catherine (Kitty) Clive," *Restoration and Eighteenth Century Theatre Research* 9 (May 1970): 51–58, and "Kitty Clive as Dramatist," *Durham University Journal,* n.s. 32 (March 1971): 125–32.

22. For her benefits in 1760, 1761, 1763, and 1765 Clive wrote four other afterpieces—*Every Woman in Her Humour, The Island of Slaves, Sketch of a Fine Lady's Return from a Rout,* and *The Faithful Irishwoman.* None of these was performed more than twice, and none was printed.

## Chapter 6

1. Aphra Behn, *Works,* ed. Montague Summers, 6 vols. (London: William Heinemann, 1915), 6: 131.

2. Ibid., p. 9.

3. Ibid., p. 123.

4. Katherine Philips, *Poems* (London: for H. Herringman, 1667), sig. b2$^v$.

5. Behn, *Works,* 6:9.

6. Hugh MacDonald, introduction to *A Journal From Parnassus* (London: P. J. Dobell, 1937), p. vii. MacDonald lists and describes a number of these "sessions."

7. *Journal From Parnassus,* pp. 25–27.

8. *Poems on Affairs of State: From the time of Oliver Cromwell, to the Abdication of K. James the Second* (London, 1697), pp. 220–21.

9. Trajano Boccalini, *Advertisements From Parnassus,* 2 vols. (London: for Richard Smith, 1704), 1: 51.

10. From the issue for September 1738, p. 469.

11. *Scanderbeg* list (London: for W. Reeve, 1747), p. 189.

12. Arthur Bedford, *A Serious Remonstrance In Behalf of the Christian Religion Against The Horrid Blasphemies and Impieties which are still used in the English Play-Houses* (London: John Darby, 1719), p. 209.

13. See chap. 2.

14. For discussion of the identification of Phoebe Clinket see Myra Reynolds's introduction to Winchilsea's *Poems* (Chicago: University of Chicago Press, 1903), pp. lxii–lxx; George Sherburn, "The Fortunes and Misfortunes of *Three Hours After Marriage*," *Modern Philology* 24 (1926): 91–109; Dane Farnsworth Smith, *Plays About the Theatre in England* (London: Oxford University Press, 1936), pp. 103–08; John Wilson Bowyer, *The Celebrated Mrs. Centlivre* (1952; reprint ed., New York: Greenwood, 1968), pp. 194–206. It seems obvious, although I have not seen it commented on, that the name Phoebe was chosen to remind the audience of the name Finch. Convincing arguments that Clinket is a generalized satire are found in Jean Gagen, *The New Woman* (New York: Twayne, 1954), p. 81, and in the introduction by Richard Morton and William M. Peterson to their edition of *Three Hours After Marriage* (Painesville, Ohio: Lake Erie College Press, 1961). The play is also available in the Augustan Reprint Society series, nos. 91–92, with an introduction by John Harrington Smith (Los Angeles, Calif.: William Andrews Clark Memorial Library, University of California, 1961).

15. Judith Milhous and Robert D. Hume, "Lost English Plays, 1660–1700," *Harvard Library Bulletin* 25 (1977): 15, suggest that the lost play *The Poetess* (1667) may have been a "topical burlesque" of the Duchess of Newcastle. If so, it probably falls into this category of plays satirizing *femmes savantes*.

16. Philips, *Poems*, sig. c1$^r$.

17. Behn, *Works*, 6: 117.

18. Ibid., p. 119.

19. Richard Steele, *The Lucubrations of Isaac Bickerstaff Esq.*, 4 vols. (London: Charles Lillie and John Morphew, 1713), 1: 167.

20. Philips, *Poems*, sig. c2$^v$.

21. Ibid., sig. d1$^r$.

## Chapter 7

1. Quoted by Philip Webster Souers, *The Matchless Orinda* (1931; reprint ed., New York: Johnson, 1968), p. 171, n. 1.

2. Katherine Philips, *Poems* (London: for H. Herringman, 1667), sigs. a1$^v$-a2$^r$.

3. Samuel Richardson, *Sir Charles Grandison*, The Shakespeare Head Edition (Oxford: Basil Blackwell, 1931), 2:221.

4. The poem prefaces Vol 1 of Haywood's *Secret Histories, Novels, and Poems* (London: for A. Bettesworth, 1732).

5. Robert Adams Day, *Told in Letters* (Ann Arbor, Mich.: University of Michigan Press, 1966), p. 43.

6. Jess Byrd, introduction to *The Busie Body,* Augustan Society Reprints, no. 19 (Los Angeles, Calif.: William Andrews Clark Memorial Library, University of California, 1949), p. i.

7. John Duncombe, *The Feminiad* (London: for M. Cooper, 1754), pp. 14–15.

8. *Their Majesties' Servants,* ed. Robert W. Lowe (London, 1888; reprint ed., New York: AMS Press, 1968), 1:239.

9. Edmund Gosse, *Seventeenth Century Studies* (1883; reprint ed., New York: Dodd, Mead, 1897), pp. 229–30.

10. Sarah Fyge Egerton, *Poems on Several Occasions, Together with a Pastoral* (London: J. Nutt, 1706), sig. A3ʳ. Egerton, though not a playwright herself, was a friend of Pix and Centlivre.

11. As Jean Gagen amply demonstrates in *The New Woman* (New York: Twayne, 1954), passim.

12. Several commentators have noted this effect of social exclusion. James Sutherland, for example, in *English Literature of the Late Seventeenth Century* (Oxford: Oxford University Press, 1969), points out that Restoration noblemen and gentlemen "helped professional authors like Dryden and Shadwell with criticism and advice, and by giving them an entrée into that polite and fashionable world they mirrored in their plays. . . . Such ready access to the arbiters of contemporary elegance undoubtedly refined the manners of much Restoration literature. When circumstances made such access difficult, as with Mrs. Behn, we can at once feel the difference of tone" (p. 27). Cf. Horace Walpole: "Why are there so few genteel comedies, but because most comedies are written by men not of that sphere? Etherege, Congreve, Vanbrugh, and Cibber wrote genteel comedy, because they lived in the best company . . . Wycherley, Dryden, Mrs. Centlivre, &c., wrote as if they had only lived in the 'Rose Tavern.' " *Letters,* ed. Peter Cunningham (London, 1857–59), 9:96.

# Bibliography

Aitken, George A. *The Life of Richard Steele.* 2 vols. 1889; reprint ed., New York: Greenwood, 1968.

Amhurst, Nicholas. *Poems on Several Occasions.* London: for R. Francklin, 1720.

Anderson, Paul Bunyan. "Innocence and Artifice: or, Mrs. Centlivre and *The Female Tatler.*" *Philological Quarterly* 16 (1937): 358–75.

———. "Mistress Delariviere Manley's Biography." *Modern Philology* 33 (1936): 261–78.

———. "Mrs. Manley's Texts of Three of Lady Winchilsea's Poems." *MLN* 45 (1930): 95–99.

*Animadversions on Mr. Congreve's Late Answer to Mr. Collier.* London: for John Nutt, 1698.

"The Apotheosis of Milton." *The Gentleman's Magazine* 8 (1738): 469.

Ariadne [pseud.] *She Ventures and He Wins.* London: for Hen. Rhodes, 1696.

Ashley, Leonard. *Colley Cibber.* New York: Twayne, 1965.

Astell, Mary. *A Serious Proposal to the Ladies, for the Advancement of their True and Greatest Interest.* 2d ed. London: for R. Wilkin, 1695.

Aubert, Mrs. *Harlequin-Hydaspes; or, The Greshamite.* London: J. Roberts, 1719.

Aubin, Penelope. *Histories and Novels.* 3 vols. London: D. Midwinter, 1739.

———. *The Life and Adventures of the Lady Lucy.* Introduction by Josephine Grieder. Foundations of the Novel, vol. 43. New York: Garland, 1973.

————. *The Life of Madam de Beaumont, a French Lady and The Strange Adventures of the Count de Vinevil and His Family.* Introduction by Josephine Grieder. Foundations of the Novel, vol. 36. New York: Garland, 1973.

————. *The Masquerade; or, The Humorous Cuckold.* n.p., 1734.

Aubrey, John. *Brief Lives.* Edited by Andrew Clark. 2 vols. Oxford: At the Clarendon Press, 1898.

Avery, Emmett L., et al. *The London Stage, 1660–1800.* 5 pts. in 11 vols. Carbondale, Ill.: Southern Illinois University Press, 1960–68.

Ballard, George. *Memoirs of Several Ladies of Great Britain.* Oxford: W. Jackson, 1752.

Barker, Richard Hindry. *Mr. Cibber of Drury Lane.* 1939; reprint ed., New York: AMS Press, 1966.

Bateson, F. W. *"The Double Gallant* of Colley Cibber." *Review of English Studies* 1 (1925): 343–46.

————. *English Comic Drama 1700–1750.* 1929; reprint ed., New York: Russell and Russell, 1963.

Bedford, Arthur. *The Evil and Danger of Stage Plays.* London: W. Bonny and Henry Mortlock, 1706.

————. *A Serious Remonstrance in Behalf of the Christian Religion.* London: John Darby, 1719.

Behn, Aphra. *The Histories and Novels.* London: S. Briscoe, 1696.

————. *The Novels.* Edited by Ernest A. Baker. London: George Routledge, 1905.

————. *The Plays, Histories, and Novels.* 6 vols. London: Pearson, 1871.

————. *The Rover.* Edited by Frederick M. Link. Regents Restoration Drama Series. Lincoln, Neb.: University of Nebraska Press, 1967.

————. *Works.* Edited by Montague Summers. 6 vols. London: William Heinemann, 1915.

Bentley, Gerald Eades. *The Jacobean and Caroline Stage.* 7 vols. Oxford: At the Clarendon Press, 1941–68.

Bernikow, Louise, ed. *The World Split Open: Four Centuries of Women Poets in England and America, 1552–1950.* New York: Random House, Vintage Books, 1974.

Boas, F. S. *An Introduction to Eighteenth-Century Drama 1700–1780.* 1953; reprint ed., Oxford: Oxford University Press, 1965.

Boccalini, Trajano. *Advertisements from Parnassus.* Translated and adapted by N. N. 2 vols. London: for Richard Smith, 1704.

Boothby, Frances. *Marcelia; or, The Treacherous Friend.* London: for Will. Cademan, 1670.

Bowers, Fredson. "Underprinting in Mary Pix, *The Spanish Wives* (1696)." *Library,* 5th ser. 9 (1954): 248–54.

Bowyer, John Wilson. *The Celebrated Mrs. Centlivre.* 1952; reprint ed., New York: Greenwood, 1968.

———. "Susanna Freeman Centlivre." *MLN* 43 (1928): 78–80.

Boyd, Elizabeth. *Don Sancho; or, The Students Whim, with Minerva's Triumph, A Masque.* London: for the author, 1739.

Brower, Reuben A. "Lady Winchilsea and the Poetic Tradition of the Seventeenth Century." *Studies in Philology* 42 (1945): 61–80.

Brown, Tom. *Works.* 9th ed. 4 vols. London: for Al. Wilde, 1760.

Bullough, Geoffrey. *Narrative and Dramatic Sources of Shakespeare.* 8 vols. New York: Columbia University Press, 1957–75.

Burnaby, William. *The Dramatic Works.* Edited by F. E. Budd. London: Scholartis Press, 1931.

Cameron, W. J. *New Light on Aphra Behn.* Auckland: University of Auckland Press, 1961.

Cary, Elizabeth, Lady Falkland. *The Tragedy of Mariam.* Edited by A. C. Dunstan and W. W. Greg. Malone Society Reprints. Oxford: Oxford University Press, 1914.

Cavendish, Lady Jane, and Brackley, Lady Elizabeth. "The Concealed Fansyes." Edited by Nathan Comfort Starr. *PMLA* 46 (1931): 802–38.

Centlivre, Susanna. *A Bold Stroke for a Wife.* Edited by Thalia Stathas. Regents Restoration Drama Series. Lincoln, Nebraska: University of Nebraska Press, 1968.

———. *The Busie Body.* Introduction by Jess Byrd. Augustan Society Reprints, no. 19. Los Angeles, Calif.: William Andrews Clark Memorial Library, University of California, 1949.

———. *The Dramatic Works.* 3 vols. London: Pearson, 1872.

———. *A Woman's Case: in an Epistle to Charles Joye, Esq; Deputy-Governor of the South-Sea.* London: for E. Curll, 1720.

Charke, Charlotte. *The Art of Management; or, Tragedy Expell'd.* London: W. Rayner, 1735.

———. *A Narrative of the Life of Mrs. Charlotte Charke.* London: for W. Reeve, 1755.

Chetwood, W. R. *The British Theatre*. London: for R. Baldwin, 1752.

Cibber, Colley. *Apology*. Edited by B. R. S. Fone. Ann Arbor, Mich.: University of Michigan Press, 1968.

———. *The Dramatic Works*. 5 vols. London: for J. Rivington, 1777.

Clive, Catherine. *The Rehearsal; or, Bays in Petticoats*. London: for R. Dodsley, 1753.

*A Collection of the Most Esteemed Farces and Entertainments Performed on the British Stage*. 6 vols. Edinburgh: S. Doig, 1792.

Connely, Willard. *Sir Richard Steele*. 1934; reprint ed., Port Washington, N.Y.: Kennikat, 1967.

Cooke, William. *Memoirs of Charles Macklin*. 1804; reprint ed., New York: Benjamin Blom, 1972.

Cooper, Elizabeth. *The Muses Library; Or a Series of English Poetry, From the Saxons, to the Reign of King Charles II*. London: for J. Wilcox, 1737.

———. *The Rival Widows; or, Fair Libertine*. London: for T. Woodward, 1735.

*The Court Legacy*. London: J. Dormer, 1733.

Cumberland, Richard, ed. *The British Drama*. 14 vols. London: C. Cooke, 1817.

Cunliffe, John W. *The Influence of Seneca on Elizabethan Tragedy*. London: Macmillan, 1893.

Davies, John, of Hereford. *The Complete Works*. Edited by Alexander Grosart. 2 vols. Edinburgh: Edinburgh University Press, 1878.

Davys, Mary. *Familiar Letters Betwixt a Gentleman and a Lady*. Introduction by Robert A. Day. Augustan Society Reprints, no. 54. Los Angeles, Calif.: William Andrews Clark Memorial Library, University of California, 1955.

———. *The Northern Heiress; or, The Humours of York*. London: H. Meere, 1716.

———. *Works*. 2 vols. London: H. Woodfall, 1725.

Day, Robert Adams. "Aphra Behn's First Biography." *Studies in Bibliography* 22 (1969): 227–40.

———. *Told in Letters: Epistolary Fiction Before Richardson*. Ann Arbor, Mich.: University of Michigan Press, 1966.

Doran, John. *"Their Majesties' Servants." Annals of the English Stage, from Thomas Betterton to Edmund Kean*. Edited and revised by Robert Lowe, 3 vols. 1888; reprint ed., New York: AMS Press, 1968.

Dowden, Edward. *Essays Modern and Elizabethan.* 1910; reprint ed., Freeport, N. Y.: Books for Libraries Press, 1970.

Downes, John. *Roscius Anglicanus, Or, An Historical Review of the Stage From 1660 to 1706.* Preface by Joseph Knight. London: J. W. Jarvis, 1886.

Dryden, John. *Sir Martin Mar-all; or, The Feigned Innocence.* London: for H. Herringman, 1668.

Duchovnay, Gerald. "Aphra Behn's Religion." *Notes and Queries,* n.s. 23 (1976), 235–37.

Duffy, Maureen. *The Passionate Shepherdess: Aphra Behn 1640–89.* London: Jonathan Cape, 1977.

Duncombe, John. *The Feminiad.* London: for M. Cooper, 1754.

Dunstan, Arthur Cyril. *Examination of Two English Dramas.* Königsberg: Hartungsche Buchdruckerei, 1908.

Edmunds, James M. "An Example of Early Sentimentalism." *MLN* 48 (1933): 94–97.

Edwards, George Graveley. *The Wild Girl.* St. Albans, Herts.: W. Cartmel, 1949.

Egerton, Sarah Fyge. *Poems on Several Occasions, Together with a Pastoral.* London: J. Nutt, 1706.

Egerton, William. *Faithful Memoirs of the Life, Amours and Performances, of That justly Celebrated, and most Eminent Actress of her Time, Mrs. Anne Oldfield.* London, 1731.

Eliot, T. S. "Apology for the Countess of Pembroke." In *The Use of Poetry and the Use of Criticism.* London: Faber and Faber, 1933.

Elizabeth I, Queen. *Poems.* Edited by Leicester Bradner. Providence, R.I.: Brown University Press, 1964.

Elwood, John R. "The Stage Career of Eliza Haywood." *Theatre Survey* 5 (1964): 107–16.

———. "Swift's 'Corinna.' " *Notes and Queries* 200 (1955): 529–30.

Ephelia [pseud.] *Female Poems on Several Occasions.* London: William Downing, 1679.

*An Essay In Defence of the Female Sex.* London: for A. Roper and E. Wilkinson, 1696.

Evelyn, John. *Diary.* Edited by E. S. de Beer. 6 vols. Oxford: At the Clarendon Press, 1955.

*The Faithful General.* London: R. Wellington, 1706.

*Familiar Letters of Love, Gallantry, And several other Occasions: by the Wits of the last and present Age.* 6th ed. 2 vols. London: S. Briscoe, 1724.

Farquhar, George. *The Complete Works.* Edited by Charles Stonehill. 2 vols. London: Nonesuch Press, 1930.

Faure, Jacqueline. "Two Poems by Susanna Centlivre." *The Book Collector* 10 (1961): 68–69.

*The Female Tatler.* 8 July 1709, 10 October 1709, 14 December 1709.

Ferrier, Susan. *The Works.* Holyrood edition. 4 vols. London: Eveleigh Nash and Grayson, 1929.

Fielding, Henry. *The Author's Farce.* Edited by Charles B. Woods. Regents Restoration Drama Series. Lincoln, Neb.: University of Nebraska Press, 1966.

—————. *The Historical Register For the Year 1736 and Eurydice Hissed.* Edited by William W. Appleton. Regents Restoration Drama Series. Lincoln, Neb.: University of Nebraska Press, 1967.

Fisher, Dorothea Canfield. *Corneille and Racine in England.* New York: Columbia University Press, 1904.

Fitzgerald, Percy. *The Life of Mrs. Catherine Clive.* London: A. Reader, 1888.

Fleming, Alison. "Catherine Trotter—the Scots Sappho." *The Scots Magazine* 33 (1940): 305–14.

Frushell, Richard C. "Kitty Clive as Dramatist." *Durham University Journal,* n.s. 32 (March 1971): 125–32.

—————. "The Textual Relationship and Biographical Significance of Two Petite Pièces by Mrs. Catherine (Kitty) Clive." *Restoration and Eighteenth Century Theatre Research* 9 (May 1970): 51–58.

Fullerton, Lady Georgiana. *The Life of Elisabeth Lady Falkland.* London: Burns and Oates, 1883.

Gagen, Jean. "Honor and Fame in the Works of the Duchess of Newcastle." *Studies in Philology* 56 (1959): 519–38.

—————. *The New Woman: Her Emergence in English Drama 1600–1730.* New York: Twayne, 1954.

Gardiner, Harold C. *Mysteries' End: An Investigation of the Last Days of the Medieval Religious Stage.* Yale Studies in English, vol. 103. New Haven, Conn.: Yale University Press, 1946.

Gay, John, Pope, Alexander, and Arbuthnot, John. *Three Hours After Marriage.* London: Bernard Lintot, 1717.

————. *Three Hours After Marriage.* Edited by John Harrington Smith. Augustan Society Reprints, nos. 91–92. Los Angeles, Calif.: University of California Press, 1961.

————. *Three Hours After Marriage.* Edited by Richard Morton and William Peterson. Painesville, Ohio: Lake Erie College Press, 1961.

Gildon, Charles. *A Comparison Between the Two Stages.* London, 1702.

————. *The Lives and Characters of the English Dramatick Poets.* London: for Nich. Cox and William Turner, 1699.

Gosse, Edmund. "Catharine Trotter, the Precursor of the Bluestockings." *Transactions of the Royal Society of Literature,* 2d ser. 34 (1916): 87–118.

————. *Gossip in a Library.* London: W. Heinemann, 1891.

————. "The Matchless Orinda." In *Seventeenth Century Studies.* 1883; reprint ed., New York: Dodd, Mead, 1897.

Gould, Robert. *Poems Chiefly consisting of Satyrs and Satyrical Epistles.* London, 1689.

Goulianos, Joan, ed. *By a Woman Writt: Literature from Six Centuries by and about Women.* Indianapolis, Ind.: Bobbs-Merrill, 1973.

Grant, Douglas. *Margaret the First.* Toronto: University of Toronto Press, 1957.

Greg, W. W., ed. *The Trial and Flagellation with Other Studies in the Chester Cycle.* Oxford: Oxford University Press, 1935.

Hahn, Emily. *Purple Passage.* Garden City, N. Y.: Doubleday, 1950.

Halliwell, James O. *A Dictionary of Old English Plays.* London: J. R. Smith, 1860.

Hammond, Anthony. *A New Miscellany of Original Poems, Translations and Imitations By the most eminent Hands.* London: for T. Jauncy, 1720.

Harbage, Alfred. *Annals of English Drama 975–1700.* 2d ed., rev. S. Schoenbaum. Philadelphia: University of Pennsylvania Press, 1964.

————. *Cavalier Drama.* 1936; reprint ed., New York: Russell and Russell, 1964.

Haywood, Eliza. *The Fair Captive.* London: for T. Jauncy and H. Cole, 1721.

————. *The Female Spectator.* 5th ed. 4 vols. London: for T. Gardner, 1775.

————. *The Female Spectator.* Selections edited by Mary Priestley. London: John Lane, 1929.

————. *Frederick, Duke of Brunswick-Lunenburgh.* London: for W. Mears and J. Brindley, 1729.

————. *The Opera of Operas; or, Tom Thumb the Great.* With William Hatchett. London: for William Rayner, 1733.

————. *Secret Histories, Novels, and Poems.* 3d ed. 4 vols. London: for A. Bettesworth, 1732.

————. *A Wife to Be Let.* London: for D. Browne, 1735.

Hazlitt, William. *Lectures on the English Comic Writers.* London: Taylor and Hessey, 1819.

————. *A View of the English Stage; or, A Series of Dramatic Criticisms.* London: Robert Stodart, 1818.

Hipwell, Daniel. "Mary de la Rivière Manley." *Notes and Queries,* 7th ser. 8 (1889): 156–57.

Hoper, Mrs. *Queen Tragedy Restor'd.* London: for W. Owen, 1749.

Horner, Joyce M. "The English Women Novelists and their Connections with the Feminist Movement (1688–1797)." *Smith College Studies in Modern Languages* 11, nos. 1–3 (1930): 1–152.

Hughes, Helen Sard. "Lady Winchilsea and Her Friends." *London Mercury* 19 (1929): 624–35.

Hughes, Leo, and Scouten, A. H., eds. *Ten English Farces.* Austin, Texas: University of Texas Press, 1948.

Hume, Robert D. *The Development of English Drama in the Late Seventeenth Century.* Oxford: Oxford University Press, 1976.

*An Impartial History of the Life, Character, Amours, Travels, and Transactions of Mr. John Barber, City-Printer, Common-Councilman, and Lord Mayor of London.* London: for E. Curll, 1741.

Jacob, Giles. *The Poetical Register; or, The Lives and Characters of all the English Poets.* 2 vols. London: A. Bettesworth, W. Taylor, and J. Batley, 1719.

Jerrold, Walter, and Jerrold, Clare. *Five Queer Women.* London: Brentano's, 1929.

Jonson, Ben. *Works.* Edited by C. H. Herford and Percy and Evelyn Simpson. 11 vols. Oxford: Clarendon Press, 1925–52.

*A Journal From Parnassus.* Introduction by Hugh MacDonald. London: P. J. Dobell, 1937.

Killigrew, Anne. *Poems.* Introduction by Richard Morton. Gainesville, Fla.: Scholars' Facsimiles, 1967.

Killigrew, Thomas. *Comedies and Tragedies.* 1664; reprint ed., New York: B. Blom, 1967.

Kline, Richard B. "Anne Oldfield and Mary de la Rivière Manley: The Unnoticed Reconciliation." *Restoration and Eighteenth Century Theatre Research* 14 (November, 1975): 53–58.

*Lady Alimony.* In vol. 14 of *A Select Collection of Old English Plays.* Edited by Robert Dodsley. 4th ed., rev. W. Carew Hazlitt. 1874–76; reprint ed., New York: Benjamin Blom, 1964.

*The Lady Falkland Her Life.* Edited by Richard Simpson. London: Catholic Publishing Company, 1861.

Langbaine, Gerard. *An Account of the English Dramatick Poets.* London: L.L. for George West, 1691.

*The Laureat: or the Right Side of Colley Cibber.* London: J. Roberts, 1740.

Leapor, Mary. *Poems upon Several Occasions.* 2 vols. London: J. Roberts, 1748–51.

*Letters and Poems in Honour of the Incomparable Princess, Margaret, Dutchess of Newcastle.* London: Thomas Newcombe, 1676.

*Letters of Wit, Politicks and Morality.* London: for J. Hartley, W. Turner, and Tho. Hodgson, 1701.

Link, Frederick M. *Aphra Behn,* New York: Twayne, 1968.

Loftis, John. *The Spanish Plays of Neoclassical England.* New Haven, Conn.: Yale University Press, 1973.

―――. *Steele at Drury Lane.* Berkeley, Calif.: University of California Press, 1952.

Lumley, Lady Jane. *Iphigeneia at Aulis.* Edited by Harold H. Child. Malone Society Reprints. London: Chiswick Press, 1909.

Lynch, Kathleen M. *The Social Mode of Restoration Comedy.* New York: MacMillan, 1926.

M., W. *The Female Wits; or, The Triumvirate of Poets at Rehearsal.* N.p., n.d.

―――. *The Female Wits.* Introduction by Lucyle Hook. Augustan Society Reprints, no. 124. Los Angeles, Calif.: William Andrews Clark Memorial Library, University of California, 1967.

McBurney, William H. "Mrs. Mary Davys: Forerunner of Fielding." *PMLA* 74 (1959): 348–55.

————. "Mrs. Penelope Aubin and the Early Eighteenth-Century English Novel." *The Huntington Library Quarterly* 20 (1957): 245–67.

MacKenzie, John H. "Susan Centlivre." *Notes and Queries* 198 (1953): 386–90.

McKillop, Alan D. "Mrs. Centlivre's *The Wonder:*—A Variant Imprint." *The Book Collector* 7 (1958): 79–80.

Manley, Delariviere. *The Adventures of Rivella; or, The History of the Author of the Atalantis.* London, 1714.

————. *Almyna; or, The Arabian Vow.* London: for William Turner, 1707.

————. *The Lost Lover; or, The Jealous Husband.* London: for R. Bentley, 1696.

————. *Lucius, the First Christian King of Britain.* London: for John Barber, 1717.

————. *The Power of Love: In Seven Novels.* London: for John Barber, 1720.

————. *The Royal Mischief.* London: for R. Bentley, F. Saunders, and J. Knapton, 1696.

————. *Secret Memoirs and Manners of Several Persons of Quality of Both Sexes. From the New Atalantis, An Island in the Mediterranean,* 7th ed. 4 vols. London: J. Watson, 1736.

Milhous, Judith, and Hume, Robert D. "Lost English Plays, 1660–1700." *Harvard Library Bulletin* 25 (1977): 5–33.

Moore, C. A. "A Note of the Biography of Mrs. Eliza Haywood." *MLN* 33 (1918): 248–50.

Murdock, Kenneth B. *The Sun at Noon.* New York: MacMillan, 1939.

Needham, Gwendolyn B. "Mary de la Rivière Manley, Tory Defender." *The Huntington Library Quarterly* 12 (1949): 253–88.

————. "Mrs. Manley: An Eighteenth-Century Wife of Bath." *The Huntington Library Quarterly* 14 (1951): 259–84.

Neill, D. G. "A Poem by Mrs. Centlivre." *The Book Collector* 7 (1958): 189–90.

Newcastle, Margaret Cavendish, Duchess of. *The Life of William Cavendish, Duke of Newcastle.* Edited by C. H. Firth. London: John C. Nimmo, 1886.

————. *Natures Pictures Drawn By Fancies Pencil to the Life.* London: for J. Martin and J. Allestrye, 1656.

———. *Orations of Divers Sorts, Accomodated to Divers Places.* London, 1662.

———. *Philosophical and Physical Opinions.* London: William Wilson, 1662.

———. *Plays.* London: A. Warren, 1662.

———. *Plays, Never before Printed.* London: A. Maxwell, 1668.

———. *The Worlds Olio.* London: for J. Martin and J. Allestrye, 1635.

Newcastle, William Cavendish, Duke of. *A Pleasante & Merrye Humor off A Roge.* Edited by Francis Needham. *Welbeck Miscellany,* 1 (1933).

Nicoll, Allardyce. *A History of English Drama 1660–1900.* 4th ed. 6 vols. Cambridge: Cambridge University Press, 1952–59.

*The Nine Muses, Or, Poems Written By Nine severall Ladies Upon the Death of the late Famous John Dryden, Esq.* London: for Richard Basset, 1700.

Norton, J. E. "Some Uncollected Authors: Susanna Centlivre." *The Book Collector* 6 (1957): 172–78, 280–85.

Oman, Carola. *Henrietta Maria.* London: Hodder and Stoughton, 1936.

*Original and Genuine Letters sent to the Tatler and Spectator, During the Time those Works were publishing. None of which have been before Printed.* 2 vols. London: R. Harbin, 1725.

Peavy, Charles D. "The Chimerical Career of Charlotte Charke." *Restoration and Eighteenth Century Theatre Research* 8 (May 1969): 1–12.

Pembroke, Mary Herbert, Countess of. *Antonie.* Edited by Alice Luce. Weimar: E. Felber, 1897.

———. *The Psalms of Sir Philip Sidney and the Countess of Pembroke.* Edited by J. C. A. Rathmell. Garden City, N. Y.: Doubleday, 1963.

———. *"The Triumph of Death" and Other Unpublished Poems.* Edited by G. F. Waller. Salzburg: Institut für Englische Sprache und Literatur, 1977.

*Pepys on the Restoration Stage.* Edited by Helen McAfee. New Haven, Conn.: Yale University Press, 1916.

Perry, Henry Ten Eyck. *The First Duchess of Newcastle and Her Husband as Figures in Literary History.* Boston: Ginn, 1918.

Philips, Katherine. *Poems . . . To which is added Monsieur Corneille's*

*Pompey & Horace, Tragedies.* London: for H. Herringman, 1667.

Pilkington, Letitia. *Memoirs.* Introduction by Iris Barry. London: G. Routledge, 1928.

Pix, Mary. *The Adventures in Madrid.* London: for James Knapton, Bernard Lintott, and B. Bragg, n.d.

―――. *The Beau Defeated; or, The Lucky Younger Brother.* London: for W. Turner and R. Basset, n.d.

―――. *The Conquest of Spain.* London: for Richard Wellington, 1705.

―――. *The Czar of Muscovy.* London: Bernard Lintott, 1701.

―――. *The Deceiver Deceived.* London: for R. Basset, 1698.

―――. *The Different Widows; or, Intrigue All-A-Mode.* London: for Henry Player and Bernard Lintott, n.d.

―――. *The Double Distress.* London: for R. Wellington and Bernard Lintott, 1701.

―――. *The False Friend; or, The Fate of Disobedience.* London: for Richard Basset, 1699.

―――. *Ibrahim, the Thirteenth Emperour of the Turks.* London: for John Harding, 1696.

―――. *The Innocent Mistress.* London: J. Orme, 1697.

―――. *Queen Catharine; or, The Ruines of Love.* London: for William Turner, 1698.

―――. *The Spanish Wives.* London: for R. Wellington, 1696.

*Poems on Affairs of State: From the time of Oliver Cromwell, to the Abdication of K. James the Second. Written by the greatest Wits of the Age.* N.p., 1697.

Pollard, A. W., and Redgrave, G. R. *A Short-Title Catalogue of Books Printed in England, Scotland, and Ireland 1475–1640.* 1926; reprint ed., London: The Bibliographical Society, 1946.

Polwhele, Elizabeth. *The Frolicks or The Lawyer Cheated.* Edited by Judith Milhous and Robert D. Hume. Ithaca, N.Y.: Cornell University Press, 1977.

Pope, Alexander. *The Dunciad.* Edited by James Sutherland. 3d. ed., rev. London: Methuen, 1963.

―――. *The Prose Works.* Edited by Norman Ault. Oxford: B. Blackwell, 1936.

Powell, George. *Imposture Defeated; or, A Trick to Cheat the Devil.* London: for Richard Wellington, 1698.

Power, Eileen. *Medieval English Nunneries c. 1275–1535*. Cambridge: At the University Press, 1922.

——. *Medieval Women*. Cambridge: At the University Press, 1975.

Randall, John. *The Disappointment*. London: for S. Slow, 1732.

Rees, Joan. *Samuel Daniel*. Liverpool: Liverpool University Press, 1964.

Reynolds, Myra. *The Learned Lady in England 1650–1760*. Boston: Houghton Mifflin, 1920.

Richardson, Samuel. *Sir Charles Grandison*. The Shakespeare Head Edition. 6 vols. Oxford: Basil Blackwell, 1931.

Rollins, Hyder, ed. *A Poetical Rhapsody*. 2 vols. Cambridge, Mass.: Harvard University Press, 1931.

*Roving Husband Reclaimed, The*. London: B. Bragg, 1706.

Rowe, Nicholas. *The Miscellaneous Works*. 3rd ed. London: W. Feales, 1733.

Sackville-West, Victoria. *Aphra Behn*. New York: Viking, 1928.

Saintsbury, George, ed. *Minor Poets of the Caroline Period*. 3 vols. Oxford: At the Clarendon Press, 1905.

Salter, F. M. *Mediaeval Drama in Chester*. Toronto: University of Toronto Press, 1955.

*Satyr upon the Present Times, A*. London: J. Morphew, 1717.

Schorer, Mark. "*She Stoops to Conquer:* A Parallel." *MLN* 48 (1933): 91–94, 486.

Seronsy, Cecil. *Samuel Daniel*. New York: Twayne, 1967.

*The Session of the Poets, Holden at the Foot of Parnassus-Hill*. London: for E. Whitlock, 1696.

Sherbo, Arthur. *English Sentimental Drama*. East Lansing, Mich.: Michigan State University Press, 1957.

Sherburn, George. "The Fortunes and Misfortunes of *Three Hours After Marriage*." *Modern Philology* 24 (1926): 91–109.

Sidney, Sir Philip. *The Complete Works*. Edited by Albert Feuillerat. 4 vols. Cambridge: Cambridge University Press, 1912–26.

Smith, Dane Farnsworth. *Plays About the Theatre in England*. London: Oxford University Press, 1936.

Smith, Lucy Toulmin, ed. *York Plays*. Oxford: At the Clarendon Press, 1885.

Souers, Philip Webster. *The Matchless Orinda*. 1931; reprint ed., New York: Johnson, 1968.

Southerne, Thomas. *Oroonoko: A Tragedy*. London: for H. Playford, 1696.

Stauffer, Donald A. "A Deep and Sad Passion." In *The Parrott Presentation Volume*. Edited by Hardin Craig. 1935; reprint ed., New York: Russell and Russell, 1967.

Steele, Richard. *Correspondence*. Edited by Rae Blanchard. London: Oxford University Press, 1941.

———. *The Lucubrations of Isaac Bickerstaff Esq*. 4 vols. London: Charles Lillie and John Morphew, 1713.

Strange, Sally Minter. "Charlotte Charke: Transvestite or Conjuror?" *Restoration and Eighteenth Century Theatre Research* 15 (November, 1976): 54–59.

Straus, Ralph. *The Unspeakable Curll*. London: Chapman and Hall, 1927.

Sutherland, James. *English Literature in the Late Seventeenth Century*. The Oxford History of English Literature, Vol. 6. Oxford: Oxford University Press, 1969.

———. "The Progress of Error: Mrs. Centlivre and the Biographers." *Review of English Studies* 18 (1942): 167–82.

Swift, Jonathan. *Journal to Stella*. Edited by Harold Williams. 2 vols. Oxford: Clarendon Press, 1948.

———. *Poems*. Edited by Harold Williams. 3 vols. Oxford: Clarendon Press, 1937.

Thorn-Drury, G., ed. *A Little Ark containing Sundry Pieces of Seventeenth-Century Verse*. London: P. J. and A. E. Dobell, 1921.

———. "An Unrecorded Play-Title." *Review of English Studies* 6 (1930): 316–18.

*Three Centuries of English and American Plays: A Checklist*. Edited by G. William Berquist. New York: Hafner, 1963.

*Times*. (London) 8 June 1954, 14 June 1954, 18 August 1954.

Tolhurst, J. B. L., *The Ordinale and Customary of the Benedictine Nuns of Barking Abbey*. 2 vols. London: Henry Bradshaw Society, 1927–28.

Trotter, Catherine. *Agnes de Castro*. London: for H. Rhodes, 1696.

———. *Fatal Friendship*. London: for Frances Saunders, 1698.

———. *Love at a Loss; or, Most Votes Carry It*. London: for William Turner, 1701.

————. *Olinda's Adventures; Or the Amours of a Young Lady.* Introduction by Robert Adams Day. Augustan Society Reprints, no 138. Los Angeles: William Andrews Clark Memorial Library, University of California, 1969.

————. *The Revolution of Sweden.* London: for J. Knapton, 1706.

————. *The Unhappy Penitent.* London: for William Turner, 1701.

————. *The Works . . . Theological, Moral, Dramatic, and Poetical.* With an account of the life of the author by Thomas Birch. 2 vols. London: for J. and P. Knapton, 1751.

*Two Centuries of Testimony in favour of Mrs. Aphra Behn.* London: J. Pearson, 1872.

*Two Old Comedies The Belle's Stratagem and The Wonder Reduced and Re-arranged by Augustin Daly For Production at Daly's Theatre During the Season 1893–94.* New York, 1893.

Valency, Maurice J. *The Tragedies of Herod and Mariamne.* New York: Columbia University Press, 1940.

Victor, Benjamin. *The History of the Theatres of London and Dublin From the Year 1730 to the present Time.* 2 vols. London: for T. Davies, 1761.

————. *Original Letters, Dramatic Pieces, and Poems.* 3 vols. London: for T. Becket, 1776.

Waddell, Helen. "Eccentric Englishwomen VIII: Mrs. Charke." *The Spectator* 158 (1937): 1047–48.

Walpole, Horace. *Letters.* Edited by Peter Cunningham. 9 vols. London, 1857–59.

Ward, Adolphus William. *A History of English Dramatic Literature to the Death of Queen Anne.* 3 vols. 1899; reprint ed., New York: Octagon Books, 1966.

Weddell, Mrs. *The City Farce.* London: for G. Hawkins, 1737.

————. *Incle and Yarico.* London: T. Cooper, 1742.

Wells, Staring B., ed. *A Comparison Between the Two Stages.* Princeton, N.J.: Princeton University Press, 1942.

Welsford, Enid. *The Court Masque.* Cambridge: Cambridge University Press, 1927.

Whicher, George Frisbie. *The Life and Romances of Mrs. Eliza Haywood.* New York: Columbia University Press, 1915.

Whincop, Thomas. *Scanderbeg: or, Love and Liberty. To which are added A List of all the Dramatic Authors, with some Account of their*

*Lives; and of all the Dramatic Pieces ever published in the English Language, to the Year 1747.* London: for W. Reeve, 1747.

Wilson, Mona. *Sir Philip Sidney.* London: Duckworth, 1931.

Winchilsea, Anne Finch, Countess of. *Miscellany Poems, on Several Occasions.* London: for J. B., 1713.

————. *The Poems.* Edited by Myra Reynolds. Chicago: University of Chicago Press, 1903.

Winton, Calhoun. "Steele, Mrs. Manley, and John Lacy." *Philological Quarterly* 42 (1963): 272–75.

Wiseman, Jane. *Antiochus the Great; or, The Fatal Relapse.* London: for William Turner, 1702.

Witherspoon, Alexander. *The Influence of Robert Garnier on Elizabethan Drama.* New Haven: Yale University Press, 1924.

Wood, F. T. *"The Disappointment." Review of English Studies* 5 (1929): 66–69.

Woodcock, George. *The Incomparable Aphra.* London: Boardman, 1948.

Woolf, Virginia. *The Common Reader.* New York: Harcourt, Brace, 1925.

————. *A Room of One's Own.* New York: Harcourt, Brace, 1929.

Young, Frances Berkeley. *Mary Sidney Countess of Pembroke.* London: David Nutt, 1912.

Young, Karl. *The Drama of the Medieval Church.* 2 vols. Oxford: Clarendon Press, 1933.

————. "The Harrowing of Hell in Liturgical Drama." *Transactions of the Wisconsin Academy of Sciences, Arts, and Letters* 16 (1910): 888–947.

————. "The Records of the York Play of the *Pater Noster.*" *Speculum* 7 (1932): 540–546.

# Index